★ ★ ★ ★ ★ ★

TRUMP RULES

WAYNE ALLYN ROOT

Redwood Publishing, LLC

Published by Redwood Publishing, LLC
Orange County, California
info@redwooddigitalpublishing.com
www.redwooddigitalpublishing.com

Printed in the United States of America

First Printing, 2020

ISBN 978-1-952106-66-8 (hardcover)
ISBN 978-1-952106-67-5 (paperback)
ISBN 978-1-952106-68-2 (ebook)

Library of Congress Control Number: 2020918883

Book Design by Redwood Publishing, LLC
Cover Design by Graphique Designs, LLC
Front Cover Photo by Mandel Ngan, Getty Images
(Image #: 1020992412, Licensed From Getty Images)

"Eat your Wheaties. Lock your seat belt. Take a deep breath. Put on your goggles. You're about to start a wild ride with the remarkable TRUMP RULES."
—Wayne Allyn Root

CONTENTS

SECTION 3   TRUMP SQUARED

SECTION 4   PROOF THE TRUMP RULES
WORK FOR ANYONE

INTRODUCTION

Why I Wrote This Book

"And in many ways, Root is the Las Vegas version of Trump . . ."

The Daily Beast

B efore I tell you about *Trump and me,* I want to explain the purpose of this book. This book explains the rules, principles, and traits of Donald J. Trump. Whether you love him or hate him, Trump's success is unquestionable. He may be the only human being in history to achieve mega wealth and mega success in business . . . real estate . . . branding . . . celebrity . . . television . . . and politics. He is, after all, a billionaire CEO, builder of skyscrapers, the luxury brand name in the world, TV star, mega celebrity, the president of the United States, commander of the US military, and leader of the free world. I would argue no one in history has ever walked on this earth with every one of those titles.

I've studied Trump my entire adult life and applied his traits, principles, and rules to my life. That's why I wrote this book. I'm not a billionaire. I'm a small businessman. But I'm a witness. Everyone can benefit from the TRUMP RULES.

These rules work for anyone and everyone. I'm living proof. This book will show you how Trump applied them to his life and how I applied them to my life. It doesn't matter if you're white or black, man or woman, rich or poor, big businessman or small businessman, Republican or Democrat. These TRUMP RULES work. Period. They will improve your life. They will supercharge your level of success. They will make you more money. They will make you better at whatever you do. Study them and live them— whether you love Trump or hate Trump, you can learn from his TRUMP RULES.

What's my story? I was just a kid from the streets of New York— like Trump. Smart, ambitious, and a hustler. I saw Trump and I said to myself, *I want to study Trump, learn from Trump, be like Trump.* It's been quite a ride. Other than being a good talker and a hustler who is willing to work 24/7/365, I have few talents in life. Yet, I took these TRUMP RULES and achieved outsized and unimaginable success. My story is actually remarkable.

Yes, Trump's rules worked for Trump. Yes, they made Trump a billionaire. But I'm living proof they can work for anyone, even if you start at the bottom and you don't have any special talents. I'm like a living, breathing, blinking Las Vegas neon sign for the real-world application and success of the TRUMP RULES.

These rules work for big businesses and billionaires. They work for small businesses and millionaires. They work for Ivy Leaguers. They work for blue collar sons of butchers, bakers, and candlestick makers. I learned early in life from Donald Trump (and other heroes of mine like Winston Churchill) that a little self-promotion is a great thing. As a New Yorker, self-promotion comes naturally. Or, as Mohammed Ali said, "It ain't bragging if you can back it up."

There is a Chinese proverb that goes something like this: *Tell me, I hear. Show me, I understand.* So, to show you that the TRUMP RULES can change your life, I'm going to share my story, inspired every step of the way by the TRUMP RULES.

There is no better way to understand how modeling Trump and the TRUMP RULES can change your life than to show you exactly how it changed mine. Hopefully, it will also give you the confidence to apply these rules to your own life without fearing failure or criticism. After all, isn't that what reading a book like this is all about!

If I can do it, *ANYONE* can! And that includes YOU!

I've led an amazing life. Some might call it a fairy tale. But like Trump, it's been up and down. I've suffered my share of failures and disappointments. Actually, like Trump, I've failed so many times, I've lost track of all my failures. But who cares? What matters, what people remember in the end, are the successes and achievements, not the failures. What they remember is that, like Trump, I never gave up. I was relentless! I absorbed the losses, got back up, dusted myself off, and used the lessons learned to get back in the game and kick ass! That's the definition of #WINNING.

It's no coincidence I've turned lemons into lemonade so many times. I learned by studying the one and only "Donald" at the most sensitive and impressionable time of my life—my formative college and early, post-college years. It's no mistake or coincidence that we have a lot in common in the way we think and act. You learn a lot by modeling somebody's life. Pretty soon you're like, "brothers from another mother."

The results have been similar, too. Lots of amazing success, some could be even described as miraculous. But also, lots of failures along the way. Why? Because what I learned from Trump is to attack life, live life on the edge, treat it like a high-wire act. *No risk, no reward.* Based on watching and modeling Trump's mindset, I became a combination riverboat gambler, Texas oil wildcatter, and Wild West gunslinger.

When you roll the dice as a combination of those three, there will be failures. Bad failures. B-I-G failures. Egg on your face kind of failures. Run and hide kind of failures. The agony of defeat.

But I also learned that if you hang in there and don't give up, there will be the thrill of victory, too. Not just victory, but unimaginable success. Big-time, attention-getting, over-sized success! Success as big as the Great State of Texas!

But while "The Donald" and I have similarities, it is important to note that we started from very different places.

What Donald Trump has accomplished is amazing. But our upbringings and starting points are from vastly different worlds. Trump inherited from his father, Fred Trump, a legacy of success and outsized achievement in the middle-class outer boroughs of New York. You might call what he inherited, *success in the minor leagues.* But the amazing Donald J. Trump wasn't willing to settle for success in the minor leagues—he was destined for the majors.

In Trump's world, the major leagues were the dog-eat-dog world of Manhattan real estate. Trump became the Super Bowl M.V.P. of the Big Apple, the king of the toughest place on earth to make it big. But for Donald J. Trump, even that wasn't enough. After conquering New York, he set out to conquer America . . . and he did it. As a matter of fact, he became the leader of the free world. I don't think it's a stretch to say that Trump, for better or worse, is now the most famous person in the world. Not just living today, but perhaps ever. Outside of Jesus himself, and maybe Mohammed, whose name has been on more lips in world history? Who has ever had more people talking about him? The split is probably equal—Trump lovers versus haters. Some see him as a hero. Some see him as superman. Some see him as almost a God. Some see him as the devil himself. But one thing is certain—everyone is talking about Trump.

Remember this. In the days of Jesus, Mohammed, and other historical figures, there was no 24/7 news cycle, or television, or the Internet, or social media. So, I think it's pretty clear Trump is really one of the most talked about persons *ever*.

But, I also don't think it's a stretch to say he is also one of the most controversial persons ever.

Trump took a foundation of very nice wealth and success and turned it into a one-in-a-billion legendary success for the ages. Trump's success is literally *biblical*. To complete the analogy, it's King Solomon or King David kind of success.

The fact of the matter is that I, undoubtedly like most of you, started in a very different place than Donald Trump. I am an SOB (Son of a Butcher) and started with nothing—no money, no connections, no wealthy father, no training from someone who knew how to achieve success. If I wanted a nice piece of bologna, I was connected (with a certain butcher)—but other than that, I didn't know a soul who could give me even a tiny head start, supercharge my career, or teach me anything about how to achieve wealth or celebrity. Don't get me wrong. My parents gave me encouragement and made sure that I had the opportunity for a first-class education, which I took full advantage of. But other than that, I was starting at the very bottom of the barrel.

Trump started on the 3rd floor of a very nice upper-middle-class building with a doorman, and worked his way up to the 70th story penthouse of a Fifth Avenue skyscraper. Literally—it's called Trump Tower. My start was more like the basement, maybe not of a slum building, but not far from it.

But that's okay. That is what makes this book so remarkable and why I feel it is so important for you, the reader. You see, I am living proof that the TRUMP RULES work—**no matter where you start.** Trump used these rules to become a billionaire celebrity, "the King of New York," the star of *Celebrity Apprentice*, the commander in chief of the United States military, and the leader of the free world. I started out with nothing and used these rules to become a self-made millionaire by the age of twenty-nine, and achieve some fairly significant success in multiple fields.

I used the same rules, learned from studying and modeling Trump, to become a successful small businessman (versus billionaire business mogul Trump) . . .

> to become a moderately successful sports gaming industry CEO (versus casino mogul CEO Trump) . . .

> to become a moderately successful TV host (versus mega TV celebrity Trump) . . .

> to become a moderately successful TV creator and reality TV show producer (versus *Celebrity Apprentice* mega-hit TV producer Trump) . . .

> to become a moderately successful best-selling author (versus #1 New York Times bestseller Trump) . . .

> to become a moderately successful national politician and Libertarian vice presidential nominee on my first try at national politics (versus the president of the United States Donald J. Trump).

Trump wound up with a star on the Hollywood Walk of Fame. I wound up with my own 180-pound granite star on the Las Vegas Walk of Stars (on Las Vegas Boulevard; in front of Paris Resort & Casino).

As a bonus, I raised a daughter, Dakota Root, who graduated Ivy League Harvard University and Oxford University, just like Trump's daughter, Ivanka, who graduated Ivy League Penn and Wharton.

Do you sense a pattern here?

While we've lived our lives in similar careers and industries, the fact is, Trump invented and perfected the TRUMP RULES. He's the founder and expert. I just borrowed them. I'm no Trump. But it's been one heck of a wild ride for an ordinary blue-collar SOB from a dead-end street on the Bronx borderline. I used the TRUMP RULES to take my success further than anyone (including me) could ever imagine.

Since I started from such a different place and was just doing my best to copy Trump's rules, I never achieved his phenomenal, earth-shattering, world-class level of success. At least not yet.

I'm sure you won't be surprised to hear I intend to keep trying, as long as I'm "above ground."

Don't misunderstand; I believe my "moderate success" is a huge positive for all of you reading this book. Trump's success is so outsized, most would be turned off by the impossibility of it all and be too intimidated to even try. What are the odds that "Jack or Jenny from the block" will become a billionaire, or leader of the free world? I'm no math whiz kid, but it's not a very high probability. There are only a handful of Trumps in the world. That level of success intimidates most people. So, they don't even try.

But my level of success, using the exact same rules as Trump, is actually realistic, achievable, and doable for everyone reading this book. My dreams aren't ridiculous, or intimidating, or unimaginable. If, thanks to the TRUMP RULES, I was able to achieve my dreams, I believe that's proof positive that you can too.

But you have to try. And you have to set specific goals. Aim high, shoot for the stars. And work your butt off. It all begins with one step. An ancient Chinese proverb says, "A journey of a thousand miles begins with one step."

This book is your first step. Run with it!

SECTION I

Getting to Know Trump and Me

★ ★ ★ ★ ★ ★

——————— CHAPTER ONE ———————

Trump and Me

"'Wayne is one of my biggest fans, one of my biggest supporters, and he takes care of me in Vegas,' Trump told [Geraldo] Rivera."

———

Excerpt from *The Grifter's Club: Trump, Mar-a-Lago, and the Selling of the Presidency*

I started life as a blue-collar SOB (Son of a Butcher). As a dead-end kid from the mean streets of New York (I literally lived next door to a dead end), I was born and raised on the Bronx borderline, in a rough, dangerous, crime-ridden town called Mt. Vernon.

For me, in the 1980s, there were two dynamic, larger-than-life figures. This was the decade during which I attended and graduated college and then started my career. Those two figures whom I loved, respected, learned from, and looked at as mentors were Ronald Reagan and Donald Trump. I built my life around what I learned from watching them in action.

Keep in mind, I never met either of them during that time. I only watched and learned from afar. Reagan was a "father figure." I loved him like I loved my own dad. But Trump was like a very cool older brother. I wanted to *be like Trump.*

Reagan was a Republican president. Trump was a New York business mogul. My life was immersed in business and Republican politics. These two were my favorite superheroes, along with an "assist" to George Steinbrenner—another high-profile, controversial, in-your-face, larger-than-life billionaire New York business mogul. Steinbrenner owned the New York Yankees, my favorite childhood team. He was very much an older version of Trump. But more about that later.

My goal was to achieve success in politics and business, like Reagan and Trump. I studied intently, listened, learned, and modeled my life after them. I recognized a life like Trump's was the more realistic goal. I set my sights on being a New York business mogul. Trump was "ground zero." I decided to *be like Trump* in every way.

There is so much to learn from President Donald Trump— whether you love him or hate him. Trump isn't just a person. He is a brand. He is a philosophy. He is a strategy. He is a force of nature: An earthquake, tornado, and tsunami rolled into one.

Most importantly, Trump is a metaphor for life. Trump is a style of attacking business, career, politics, and life with an energy, passion, abandon, and enthusiasm known to only the ultra-successful. Trump is the eradication of fear.

I was no fan of President Obama. Actually, to be fair and honest, I was diametrically opposed to everything for which Obama stood. Fortunately, Obama's success was limited (by President Trump, who is busy erasing pretty much everything Obama did). Yes, Obama became president of the United States. How cool is that? But before that, he was an unknown community organizer and lost a race for Congress.

Obama was so unknown and unsuccessful, that when my Columbia University Class of '83 met for our twentieth reunion in

2003, Obama wasn't even on the radar. Yes, I was a college classmate of Obama, same year, both Pre-Law, both Political Science majors. Obama was only five years away from becoming president of the United States and no one even *considered* him as a speaker at our reunion. I was, however, one of the speakers that weekend. In 2003, few people had ever heard of Obama. He was a nobody with literally no success . . . and then suddenly, he was President. I call that a *one-hit wonder*.

Despite that, I learned valuable lessons from studying Obama. There is much to learn from someone who has catapulted somehow, someway, to mega-success. I study winners to learn from them (whether I personally like them or dislike them doesn't matter). There is plenty to learn from even a *one-hit wonder* like Obama. Let's give Obama credit. It takes great talent, skills, vision, and timing to navigate from a *nobody* (literally) to president of the United States in five short years.

But compare that to President Donald J. Trump. Here's a man who has achieved the rare Triple Crown: Mega-wealth, celebrity, and success, all at the highest levels ever seen in world history. Trump is truly one-in-a-billion. Becoming a billionaire in the business world alone is a remarkable feat. It's quite literally one-in-a-billion. But few billionaires in world history have ever achieved Trump's level of celebrity. None of them ever created the brand name for luxury in the world. None of them ever conquered Hollywood and created one of the most watched reality shows perhaps in television history. And only one has ever become president of the United States. Amazing. Yes, of course, Trump has had a few failures along the way. I'll discuss them in detail in a later chapter. But all things considered, I think I can make the case that Donald J. Trump is the most successful person ever. Trump wins the Triple Crown, the Three Peat; he's the Champion of Champions.

Trump has achieved awe-inspiring levels of success in business, entrepreneurship, real estate in particular, branding, celebrity, publishing, television, and now, of course, politics. He has been arguably, at various times, the greatest in the world at each of those. There really has never been anyone else like him, ever.

I've personally been a student of Donald Trump's life since this blue-collar son of a butcher graduated Columbia University thirty-six years ago. In 1983 (the year of my college graduation), Trump was an American icon. He was the hero, mentor, and role model of this kid from the streets of New York . . . and every other kid who dreamed of making it big in business. We all wanted to be *like Trump.*

My personal case is special. Think about the timing of our parallel lives. Trump's over-the-top success ties to all the milestones of the early life of this impressionable, young, New York street kid. The biggest moment of my young life was being accepted into Columbia University. My first year in college was 1979/1980. At that moment, Trump was a brash young real estate mogul building the famous Grand Hyatt Hotel in Manhattan next to Grand Central Terminal. I was attending Columbia, only 4.6 miles away from Trump's magical construction zone. Of course, being the super ambitious young man that I was, I noticed.

During my four years at Columbia, Trump was in the headlines, day and night, for building the most grandiose building in world history—Trump Tower on Fifth Avenue. When the time I graduated and joined the business world in 1983, Trump Tower had just opened to the public. It was inaugurated on November 30, 1983. A star was born. Trump was either on the cover of the New York newspapers, or in the headlines of every gossip column in American newspapers and magazines almost every day. Trump *owned* New York.

The parallels and milestones of my life don't end there. The most important and impressionable years of my young business career were 1985 through 1988. During that time, I was achieving my own early success in New York real estate and in media. At that time, Trump bought Mar-a-Lago in Palm Beach, the most exclusive private residence in America. He was also busy shocking and amazing the entire city of New York by fixing the famous Wollman Ice Rink in Manhattan's Central Park four months early, and at $750,000 under budget. Government tried and failed for six long years to fix Wollman. Government wasted over $12 million. Trump did something no one in government could do . . . and did it in record time. His larger-than-life legend grew even larger. I really wanted to *be like Trump*.

But the best and biggest for Trump was yet to come. By 1987, he had the #1 bestselling book in America, *The Art of the Deal*. By 1988, he had bought the world-famous Plaza Hotel. And, during this entire period, 1985 to 1988, Trump built a casino gambling empire with three magnificent, high-profile hotels in Atlantic City.

Donald Trump <u>WAS</u> New York. As for me, this young, impressionable New York kid badly wanted to learn from the best, so I could become the best.

I am living proof there are remarkable lessons to be learned from Trump. I owe my success and personal achievements to the TRUMP RULES that you are about to learn in this book. I wasn't more talented or intelligent than many of the kids with whom I grew up. As you'll read about in the last chapter of this book, by modeling Trump and his penchant for promotions, media, and headlines, I managed to achieve remarkable success. If I can do it, so can you.

Dear reader, I believe YOU can apply these brilliant and unique *one-in-a-billion* rules about which you are about to read, to achieve extraordinary success at anything you choose. Let me show you how to channel your *inner Trump*.

Few people understand Trump the way I understand Trump. Up next, you'll be reading a few columns I wrote about Trump and then a chapter on how I actually met Trump. Those two chapters will prove, beyond a shadow of a doubt, that you're in the right place at the right time. While it may not be a TRUMP RULE, one of the facts I have learned about life that is proven by these next chapters is that, "timing is not just important . . . it is everything." The fact that you are reading this book right now puts you in the right place at the right time.

Next, you'll read the actual TRUMP RULES chapters and learn how you can apply these brilliant, common sense rules to your own life. Few will ever become as wealthy as President Trump. But everyone can learn something from Trump to make their lives better, to get the job they want, start the business they want, or find the investors they need. This isn't about becoming a billionaire, or becoming president. It's about becoming the best you can possibly be. It's about turning dreams into reality. But we all have different dreams.

This book is dedicated to teaching you how to apply these priceless one-in-a-billion rules to your own personal life and career. These TRUMP RULES are a magical roadmap, guiding you along the route (or in this case, ROOT) to your personal unimagined success.

Buckle your seatbelt. Together, we're going on a magical, high-speed, adrenaline-rush journey!

———————— CHAPTER TWO ————————

My Story
How I Met Donald J. Trump

*"People have built entire careers by gaining
access to the MAGA brand . . . Wayne Allyn Root
was one . . . . Root owes his career
to Trump . . .."*

———

Excerpt from *The Grifter's Club: Trump, Mar-a-
Lago, and the Selling of the Presidency*

All the years I spent studying, watching, and learning from Donald Trump was from afar. During those years, I never met or saw him in person. Not even once.

The story of how we finally met is exhibit A for what makes Trump *Trump*.

I was watching a movie on HBO while working out in my home gym one day in the spring of 2015. I work out two hours a day, every day. The only way to get through a long, grueling workout is with a movie. I start the workout when the movie starts, and I end the workout when the movie ends. It's a great way to get through a two-hour workout (and take your mind off the pain).

Well, on this day, I happened to watch *Bullworth*. The old movie from the 1990s starring Warren Beatty as a US Senator running for re-election. Beatty's character looks like a surefire loser until he starts saying whatever is on his mind, no matter who it offends. If it's the raw truth, he says it. And, of course, that's refreshing to voters. He's saying exactly what most people are thinking, but are too afraid to say out loud. Suddenly, Warren Beatty becomes a phenomenon. Suddenly, he attracts huge crowds and standing ovations. Suddenly, he's in all the headlines. He not only wins his Senate race resoundingly, he becomes a frontrunner for president of the United States.

A lightbulb went off. I thought, *THAT'S DONALD TRUMP!*

I wrote the commentary about Trump as our real-life Bullworth. I wrote that he could be our next president because people are sick of BS and "politics as usual." They want truth—even if it hurts or offends. Trump can be that guy.

The next day, I noticed an email from "The Office of Donald J. Trump." I assumed it was a mass mailing with a sales pitch for some Trump product or a new book. But when I opened it up, it was a personal note from Donald Trump *himself. To me.*

He had read my "Bullworth" column and loved it. He wanted to thank me for it.

I've been in politics my entire life—literally. I started my political career at age three, handing out campaign literature for Barry Goldwater, in my father's arms, in front of a supermarket in Mt. Vernon, NY. I had worked directly for major political candidates since I was a teenager. I had written hundreds of commentaries about different Republican politicians for many years. Not once, in all those years, had any of them ever contacted me to say they read it . . . they enjoyed it . . . or to thank me. Only Donald J. Trump.

No Senate or Congressional or Governor candidate . . . *let alone a presidential candidate* . . . had ever contacted me to thank me for a nice column about them.

Only Trump.

He's one smart cookie. Brilliant. This one story sums up so much of the TRUMP RULES. Trump understands how to become successful. How to win at anything in life. Add the following to the more formal and in-depth chapters on the TRUMP RULES you'll read about later in this book.

First, out-work and out-hustle your competition.

Trump was busy running a business empire . . . and producing and starring in one of the most popular reality TV shows ever . . . and writing bestselling business books . . . and running for president, too. Yet, he found time to read my column. And then found time to track down my contact info and send me a personalized handwritten note. *Really?*

All the experts said he couldn't win the presidency. They said he couldn't beat out sixteen of the most professional and poised politicians in history—all running for the GOP nomination. And, if by some miracle, he won the GOP primary, they said he could never beat out the most famous brand name in the history of politics, Hillary Clinton, in the general election.

I wrote plenty of commentaries and articles about the other sixteen supposedly brilliant GOP presidential candidates but never heard a single word from any of them. I guess they had no time to read my column. *Trump did.* And, if they did read the column, none of them probably even thought about sending a thank you note to the author. *Trump did.*

The reality is, I've written hundreds of columns about politicians. Trump is the first and only one to ever send me a thank you note. That about says it all.

The experts claimed Trump was mean and nasty and offensive, and don't forget "selfish." *Really?* Well none of the supposedly nice guys, like Jeb Bush, ever took the time to send me a note. *Only Trump.*

He's either the nicest, most thoughtful, selfless politician of all time . . . or he's calculating, and faking sincerity. Does it matter? Then the rest of them should fake it, too. Because it works! I joined the Trump bandwagon that day and never left.

Secondly, you win in business, politics, and life with *personality*.

Trump showed personality with that note. I've met all the leading GOP politicians of the last thirty years. I have photos with all of them on my office walls. They were all duds. No personality. No energy. No charisma. No spark. Only Trump and Reagan had personality. It's no surprise they both won.

P.S. I'll admit on the Democrat side, there have been three presidential candidates with enormous charisma and personality— JFK, Bill Clinton, and Obama. It's no surprise they all won. Personality wins elections, not issues.

Third, you win by being relentless.

Trump epitomizes relentless (and tireless). He rarely sleeps. He is a human hurricane . . . tornado . . . human energizer bunny. He is a man in motion. He is always moving, selling, promoting, and pitching. I can picture him writing thank you notes at 3 a.m., between conference calls in the middle of the night with business partners in China and Israel.

Fourth, Trump understands the philosophy of Dale Carnegie who wrote the bestselling book, *How to Win Friends and Influence People*.

By sending out thank you notes, he builds a reservoir of goodwill and an army of fans. How can anyone not root for a guy running for president who takes the time to send you a thank you note? Trump understands what Dale Carnegie understood—make people around you feel good and they'll do anything for you!

My grandfather put it slightly differently . . . My grandfather, Simon Reis, was a Jewish German immigrant who arrived penniless in New York in the 1920s. He became a very successful small business owner. He taught me there are only two rules in business:

#1) The customer is always right.

#2) If the customer is ever wrong, refer back to rule #1.

Trump understands that his conservative base, and conservative activists, and conservative talk show hosts (like me) who keep the base energized, motivated, and positive are among his most valuable customers. Treat them right and you become president (or anything else you want to be). Brilliant, right? So simple, yet no one else ever understood this rule.

Now, to the rest of the story. Trump's note wasn't a one-time event. He wasn't a "one-hit wonder." From that time forward, Trump sent me personal handwritten notes after each of my columns. He followed me and voraciously read *everything* I wrote.

Eventually, one day, a note came agreeing with my column advising Trump to create and release a dramatic tax cut plan that would excite conservatives. Trump, again, thanked me for my excellent advice and then followed up with a request: *"Could you write my tax plan?"*

Only Donald Trump would ask me to write his tax-cut plan. I replied, "Sure, when do you need it?" Trump replied, "Today." *Only Trump.*

I dropped everything, canceled my appointments, and wrote a conservative tax cut plan based on my many years in the trenches as a small businessman. Something I knew would excite and motivate not only conservatives, but also, all capitalists and small-business owners, the type of people who would form the foundation and backbone of Trump's GOP presidential campaign.

I recommended one low flat tax, lower than Reagan's 28% rate, keeping 100% of the deductions for mortgage and charity. I recommended Trump not touch mortgage or charitable deductions, because homeowners and churchgoers are the base of the GOP.

Within days, Trump came out with his very first tax plan. It looked pretty much like the one I had designed. A few minor changes, but it was clear he had considered what I had proposed.

Within a few weeks, Trump's top campaign officials contacted me asking if Trump could use my "Middle Class Plan for Winning the Presidency" commentary as a base for his new book. I agreed. The guy running for president is modeling his entire campaign book on my ideas? What an honor.

Remember what I said earlier. Make people around you feel important and feel good about themselves and they'll do anything for you. I went on to make over 1,500 TV and radio appearances to champion and defend Trump. Not just TV here in the USA, but I appeared on TV over thirty times in other countries on behalf of Trump—including frequent appearances on Israeli TV, Australian TV, UK TV, Romanian TV, Canadian TV, and how about this one—I appeared on an international TV network reaching every Muslim nation! Not bad for a Jewish kid from the Bronx.

I am proud to have played a small, yet crucial, part in Donald Trump's winning the presidency.

Fifth, Be a Good Listener.

A good businessman or politician, no matter how big his or her ego, must listen. Sure, Trump has a big ego. Sure, he makes all his own executive decisions. All good bosses and leaders do. But they only make those decisions after listening to others. Then, and only then, do they make the final decision. *Trump listened to my advice.* Very few

★ ★ ★

politicians listen. I've written advice to many GOP politicians. Trump was the only one to ever acknowledge reading it, he clearly listened, and then adopted at least part of it. *Bravo.*

Soon I was honored to be chosen to open Donald Trump's presidential rallies in Las Vegas. I was honored to be the opening speaker or keynote speaker at every Trump event from December 2015 to October 30, 2016. Each time I met Trump backstage, he was the exact opposite of the man the media paints. The man I met backstage was friendly, caring, listened, and spent time with each person. He cared about each of us. He appreciated what we did for him.

Most importantly, it became clear that he truly cared about working class and middle class Americans. It wasn't an act. It was *him.* The version painted by CNN and MSNBC was, and is, "FAKE NEWS."

Over a year later, I was invited to Mar-a-Lago. He hadn't seen me in the months since his election. He had personally met tens of thousands of people since then. Yet, when I walked in the door, he screamed out, "Wayne! Wayne! Come over. Join me for dinner." He was eating dinner with Don Jr, Eric, his daughter-in-law Lara, and Geraldo Rivera. He spoke to me as if we were old-time friends. He remembered everything about our prior meetings. He treated me like I was the most important person in his world. He thanked me for all my help during the election. He told his sons, "Wayne is the greatest. What a fighter for us." *Only Trump.*

That's the Trump few know.

That story is so powerful, it was told in a book about Trump published in the summer of 2020. Author Sarah Blaskey wrote a negative book about Trump titled, *The Grifter's Club.* My story of meeting Trump may have been the only positive one in the entire book. The author called me to tell me that her own father found my story to be his favorite in the book. And even in that very negative book about Trump, several quotes from chapter eight ring true:

- "People have built entire careers by gaining access to the MAGA brand . . . Wayne Allyn Root was one."
- ". . . Root owes his career to Trump . . ."
- "Root introduced Trump at his [presidential] campaign rallies in Las Vegas."
- ". . . Root is happy to admit he built his career on the coattails of a giant [Donald Trump] . . ."
- ". . . Trump was a Wayne Allyn Root fan."
- "'Wayne is one of my biggest fans, one of my biggest supporters, and he takes care of me in Las Vegas,' President Trump told [Geraldo] Rivera."
- "All the billionaires and big shots [at Mar-a-Lago] stared jealously [at Root having dinner with President Trump] . . . nosy Palm Beachers who have to beg for an audience [with the President] couldn't quite believe what happened."[1]

What an honor to have my relationship with the president of the United States featured in this book about Trump and the infamous Mar-a-Lago.

A few months later, President Trump saw Chris Ruddy, founder and CEO of Newsmax TV. Here was the conversation, as told by Ruddy as a guest on my national TV show:

"President Trump was out golfing with Rush Limbaugh . . . The first thing President Trump says [as he comes off the golf course] . . . 'I watched Wayne's show . . . I watch it all the time . . . I love Wayne . . . be sure you tell Wayne how much I love his show.'

Wayne, these are direct quotes from the president of the United States about your TV show."

—Chris Ruddy, Chairman of Newsmax TV, Presidential friend and advisor (12/5/19 on Newsmax TV)

That's my personal Trump story. It's been quite a journey. And quite an honor every step of the way. I have a funny feeling this story is only just getting started.

—— CHAPTER THREE ——

Proof Positive You Are in the Right Place at the Right Time

"... Trump was a Wayne Allyn Root fan."

Excerpt from *The Grifter's Club: Trump, Mar-a-Lago, and the Selling of the Presidency*

I'm not just any author writing about Trump. News media across the country has called me, "The Donald Trump of Las Vegas" and "The Poor Man's Donald Trump." They call me that because I think like him, speak like him, act like him. For three years, from 2017 to 2020, I hosted a popular primetime television show on Newsmax TV, reaching, at its peak, seventy million homes. Whatever I said on my Newsmax TV show ... in the next day or two, it was often heard coming out of Trump's mouth. I know this guy. I understand this guy. We think so much alike, it's scary. I often know what President

Trump is going to say, before it comes out of his mouth. I have a keen understanding of what makes him tick. I understand what rules and traits made him successful—because I studied him, copied him, and later applied those rules and traits to my life.

Before you begin studying these priceless TRUMP RULES that will change your life, I want to set the tone. I want to first show PROOF POSITIVE that you're reading the right book. That you're in the right place, at the right time. That you're reading a book written by a guy who understands—like no other—what makes Trump *Trump*.

So, upcoming are just a sampling of op-eds that I wrote about Donald Trump, predicting who he was, and that he'd become President, long before anyone else understood what was about to happen. Let's start with my op-ed at Fox News on the day Trump announced for president, when no one gave him the slightest chance, when Trump's poll ratings were at one to two percent, when critics called him a "racist," when literally every corporate sponsor and partner abandoned him.

DONALD TRUMP FOR PRESIDENT? THE 2016 RACE JUST GOT FUN

By Wayne Allyn Root

I know. I know. "Trump is flawed," the critics say. "He is a clown." "He is a buffoon." "He's divorced . . . twice." "He has business bankruptcies." Yes, all true. And Reagan was a failed B-movie actor who played second fiddle to a chimp. Heck, Reagan had a failed Vegas lounge act that closed in a week. Reagan was rejected by United Artists executives to *PLAY* the part of a president. Two years later he was Governor of

California. Then he went onto become the man polls show is regarded as our greatest modern president. Could Donald Trump be "Reagan-Part Deux?"

Yes, Donald Trump is flawed. But ironically, he may be the perfect candidate at the perfect time. Why? Because he says whatever is on his mind. He has no filters. He doesn't care about political correctness. He doesn't answer to anyone—not donors, not handlers, not consultants, not pollsters and God bless him—not the media. Donald Trump is his own man. Trump says whatever he wants because he is worth $9 billion.

"The Donald" doesn't need any donations. He doesn't need the support of fat cat donors or multi-national corporations like the other GOP candidates. He doesn't need scandalous donations (a.k.a. bribes) from foreign governments like Hillary Clinton. Hillary is greedy. We know she thinks of herself as broke. Her hubby Bill says he's still worried about "paying the bills." Desperate people do desperate things. But Donald Trump has $9 billion. He never has to do desperate things. He has 9 billion reasons to say whatever he wants- and let the chips fall where they may.

Donald Trump is free to become "Bullworth."

Remember that 1998 movie starring Warren Beatty as US Senator Bullworth? He didn't give a damn what people thought anymore, so he said whatever he wanted. He told the truth and let the chips fall where they may. Bullworth stood at the pulpit of a black church and told black voters that the Democratic Party and their politicians claim to want to help you, make all kinds of promises, but they are all lying to get your vote. Then after the election they're nowhere to be found. They never keep those promises. Why? "Because you don't donate enough money," Bullworth admitted. "What's the proof?" Bullworth asked. "Half your kids are unemployed, the other half are in prison." The truth hasn't changed since 1998.

Bullworth dared to tell the truth. And the people loved it! Not only was Bullworth re-elected, he became an instant media sensation and the shocking favorite of voters for President. Honesty is *that* refreshing. Can real-life imitate art? We are about to find out.

Donald Trump is the real-life Bullworth. When voters listen to the raw truth of Trump next to the "mainstream, establishment candidates" who tell lie after lie to get elected, Donald will shine by comparison. Suddenly it will all become clear- the lies and B.S. aren't working. The other candidates are scamming you, bribing you, placating you. It's time for someone willing to tell it like it is. It's time for a real-life Bullworth.

Maybe, just maybe, Trump will admit out loud the damage Obama has done to our economy with his socialist policies. It's time for a politician to ask what socialism did for Greece, or Spain, or Italy, or France, or miserable Cuba? Or Venezuela with food and toilet paper shortages. And what has over 50 straight years of Democrat leadership done for bankrupt crime-ridden hellholes like Detroit, Chicago or Baltimore? I'm betting Trump is the guy willing to tell the truth.

Maybe he'll admit there is no recovery. It's all a lie. A mirage. The numbers are gamed. It's all created with fake money printing by the Fed; artificially low interest rates; and half the country being propped up by government checks.

Maybe he'll admit that the border is wide open and the illegals flowing across will destroy middle class jobs and drown our nation under a tsunami of welfare, food stamps, free healthcare and the costs for cops, courts and prison. Maybe Trump will tell you that anyone who says illegal immigration is good for the economy is a liar.

Maybe he'll admit that our open border will soon lead to a terrible terrorist attack. Maybe he'll ask out loud "What kind of president would purposely leave the border open?"

Maybe he'll admit the taxes aren't "historically low" as Obama claims. The taxes are in fact "too damn high." High taxes are killing entrepreneurship and jobs. If billion dollar corporations are so damaged by the 35% corporate tax rate they are forced to escape America with "inversions," then why isn't any politician admitting the 43.8% top individual tax rate is damaging taxpayers and killing even more jobs? Maybe the average taxpayer needs an inversion too! I'm betting Trump is the guy to say it.

Maybe he'll admit public schools are failing and dumbing-down our children. Your kids are not learning. They are not prepared to compete in the global marketplace. And the problem isn't money. We already spend too much on education. The problem is teachers unions and bad teachers who can't be fired.

Maybe he'll admit we have too many government employees and they are paid way too much. Their obscene pensions are bankrupting cities, counties, states and our entire federal government. Those pensions can never be paid in full. Someone needs to admit that. I'm betting Trump will be that guy.

Maybe he'll admit there are no quality jobs because of thousands of pages of new regulations . . . and Obamacare's 2.1 million words of regulations . . . and insane EPA mandates . . . and thousands of more "climate change" regulations coming down the pike.

Trump has already bravely pointed out that black unemployment is twice as high as white unemployment, thereby proving Obama has been a terrible president for the same black Americans he claims to support.

Maybe Trump will point out we have absolutely no plan to stop ISIS and they are winning.

Maybe Trump will point out that Obama's policies are bad for Israel and Jewish voters are crazy to support Obama.

Maybe, just maybe America is ready to hear the truth. And Donald Trump is just the man to tell it like it is.

Will Trump win the presidency? The jury is still out. But he will be a breath of fresh air. He will wake the voters up. A real-life Bullworth has arrived. Donald Trump will certainly make the 2016 race for president fun. *I can't wait.*[2]

Originally published for Fox News on June 16, 2015.

★★★

More proof I understand Donald Trump in a unique way . . .

My op-ed at Fox News from July 2, 2015 . . . two weeks after Trump declared he was running for president. At this very moment, Trump was embroiled in his "Hispanic racism" controversy. Yet, I boldly predicted he'd become president, as well as the greatest Hispanic and Black jobs creator ever. Who else made this exact prediction at any time before Trump's election? No one on the planet earth . . . and eventually he did create the lowest Black and Hispanic unemployment in history.

DONALD TRUMP—THE FIRST HISPANIC PRESIDENT

By Wayne Allyn Root

Funny headline, huh? Because of course Donald Trump isn't Hispanic. More importantly, the Hispanic world seems at war with Trump over his recent comments about "Mexico and Central America sending us their worst citizens, not their best." And corporate America is running away from "The Donald" and his controversial comments, fearing a Hispanic backlash.

So how can anyone even hint that Donald Trump could be a great president for Hispanics?

My father taught me, "Don't worry about what someone says, watch what they do." Donald Trump's words don't matter. Watch what he does. He is the only guy running for president who knows how to create millions of jobs and make billions of dollars.

So, let me ask you this- If Donald Trump offends Hispanics with his words . . . but turns around the US economy, creates millions of jobs for everyone, but especially for Hispanics . . . not just crappy low wage part-time jobs, but good paying full-time jobs . . . then isn't he a better president for Hispanics than someone who says nice things, compliments them all day long, but produces a crappy economy with no good jobs?

So, Donald Trump could yet become our "First Hispanic President" through deeds, not words. That's how Donald Trump can win the presidency- even after his inartfully-stated comments about Hispanics. You see what matters are deeds, not words. What everyone should worry about is real performance, not false promises to get your vote.

What exactly has Obama done for anyone, other than a world record for most government handouts ever? Is that what Hispanics want? Government checks in order to survive? Is that what black Americans want? Is that what women want? Is that what gays want?

Because despite all the flowery talk . . . and flowery promises . . . and propaganda about creating millions of jobs- the reality is . . . *there aren't any.* I have "boots on the ground" and I'm telling you there are no real jobs. Just crappy low wage part-time jobs that require food stamps and free healthcare just to survive.

Take Thursday's jobs report.[3] Part time jobs were up by 161,000, while full-time jobs were **down** by 349,000. More proof that all of Obama's flowery words won't get you a good job.

Maybe it's time to stop worrying about what someone says, but instead watch what he does.

Obama's fancy words have nothing to do with performance. That could be why the number of Americans on food stamps hit an all-time record under Obama.[4]

That could be why the number of Americans on welfare hit an all-time record under Obama.[5]

That could be why the poverty level under Obama broke a 50- year old record.[6]

That could be why as of Thursday's job report, more people are unemployed under Obama (93,626,000) than at any time in history.[7]

Obama talks big and flowery, but his actions result in a horrible miserable life for average Americans.

Look at the polls. Donald Trump is more popular than ever. Why?[8]

His words that offended Hispanics have excited and inspired millions of middle class native-born Americans who are thrilled someone is finally telling the truth (although perhaps a bit too harshly and stated inartfully) and putting American citizens first over foreigners or illegal aliens.

Donald Trump "the underdog" really can win the presidency. Americans love an underdog. NBC, Univision, Macy's and the PGA Golf Tour are all turning Trump into a lovable underdog.

Ironically, they are turning a billionaire into "the little guy fighting the big corporations."

Now Trump needs to "strike while the iron is hot." He needs to spend a huge sum of money (say $100 million) *fast* on a national TV advertising campaign. And what he should say is . . .

"I am the Hispanic president because I'll create more jobs for Hispanics than any president in history.

"And not just any jobs . . . good jobs that allow you to pay the bills and pay for health insurance and send your kids to college, without depending on government welfare to survive.

"I am the Hispanic president because I'll raise your income like no president in history.

"I am the Hispanic president because I'll raise your standard of living like no president in history.

"I am the Hispanic president because I offer opportunity, mobility and jobs, not welfare or food stamps.

"I will also become the African American president...and the female president . . . and the working man's president . . . and the gay president."

Because in the end what matters to every race and every group isn't flowery talk . . . or rhetoric . . . or propaganda . . . it's action. It's deeds. *It's jobs.*

And I'm the jobs president. Which is good for everyone. I'm the only person running for president who can deliver jobs, jobs and more jobs.

Say that and brand that theme into the minds of Americans—even Hispanic Americans—and Donald Trump can become the president of the United States.[9]

Originally published at Fox News on July 2, 2015.

***

Here is a commentary I wrote on December 17, 2015, after my *up-close and personal* Trump experience. I was his opening speaker days before at one of his first big rallies. I came away convinced Trump was going to win the presidency. And I figured out how he'd do it—with disaffected working-class and middle-class voters. Another bullseye.

EXPLAINING WHY TRUMP WILL BE PRESIDENT—UP CLOSE & PERSONAL

By Wayne Allyn Root

Donald Trump is going to be the next President. There's no stopping him now. Let me explain why— with an up close and personal Trump experience.

I am writing this column after a wild 48 hours. I returned late last night from the GOP Presidential debate, where I was a guest of the Trump campaign. The night before the debate, every GOP Presidential candidate was in Las Vegas for a rally or fundraiser with their fans. Each of them attracted 200 people here . . . 100 people there . . . 50 people here . . . 40 people there. Donald Trump on the other hand had a "small intimate gathering" for 5000 to 7000 fans!

And guess who had the honor and privilege of being the lead speaker and Master of Ceremonies? *Yours truly.*

There were only 2 speakers—Donald Trump and Wayne Allyn Root. I became the opening act for the man I believe is the next President of the United States. It was like opening for Mick Jagger and the

Rolling Stones. This wasn't a political rally . . . it was a rock concert!

That's why Trump will be the GOP nominee for President. Rubio attracts 200. Trump brings in thousands upon thousands . . . a sea of humanity. My guesstimate was between 5000 and 7000.

It's important to point out that this overflow Trump love-fest happened in Las Vegas…a town notorious for zero political interest. And that makes sense because my friends all over the country tell me about Trump rallies with 15,000 attendees . . . 18,000 . . . 20,000 . . . and more. That's what Trump brings to the table. No other GOP candidate can match this passion, intensity and love.

But here's the really interesting part. Since I was the center of the Trump universe that night, I can tell you about "the Trump phenomenon up close and personal." After the speeches by Donald and myself were over, I stayed for well over an hour taking photos with the fans. It was the experience of a lifetime. Hundreds of people said Donald and I delivered the two best political speeches they'd ever heard in their lives.

I used this opportunity to spend quality time and talk to the Trump supporters. I got to really *know* them. And what I found is the reason Donald will win the GOP nomination and eventually . . . the Presidency of the United States. The reason is Donald is the hero of working class Americans. Donald's fan base is plumbers, electricians, construction workers, taxi drivers, secretaries, hairdressers, cops, firemen and yes, in Las Vegas—casino workers. Donald is a man of the people.

I know it's ironic. It took a business mogul worth $10 billion to bring working class Americans to the GOP, but Donald did it. These people- almost to a man and woman- have either never voted before, or voted only Democrat in the past, or voted once for a Republican in their lives- Ronald Reagan.

These are Reagan Democrats and blue dog Democrats and independents. This is great news for the GOP. The media keeps saying the GOP needs to expand their tent. Well Donald Trump has done it.

While establishment types scream that Trump is "ruining the party" because he's scaring off and offending minorities, Mexicans, immigrants, Muslims, etc . . . the reality is none of those groups are coming in any significant number to any other GOP candidate. Not Cruz . . . not Rubio . . . not Bush . . . not anyone. They aren't expanding the tent by one person. They are TALKING about expanding the tent. But moderate Republicans who criticize and condemn Trump . . . and say nothing and believe in nothing . . . like Jeb Bush and John Kasich at this point have a tent with only their own wives, children and mother in it.

But Trump doesn't talk. He does it. Trump has expanded the base, not based on race or gender . . . but based on class. Why is that bad? I think expanding the tent is good, no matter who comes in. You mean that expanding the tent to include gays or women or blacks or Hispanics or Muslims is good . . . but expanding the tent to include millions of working class Americans isn't good?

Funny how when Democrats get those voters, the media says it's great. "Democrats care about the working man and woman" they say. But when Trump gets them it's suddenly a bad thing, a condemnation, a put down. I read articles across the world on Tuesday claiming that Trump attracted an "uneducated crowd" to the Vegas rally. The Boston Globe described the rally as "ugly." Really?

When they vote Democrat these same people are "middle America" "the working man" and "salt of the earth." But when they vote for a Republican the media insinuates they are low class and uneducated.

Well that mass of working class Americans is the Trump Army. This is a citizen revolution. I call it "The Trump Revolution of working class stiffs." Good people. Honest people. Hard working people. Salt of the earth. The foundation of America. Real Americans who don't want handouts, only a job and a fair chance for upward mobility. Real Americans who have never taken welfare in their lives. Real Americans who just want their kids to do better than themselves. Real Americans who pay into the system, not take out. God bless them.

And why are they so mad? Why is Trump their hero? Because he speaks for them. He speaks plain spoken, common sense, American values. He tells the raw honest truth. They are sick of the B.S. They are sick of being lied to. They are sick of political correctness. And most importantly, they are sick of being under attack.

The middle class is being murdered- and they see it, they feel it, they are living it. They are being destroyed, annihilated, slaughtered. They are being driven out of existence by Obama's socialist cabal and Hugo Chavez's Venezuela-like policies . . . combined with the establishment GOP's favoritism towards big business. Both parties have destroyed the working class and middle class of America. The government is actively working against the people. The system isn't fair. The deck is stacked against them. And they see one hero who speaks for them . . . and wants to fight for them- Donald Trump.

That's why Trump leads 41 to 14 in the latest polls. Think about that: 41 to 14. That's called an historic landslide. I witnessed first-hand what fuels this Trump phenomenon. He will combine traditional GOP voters (conservatives, Tea Party, pro-business, small business) with millions of non-traditional GOP voters- working class, union members and middle class Americans. Yes, I predict Trump will win the union vote. He will be endorsed by The Teamsters Union . . . by steel workers . . . by police and fire unions across this country.

Trump is a new kind of Republican. The kind I've been writing about for years. The kind I wrote about in my national bestseller—"The Murder of the Middle Class." The kind that forms a citizen revolution with the people that made America great—working men and women of the great American middle class. The kind of citizen revolution that fights hard and fights rough to take back this country.

On Monday night in Las Vegas, I saw it all, up close and personal. I was blessed to be a witness to a new citizen revolution. I am a witness to THE TRUMP REVOLUTION.

I am a witness to history.[10]

Originally published at TownHall on December 17, 2015.

***

Here's a piece I wrote about Trump in 2016 to keep religious Christians on board and motivated to fight hard for Trump. How true did these words turn out to be? Another bullseye.

A MESSAGE FOR CHRISTIANS ABOUT DONALD TRUMP

By Wayne Allyn Root

I am a Jew turned evangelical Christian. I am also a passionate supporter of Donald Trump.

I have a message for Christians who don't like Donald Trump: **"YOU'RE MISSING THE BOAT."**

Christians have Trump all wrong. God sends messages in many forms. You're just not listening. God is talking, but your eyes and ears are closed.

Here's a famous joke about God and how he talks to us.

"A deeply faithful Christian man is stuck on roof of home with massive flooding up to 2nd floor. A rescue rowboat comes. He says "No, I'm waiting for God. I've prayed and I know he's coming."

A 2nd rescue rowboat comes. Same response, "No, I'm waiting for God."

A 3rd rescue rowboat. Same response, "No, I'm waiting for God."

The water rises. The man drowns.

Now he's meeting God in heaven. The religious man says "Where were you God? I prayed. I was faithful. I asked you to save me. Why would you abandon me?"

God says, "Hey dummy, I sent you 3 rowboats. Are you blind?"

Did you ever consider Trump is our rowboat?

Maybe God is trying to tell us something important—that now is not the time for a "nice Christian guy" or a "gentleman" or a typical Republican powder puff. Maybe now is the time for a natural born killer, a ruthless fighter, a warrior.

Because right about now we need a miracle, or America is finished.

Maybe the rules of gentleman don't apply here. Maybe a gentleman and "all-around nice Christian" would lead us to slaughter.

Or do you want another Mitt Romney, Bob Dole, John McCain, Gerald Ford, John Boehner, Mitch McConnell, or Paul Ryan? Did any of them win? Did they lead the GOP to "the promised land?" Did they change the direction of America? No, because if you don't win, you have no say.

Paul Ryan couldn't even deliver his own state Wisconsin!

And as leader of the House, Paul Ryan rolls over to Obama like my dog rolls over for a scrap of food, or a steak bone. He's a useful idiot. Nice, but obedient.

I mean Paul Ryan . . . not my dog. My dog is actually a pretty good defender and loyal.

Maybe God is knocking on your door so loud, but you're not listening. Maybe God understands we need a "war leader" at this moment in time. Maybe God understands if we don't win this election, America is dead. It's over. The greatest nation in world history will be gone. Finished. Kaput. Adios.

And with one last breath, maybe what we need to save us at the last second, is someone *different*. Someone you haven't ever experienced before- because you weren't raised in rough and tumble New York where nothing good gets accomplished unless you're combative, aggressive, outrageous, on offense at all times, and maybe just a tad arrogant too.

Someone with a personality you've never seen on stage at your church.

Maybe, just maybe, being a nice gentlemanly Christian would not beat Hillary, and her billion dollars, and her best friends in the media, who will unleash the dogs of hell upon the GOP nominee (no matter how moderate or "gentlemanly" he is).

I guess you think God is only nice and gentlemanly. *Really?* Then you've missed the whole point of the Bible. When necessary God is a pretty tough guy. When necessary, God strikes with pain, death and destruction. When necessary, God inflicts vengeance.

Maybe you think God couldn't possibly be associated with someone like Trump. Trump is too vicious, rude and crude.

When we won WWII, was God "nice?" Were we gentlemanly when defeating Hitler? Were we gentlemanly when firebombing Germany? Were we gentlemanly when dropping atomic bombs on Japan? Is God ever "nice" on the battlefield? Or does he send us vicious SOB's like General George S. Patton, so the good guys can defeat evil?

It's pretty clear to me God sends unique people to be "war leaders." That's a different role than a pastor or church leader. God understands that.

Maybe God purposely sent Trump instead of the nice Republican powder puffs like Paul Ryan, or Mitt Romney, or John Kasich because he wants us to win.

And maybe it's time to re-define "nice." Maybe Mitt Romney and Paul Ryan aren't nice at all- because they led us to defeat. And losing again would mean the end of America. And God can't allow that.

Maybe Romney and Ryan mean well, but the road to hell is paved with good intentions.

Or maybe they're just jealous they had their chance and blew it. Maybe they'd rather help elect Hillary than allow a Trump victory that would make them look weak, feckless and incompetent.

I was reading the Bible this morning and I found the perfect verse that explains the success of Donald Trump . . ..

Isiah 40:30-31

Even the youths shall faint and be weary, And the young men shall utterly fall, But those who wait on the Lord Shall renew their strength; They shall mount up with wings like eagles, They shall run and not be weary, They shall walk and not faint.

It's almost like God created this verse for Donald Trump and this moment in history.

Trump is our energy. More energy than any candidate EVER. He took on the 16 best candidates in GOP history...all younger than him...all with better political credentials...and destroyed them with his energy. You mean that kind of energy in a 70-year old isn't inspired by God?

Trump renews our strength. Or does the all-time record turnout and all-time record votes for a GOP presidential primary candidate not define "strength?"

With Trump we mount up with wings like eagles. With Trump as our leader there is nothing we can't do. Any man that can build skyscrapers in Manhattan and vanquish 16 presidential opponents, while spending almost no money . . . can lead us to the heights of eagles.

With Trump we run, we are not weary. Just when we get tired of the fight against Obama, Hillary, big government, big business, big media, big unions . . . just when it all seems impossible to overcome the powerful forces of evil . . . along comes Trump to re-energize us.

Trump inspires us. Trump gives us hope. Trump gives us confidence in victory. Trump gives us just a touch of arrogance. Maybe God understands that's exactly what we need right at this late stage to save America.

So, let me repeat my message to Christians: **"YOU'RE MISSING THE BOAT."**

God is about miracles. We don't need a "nice guy" or a "gentleman" right now. It's the 4th quarter and we're losing 14-0. We need a miracle.

I believe Trump is our miracle. I believe Trump is our rowboat.

Except he's more like a *battleship!*

No one is saying Trump is perfect. No one is saying Trump is a perfect conservative. But he is a patriot. He is a warrior. He is a capitalist. He is the right man, at the right time.

Yes, he's a bit rude and crude and offensive. But that may make him the perfect warrior to save America, American exceptionalism, capitalism and Judeo-Christian values.

The choice should be easy for Christians. It's Trump . . . or it's the end of the America.[11]

Originally published at TownHall on June 24, 2016.

***

C'mon, admit it. These columns are uncanny.

No one, anywhere, has ever understood or made predictions about Trump this accurately.

This next column provides proof of *why* I understand Donald Trump so well. Because sometimes I feel like we're twins. I think we might be "brothers from another mother." I just came from the poor, short, Jewish side of the family.

Of course, the reason I understand Trump so well, is that I grew up studying and *modeling* Trump. I tried hard to *be like Trump*. As you can see in the following column (written the day before Trump's first-ever GOP presidential debate), I succeeded in channeling my *inner Trump*. After you finish this book, so will you.

As everyone now knows, Trump went on to win that first debate—just as I predicted. Another bullseye.

ADVICE TO DONALD TRUMP FROM A FELLOW BIG-MOUTHED NEW YORK BUSINESSMAN & POLITICIAN

By Wayne Allyn Root

I'm sure the top political consultants and experts in the world are all advising Donald Trump to "tone it down" and "act Presidential" at tonight's first GOP Presidential debate. They're telling him not to be a bomb thrower . . . not to offend anyone . . . not to be controversial . . . not to respond to fire with fire. They're telling him to play down his bigger-than-life personality. I'm sure they want him to play nice . . . and show his willingness to compromise.

This fellow New Yorker and big-mouthed businessman and politician has a response to that professional advice: *Tell them to go to hell!*

My advice should matter, simply because I've been there before. And my test run (on a much smaller scale) proves all the experts are wrong.

America wants a "Bullworth." America wants a politician that tells the truth . . . that tells it like it is . . .

38

that offends . . . that isn't afraid to hurt feelings . . . who tosses the dice . . . who throws caution and political correctness to the wind. In short Trump is wining because he is the opposite of what the experts want him to become.

Once upon a time, a bombastic, controversial, confident, outspoken, opinionated, tell-it-like-it-is, bigger than life New York businessman ran for President. He was a complete political newcomer and novice. He was an Ivy League educated, but with a cocky New York street fighter attitude. He knew business, the economy and how to create jobs. He despised the socialist policies of Obama and had the chutzpah and audacity to question Obama's college background. He warned America that Obama would badly damage the economy.

He was also known for his success in the gaming industry and reality television. He had no filter. His personality was that of a bull in a china shop. You might describe him as RELENTLESS. He ran his campaign almost by himself. He wrote his own policies and speeches.

And no one thought he had a snowball's chance in hell of winning his party's nomination.

No, I'm not talking about Donald Trump. The guy I'm talking about ran for the Libertarian Presidential nomination in 2008. **His name was Wayne Allyn Root.** *That's me.*

And despite no background or name recognition in national politics of any kind . . . I parlayed all of those Trump-like personality traits into the Libertarian Vice Presidential nomination.

Please understand I would never describe myself anything close to Donald Trump. Because there is only one Donald Trump. But the similarities really are quite funny (and maybe even a little bizarre).

I was told by experts, consultants, party insiders and delegates at our national convention that I was "too much." That I had to "tone it down." That my bigger than life, in-your-face New York personality would turn people off. That my political incorrectness and blunt, loud, emotional, opinionated style would offend Libertarians- who by nature are shy, humble and intellectual. Unless I changed, I had no chance. I heard that advice a thousand times or more.

They were all wrong. Are you listening Donald?

I decided to ignore all the advice. I decided to just be me. And it worked.

Yes, I did it on a much smaller scale (third party Presidential run), but I also started in a much worse position. I was not a household name. I didn't have a #1 rated reality TV show. I didn't have a billion dollars to spend. I was a successful entrepreneur, but not a billionaire business mogul. The experts gave me no chance to win the nomination. Zero. Zip. Nada.

But none of that mattered. The good news for Donald Trump is . . . . with all those similar Trump-like personality traits, I went out and won my party's Vice Presidential nomination in my first try at national political office.

I beat out a United States Senator (Mike Gravel) and came within a whisker of beating a 4-term US Congressman who led the impeachment of President Clinton (Bob Barr). Then I wound up on the Presidential ticket and joined Bob Barr the next day on Fox News (for the first time in my life). The experts were shocked.

What were the keys to my political success? They were pretty similar to what Trump is doing today. First, I was relentless. You might expect that from the author of "The Power of Relentless." I never let anyone stop me, slow me, or discourage me. I never worried about offending anyone- I just told the truth and let the chips fall where they may. I just kept fighting- no matter what the critics said . . . no matter what the media said . . . no matter what the experts and political consultants said. I was just me.

Secondly, just like Trump, my lifetime of experience in front of television cameras gave me a huge edge. Until the night of the Libertarian Presidential debate on national TV, I was a complete unknown. But I had an ace in the hole. I knew how to stand out in a crowd on national TV, because I'd done it my whole life- from host of five shows on CNBC (then known as Financial News Network), to star of countless TV infomercials, to Executive Producer and host of my own reality television show.

Then I went out and dominated the Libertarian presidential debate. I hit a grand slam. Like Trump, I shared the stage with a lot of candidates. With so many candidates on one stage, and so little time to make an impression, what matters most is memorable lines. No one remembers facts. They remember bigger-than-life personality. If the viewers remember a few funny or impactful one-liners, you won! And trust me, I delivered a bunch of zingers everyone was talking after the debate. And so, my life changed on that stage.

So, what will happen at that debate tonight in Cleveland? No one knows. Anything can happen on that stage. But I'll bet on Donald. He has great instincts. I'd bet when the camera lights go on, Donald will outshine the competition.

Understanding Trump's background and personality, I think it's more than likely he'll hit a grand slam with a few memorable lines everyone will be talking about the next day. Remember...Trump is the one with the advantage. There will be 9 nervous men who have never played for stakes this high on national TV. And they'll be up against a television showman and media superstar who loves the limelight, loves the media, loves TV cameras, loves pressure.

My prediction? Trump will produce the most memorable moments of the night. In a televised debate that's what matters. I'm betting Trump will cause conservatives watching at home to give standing ovations in front of their television sets. Once that happens with tens of millions watching, the narrative is set. This is Donald's chance to make a lasting impression. After that, even the media won't be able to discredit Trump. He'll be seen as a legitimate contender and potential future President of the United States.

How do I know? *Because I've seen it all before.*

So, here's my advice to Donald Trump . . ..

Ignore the experts and consultants. Go big, or go home! Be yourself. Be loud. Be colorful. Be politically incorrect. Speak the truth. Let it fly- and let the chips fall where they may. Be exactly what you were born to be- a bigger than life political disruptor. A breath of fresh air. A teller of the truth some people don't want to hear, but we all need to hear.

One more thing- be RELENTLESS. Never stop believing. Never stop fighting. Never worry about offending. Just tell the truth and be you.

I'll be rooting for you! So will much of America. Good luck Donald.[12]

Originally published at TownHall on August 6, 2015.

***

And here's the commentary I'm most proud of. Because I figured out Trump's best attribute. Above all else, the secret to Trump's one-in-a-billion success is that he is RELENTLESS! He never gives up, or gives in. He destroys all his critics, because he outlasts them.

DONALD TRUMP IS WINNING BECAUSE HE IS RELENTLESS!

By Wayne Allyn Root

The mainstream media doesn't get it. Intellectuals don't get it. Campaign consultants don't get it. John McCain doesn't get it. Maybe even Fox News anchors don't get it. How the heck is Donald Trump still in the GOP presidential race, let alone winning? How can he offend so many people, yet still sit at the top of the polls? The opinion makers and TV experts just don't understand his appeal.

Well I get it. I'm the author of a new book called, "The Power of RELENTLESS." The media and everyone that does business with me calls me "Mr. Relentless." Well I've finally found someone more relentless than me- Donald Trump. He breaks the mold. If Hollywood central casting created a "prototype" for relentless, it would be "The Donald."

My book is about winning at anything. Make no mistake about i—it's a war out there. No matter your goals or industry you're in—it's a dog eat dog competition. The broken and battered bodies lie all over the battlefield. Trust me, the weak shall never inherit the earth. My book is about the fact you've got to be tough and never give in, or give up. You've got to wear blinders and attack relentlessly. You've got to be on offense 24/7.

You can never let an obstacle slow you down. You just put your head down and attack like a bull in a china shop. You go over it, or under it, or around it, or you run right through the brick wall.

That relentless mindset is more important to success than any other factor. Relentless is more important than your IQ, your looks, your expertise, or your college degree. They don't teach it in college. But all the great leaders have it. What's the difference between a relentless billionaire and a pitbull? The pitbull *eventually* lets go!

This *"Power of RELENTLESS"* philosophy describes Donald Trump to a T. He's not just a bull in a china shop. He's a human energizer bunny- you can hit him, knock him down, blindside him, break his knees with a lead pipe. But he just keeps getting up. He's Freddie Kruger in "Nightmare on Elm Street." He's Slyvester Stallone in Rocky. He's a real-life wack-a-mole.

Donald has survived 4 business bankruptcies and come back stronger than ever. He's now worth somewhere between $4.5 billion (according to Forbes) and $10 billion (according to his FEC filing). Instead of asking during the debates about his record of bankruptcies, I think the better question would have been, "Mr. Trump, can you explain to the audience how you keep making miraculous comebacks? How you turn failures into an even bigger net worth? All of America is fascinated. In this terrible Obama economy, we all need to know your secret!"

The experts said he'd never survive his comments about Hispanics or Mexico. He took the lead.

They said he'd never survive his comments about John McCain. He expanded his lead.

Republican leaders said Trump didn't belong on the debate stage. Yet because of Trump, 24 million Americans tuned in. The "Trump Debate" was the most watched non-sports event in cable television history.[13]

The experts and focus groups I watched after Thursday's debate said he was dead after his Rosie

O'Donnell remarks and confrontation with Megyn Kelly of Fox News during the debate. Yet the latest NBC News poll post-debate out on Sunday shows Trump still up by just about 2 to 1.[14]

Since the debate, Trump has been accused of what many are calling distasteful remarks about Megan Kelly. I agree they were ill-advised. Yet Donald has African American women coming to his defense![15]

I hear Republican leaders calling for him to drop out of the race. They're all kidding themselves.

Donald Trump at this point is the world's biggest reality show. He's the most fascinating character ever on our TV screens. He's his own country code. He makes Bruce/Caitlyn Jenner seem boring. The more offensive and outrageous his comments, the more his legend grows. He may be the definition of "too big to fail."

Relentless people like Donald Trump can't be stopped or even slowed. They just keep fighting and moving forward relentlessly. That's how you win a war- inch by grueling inch. That's how you win a marathon- one step at a time. You put enough steps together and pretty soon you've defied the odds and you've run 30 miles. That's how you eat an elephant- one bite at a time. That's *"The Power of RELENTLESS."* Donald Trump understands it, his critics don't.

Times have changed. Traditional politicians are the dinosaurs. They are taxi drivers who paid $100,000 for taxi medallions. Donald Trump is Uber, who paid nothing, has no license and has taken away all their customers. The taxi drivers don't understand what's happened and why.

I checked in with an old friend this weekend. She is an intelligent, sophisticated, educated, beautiful, brilliant, female business owner- a rare Republican living in Manhattan. I wanted to get her read on Trump. Here is the response I got:

"I still feel the same. Sure, he could have kept his cool a bit more. But at the end of the day this country is now DRIVEN by disruptive technologies and innovations and in a world where Kim Kardashian's ass has its own fan club and Bruce Jenner in a Diane Von Furstenberg gown is a "valiant and brave sports hero," there is only ONE candidate who is in tune with the zeitgeist-Trump. The 'Same ole same ole' ain't gonna cut the mustard. The times they have 'a changed."

Here is my sum up of the appeal of Donald Trump:

He is a relentless disruptor and agitator.

He is a relentless rebel and renegade.

He is a relentless bad-ass.

He is relentlessly combative.

He has a relentless big mouth.

He is relentlessly offensive.

He is relentlessly controversial.

He is relentlessly politically incorrect.

He is relentlessly stubborn.

He is a relentless street fighter.

He relentlessly believes in himself, his talents, his gut instincts, his country, American exceptionalism, and capitalism.

And that's enough for millions of American patriots who've had it with "politics as usual."

There's only one problem. I thought I was "The King of Relentless." I wrote the book on the subject. I have the web site: RelentlessROOT.com. I thought I had the market cornered. That damn Donald Trump. He wins again.

Has Trump wounded himself? Sure. And he'll probably do it again. But no one should be surprised if we're all calling him "Mr. President" 18 months from now.[16]

Published at Breitbart News on August 10, 2015.

***

That's "The Power of RELENTLESS."

What is Donald J. Trump if not relentless? After four years as president, what other word best describes him? I hit another bullseye.

In another article in 2016, I branded Trump as the new Ronald Reagan of the GOP. I was on the money!

TRUMP: WELCOME BACK RONALD REAGAN!

By Wayne Allyn Root

I've argued for a year now that Donald Trump is our Reagan. That in almost every way, *Trump is Reagan, Part Deux*.

It was a lonely argument for most of the past 12 months. Not so much anymore. Donald Trump just delivered the greatest Republican Presidential address since Reagan.

Trump channeled Reagan in every way on Thursday night, while laying out his case for "making America great again."

Trump was a handsome, dynamic, charismatic, passionate, high-energy, master showman and entertainer- just like Reagan.

Trump spoke in plain, simple, straight-forward terms directly to average Americans, not over their heads- just like Reagan.

Trump appealed to working class and middle class Americans aka "The Silent Majority"- just like Reagan.

Trump mentioned specific blue-collar occupations he loves- steelworkers, carpenters, bricklayers, electricians, coal miners- just like Reagan.

Trump appealed to the values of the great American middle class as "The Law and Order President" multiple times- just like Reagan.

Trump appealed to middle class white America by promising "I will restore law and order." He pointed out dramatic increases in violent crime, drugs, inner city chaos, and attacks on police and promised to end it all- just like Reagan.

Trump defended law enforcement, military and vets- just like Reagan.

Trump declared his love for America, American exceptionalism and "America First"- just like Reagan.

Trump talked of his love for "believers, dreamers and strivers" vs. the kind of people he dislikes: negative people, critics, cynics and those who doubt the greatness of America- just like Reagan.

The heart of Trump's speech was about using a combination of massive tax cuts and killing regulation to return America to prosperity- just like Reagan.

Trump spoke of his responsibility as President- to defend and protect American citizens, not foreigners- just like Reagan.

Trump promised "I AM YOUR VOICE." Trump spoke of a system rigged against average Americans. He explained why he got into politics- to stop a system "where powerful people can beat up people who can't defend themselves." He was channeling Reagan.

Trump talked of "the dignity of working people"- just like Reagan.

Trump singled out evangelical Christians as his base and the heart of his support- just like Reagan.

Trump spent the night speaking specifically to a nation of Christians, working people, gun owners, military, police, vets, coal miners, hard hats and patriots with respect for the Constitution- he recreated _the exact_ Reagan coalition.

Trump singled out his love and support of Israel- just like Reagan.

Trump painted a picture of prosperity by promising "to make America rich again"- the same theme as Reagan.

And of course his slogan- "Make America Great Again" was Reagan's exact slogan in 1980.

But here's what is most important moving forward...

Trump must remind America of "The Reagan Miracle." It happened over 36 years ago. Most Americans have either forgotten, or weren't even born yet, or came from different countries. They weren't here. They don't know. The biased liberal media is desperate to keep them in the dark and ignorant.

Trump must point out that all Reagan did to turn the misery, malaise and depression of Jimmy Carter into the greatest economic recovery and expansion in world history was to dramatically cut taxes and regulations. *That's it*. That's all it took. It's the exact same plan as Trump (with a wall thrown in).

Make sure every American knows the Reagan record. Make sure they know Trump is Reagan, Part Deux. Repeat this magical Reagan record again and again, from now through November.

Remind Americans that Reagan's low taxes and rollback of regulations produced an era of prosperity unlike anything in history . . ..

Reagan exploded the economy with $30 trillion in goods and services created.

Net assets like stocks and real estate went up by $5 trillion- an increase of a remarkable 50%.

Reagan's low tax policies created nearly 20 million jobs in a short span, increasing US employment by a remarkable 20%.

From 1981-89 GDP per capita rose by 23%- the greatest increase in the history of America.

In one year alone the GDP increased by 6.8%- the largest increase in *50 years.*

In only 7 years the economy grew by a staggering one third.

The value of the stock market TRIPLED.

Inflation was 13.5% when Reagan took office . . . by 1983 it was 3.2%

The number of Americans earning $1 million dollars a year went up a staggering 8 times!

The economic boom lasted 92 consecutive months-the longest peacetime boom in world history. *It shattered the previous record of 58 months by almost 60%.*

Folks that is the definition of OPPORTUNITY, PROSPERITY, MOBILITY AND FREEDOM

Reagan created FREEDOM by the ton.

All it took to create the "Reagan Miracle" was lower taxes and less government regulation and interference. It's really that simple.

Trump is our new Reagan in every way.[17]

Originally published at Breitbart on July 22, 2016.

***

I was alone in that Reagan-Trump comparison in the early days of Trump's campaign. I made the comparison in hundreds of speeches and columns from the moment Trump came down that famous Trump Tower escalator. People thought I was stark raving mad. Many establishment Republicans were angry that I was "damaging the memory of Reagan." I turned out to be 100% right. Trump not only won and revitalized the GOP—just like Reagan, but he also used a *Reagan-esque* tax plan to produce the greatest economy since . . . Reagan.

I hope you get the picture now. I understand Donald Trump like no one else in the world, simply because I've spent my whole adult life studying and modeling him and his TRUMP RULES. <u>So can you.</u> That's what this book is dedicated to—teaching anyone how to *be like Trump.*

And finally . . .

Only days after Trump's election in 2016, I wrote the following commentary at Fox News. It was uncanny in its future accuracy. Trump has indeed become America's most pro-Israel president, and the greatest friend of the Jewish people, EVER. How did I know? That's the point of this book. I have *Trump's number.* I understand the man and what makes him tick. That's precisely why you are in the right place, at the right time with the TRUMP RULES.

TRUMP IS HEADED TO THE WHITE HOUSE: DID WE JUST ELECT OUR FIRST JEWISH PRESIDENT?

By Wayne Allyn Root

Just as Bill Clinton wasn't black, but he was called "America's first black president . . . .

I believe Donald Trump should be called "America's first Jewish president."

I should know. I'm an Ivy League-educated Jewish kid from New York.

Trust me, Donald Trump is as close as you can come to being our first Jewish president.

The very unique traits that have made him a billionaire and now President of the United States are as Jewish as you can get!

Let me prove Donald is our first Jewish president...

Donald is a lifelong New York businessman, who made his fortune in real estate. You can't get more Jewish than that.

Well actually you can. His winter home Mar-a-Lago is on the East Coast of South Florida.

When he bought his Florida home and turned it into a popular and exclusive country club, he specifically opened the membership up to Jews. Mar-a-Lago was the first club that ever allowed Jews in Palm Beach. Donald changed the customs of the most-wealthy, WASPY town in America to favor Jews.

Donald is family-oriented and clearly loves and dotes on all his children. He is bursting with pride at his children's success. That could be the most Jewish trait of all. To Jews, family and children are everything.

Donald is your typical Jewish parent. Donald's children are all Ivy League graduates- just like my daughter who recently graduated Magna cum Laude from Harvard.

Donald's daughter Ivanka has converted to orthodox Judaism. That makes Donald the first president in the history of America with orthodox Jewish grandkids.

Donald is handing his business over to his children. That is the goal of every Jewish businessman in history.

Donald is the most hardworking businessman I've ever met. That is a trait handed down to me by my Yiddish grandfather. I believe it is the main reason for the success of the Jewish people. I've been a workaholic, just like Donald, my entire life.

Donald has never worked for others. He owns all of his own businesses. My Jewish butcher father David Root taught me that 2 things mattered above all else in life- being a good father and always owning your own business.

Donald has more chutzpah than anyone I've ever met in my life. Chutzpah is a unique word that comes from the Yiddish language. It means you are so ambitious, you aim so high that people think you're nuts. Donald aims higher than anyone who has ever lived. Now he's President of the United States!

Donald is the most relentless person I've ever met. Relentless is a very uniquely Jewish trait. Jews are relentless fighters—we have survived thousands of years of hate, discrimination, persecution, robbery, slavery and murder. We haven't just survived... we have *thrived!* I wrote the book, "The Power of RELENTLESS." Of course it was endorsed by Mr. Relentless himself, Donald Trump.

Donald is a big success in Hollywood as a TV producer. He joins an exclusive club that is predominantly Jewish. I should know. I have created, Executive Produced and hosted hit TV shows my entire adult life.

Donald is a bigger-than-life personality. He has dynamic communication skills. He's very charismatic, opinionated, ambitious, aggressive, combative, committed and passionate about his ideas and beliefs. He says whatever is on his mind, even if it offends. All of those are traits I've seen in my Jewish friends, relatives and business partners for my entire life.

Many of Donald's political views and policies are tailor-made for Jews. He could be the most pro-Israel president in history. Donald will always stand with the Jews of Israel.

How strong are Donald's bonds to Israel? He was the Grand Marshal of the annual "Salute to Israel" parade.

The Jewish National Fund awarded Donald the "Tree of Life" award for his lifetime of support for the Jewish people and the state of Israel.

Jewish Week found that Donald has given generously for many years to Jewish charities. A professor of "American Jewish History" calls Trump's charitable giving to Jewish causes "impressive" and clearly out of the ordinary for a non-Jew.[18]

His stance on "extreme vetting" and stopping the mass importation of Muslim refugees should be welcomed and enthusiastically embraced by every American Jew. Donald's goal is the same as mine-keeping people out of our country who could commit acts of terrorism and who have an unnatural hatred and prejudice toward Jews.

One of Donald's first priorities as president is to re-negotiate the Iran deal- perhaps the worst treaty ever negotiated in US history and a danger to Israel's future survival.

Donald is the strongest anti-terrorism president possible. He understands our enemy is radical Islam. He uses the words "Islamic extremist" in the same sentence. That alone makes Donald the best friend Jews ever had.

Amazingly, who was the very first world leader to talk to Donald after his victory? Benjamin Netanyahu of Israel. Coincidence?

Speaking of best friends, many of Donald's friends, business partners, executives at the Trump organization, country club members at Maralago and trusted lawyers and advisers are Jewish. No US president has ever in history been surrounded by so many Jewish friends and advisors.

Trust me, by almost every possible measurement, we've just elected our first Jewish president.[19]

Originally published at Fox News on November 20, 2016.

***

That commentary was published by Fox News only days after Trump won the 2016 election. Was my analysis on the money, or what?

In this editorial, twelve days after his election, I predicted Trump would be the most pro-Israel US president in history. There is no question that he is. *It's not even close.*

Trump made the bold decision to move the US Embassy to

Jerusalem. Then he actually did it! Simply amazing. Previous Presidents had promised to do so, but no other President had the guts to actually make the move. Critics predicted doom: riots, anarchy, terror attacks in the aftermath. What was the response? Crickets. Nothing. Zero. Trump pulled it off! Trump was right, *again.*

And, he did it in a very Jewish way. A racial slur accuses Jews of being "tight with our money." The truth is, we are! Or perhaps, more precisely, we are logical and rational with how we spend money and want to make sure we get a fair deal and a *bang for our buck.*

When his advisors told President Trump it would cost $4 billion and four years to build an embassy in Jerusalem, President Trump told them to save the money and use an existing building. The embassy opened, not four years later, but within a few months. The remodeling of an existing building cost less than $1 million. That one decision just saved American taxpayers just about FOUR BILLION DOLLARS!

Trump had the United States withdraw from the United Nations Human Rights Council for being too negative towards Israel. This decision was long overdue, but no other US President has ever had the chutzpah to do it.

Trump unconditionally supported Israeli military operations against Iranian forces in Syria. Things are black and white in Trump's world, there's no gray. Israel is the good guy with the white hat. Bravo.

I predicted Trump would kill the Iran deal. *He did.* How did that hurt the USA? It didn't.

As I write this book, Iran's economy is collapsing and could result in regime change. Or perhaps the same regime might develop a little nicer attitude towards the USA. How great would that be for America and the world? Trump was right, *again.*

I predicted Trump would implement "extreme vetting" to keep our borders safe from terrorists and malcontents. He has.

★ ★ ★

And, although his distractors called it the "Muslim Travel Ban," in fact it banned ALL persons from seven dangerous, terror-riddled countries from entering the United States. That they were primarily Muslim countries was not because of the religion practiced in those countries, but rather based on the fact that those were the countries from which recent history and military intelligence predicted terrorists were most likely to come.

Trump is so pro-Israel, he makes all other presidents in US history seem anti-Israel. Previous Presidents were careful not to overly show bias either against or towards Israel. (Well, OK, on occasion Obama did let his hatred of Israel show through big time.) But Trump? He has no interest in *holding back*. He sees Israel as America's best friend and is unafraid of openly taking sides.

My Fox News prediction worked out pretty darn well, don't you think? President Trump is clearly "America's First Jewish President."

Am I tuned into Trump? Do I have Trump's number? Here comes the meat of this book. So now you know. You are in the right place, at the right time. I understand Trump like no one else in the world. Read the rest of this book. Focus, study, listen, learn, and model the TRUMP RULES. They will change your life.

SECTION II

Trump Rules: The Top 10

★ ★ ★ ★ ★ ★

—————— CHAPTER FOUR ——————

TRUMP RULE #1
Always #WINNING

The secret to President Donald J. Trump's remarkable, one-in-a-billion success starts with winning. Or as the younger generation calls it: **#WINNING.**

Trump is a winner. He believes in results and performance . . . he believes in the bottom line! He sets the bar high. He believes winning is everything. He doesn't worry about political correctness. He doesn't worry about who he offends. He doesn't spare feelings. He wants results. Everything else is BS. With that attitude, Trump transformed the GOP from a party of habitual losers to nonstop winners. Because . . .

Winning is contagious.

Before Trump arrived on the scene, the GOP had lost four out of the last six presidential races, and Hillary was considered a lock to defeat any GOP presidential candidate in 2016. The GOP was on the verge of losing five of seven presidential races. The experts in the media repeated, again and again, the theme that the GOP had virtually no path to electoral victory. Republicans were being consigned to the garbage heap of history as the perennial loser in national campaigns for the rest of all time. Even worse, the GOP had a losers' attitude, even in the places they were still winning—the House and Senate. During Obama's eight years as president, the GOP capitulated on almost everything Obama wanted. They rolled over quicker than a dog in heat under the leadership of people like John Boehner, Paul Ryan and Mitch McConnell—all cut from the same mode: Boring, white, country club males who had no clue how to fight relentlessly. All they knew how to do was behave nicely and roll over like a friendly dog.

They all had country-club manners, with a losers' attitude, and terrible, if not nonexistent, negotiating skills. In the heat of battle, the GOP ran up the white flag more often than France. To them, compromising meant agreeing with whatever the Democrats wanted. What's the point of winning, if you lose even when you win?

This isn't second guessing, hindsight, or even back seat driving. I'm on record. I talked about this "GOP Losers Complex" repeatedly in my books, *The Murder of the Middle Class: How to Save Yourself and Your Family from the Criminal Conspiracy of the Century*, *The Ultimate Obama Survival Guide: How to Survive, Thrive, and Prosper During Obamageddon*, *Angry White Male: How the Donald Trump Phenomenon is Changing America—and What We Can All Do to Save the Middle Class*, and *The Conscience of a Libertarian: Empowering the Citizen Revolution with God, Guns, Gold and Tax Cuts*. The GOP was a party of losers, wandering hopelessly in the desert. I was embarrassed to be a part of such a group of sad sacks, with such a lousy attitude, no confidence, no courage, no vision, no fight, and always setting the bar as low as possible.

Pre-Trump, the GOP was a beaten down party with no hope of actually lowering taxes, killing regulations, gutting Obamacare, building the wall, securing our borders, fighting back against climate change hysteria, or accomplishing anything else they claimed to support. The pre-Trump GOP was afraid of their own shadow. They did not know how to win.

Then along came Donald J. Trump.

Everything changed. Trump campaigned, talking about winning nonstop. It's all he talked about at campaign rallies. I should know. I was opening or keynote speaker at every Trump presidential event in Las Vegas in 2015 and 2016. After delivering my own opening barn-burner speech, I had a front-row seat to listen to the man himself. And, what he talked about more than anything else, was winning.

Trump repeated the word and theme about winning more than any candidate in history. It was clear that winning was what Trump thought about constantly. It was his scorecard. You win or you lose. To Trump, it is this simple—you are a winner or you are a loser. Donald J. Trump had never been a loser in his entire life. He set the bar high. He stated his lofty goals out loud. He painted a picture and made all of us think about what winning looked like. He promised his supporters, "We're going to win so much, you're going to get *tired* of winning." That, along with "Make America Great Again," became his signature lines.

The picture he painted was of a world where Republicans do nothing but win. Where Republicans actually achieve their lofty goals. Where Republican politicians don't just promise, they deliver. Where we don't settle, capitulate, or compromise by simply giving in. Where we don't feel happy to get a few crumbs at the table. He made us believe that winning isn't just possible, it is our *right*. And, the reason it's our right is because we are patriots fighting side by side with him for the very survival of the greatest country in world history. When Trump was talking, all you wanted to do was chant, "USA, USA, USA!"

Trump made us actually see and feel the victories we could achieve. Not just the election victory (which, until then, no one thought was possible), but the specific list of issues we'd win on after winning the election. *Then, he made it happen*—almost exactly as scripted.

Trump reminds me of one of my other heroes, **George Steinbrenner.** Another tough-as-nails, high-profile New York billionaire businessman with a *winning is everything* attitude. It's only a guess, but I'm willing to bet Trump watched and learned from Steinbrenner.

Like Trump, Steinbrenner was addicted to winning . . . to fighting publicly . . . to kicking ass . . . to a love of dog-eat-dog competition . . . and to results. Like Trump, either you won and produced positive results for Steinbrenner, or *you're fired!* Simple. Like Trump, George did not accept losing, or excuses. It was win first place or you're a loser. Period.

And like Trump, Steinbrenner proved this philosophy works. Not always. No one wins every battle. But more often than not, aiming for victory, clearly defining victory, clearly seeing victory before it happens, settling for nothing but victory, and making sure everyone around you knows there are no excuses, there is no other choice but victory; and this leads to amazing #WINNING.

Let's take a quick look at the George Steinbrenner story. The similarities are amazing. The results are the same—winning at a level unimaginable to mere mortals who don't understand the mindset of a Trump or a Steinbrenner.

Steinbrenner bought the New York Yankees in 1973 from CBS. They had become the laughing stock of baseball. The team did nothing but lose. The team had no stars. The cupboard was bare. The players had a lousy attitude, a look of defeat. The future looked bleak. Steinbrenner paid $8.7 million for the Yankees.

Over the next thirty-seven years of Steinbrenner's ownership and leadership, the Yankees became the winningest sports franchise in history. They made it to eleven World Series (one almost every three years of Steinbrenner's reign); won seven World Championships (almost one every five years); won the most games in all of baseball during those thirty-seven years; enjoyed twenty-one consecutive winning seasons (something no team had every done before, and will most likely never do again); and, from 1995 to 2013, made the playoffs seventeen times in those nineteen seasons.

If winning is everything, Steinbrenner is perhaps the greatest winner in the history of sports.

But, for Steinbrenner, it was about more, much more, than just winning baseball games. It was about why you were winning. It was about winning by being excellent, by being the best, and by doing your best—*or you're fired*. Sound familiar?

Like it or not, Steinbrenner judged his own *success* on accumulating wealth—on who made the most money. And at that art form, he excelled like few in history. Steinbrenner's passion for winning made everyone around him better, more successful, and wealthy beyond their wildest dreams.

His drive to be the best made him one of the wealthiest men on the planet. Sound familiar?

It made his two sons wealthy. Sound familiar?

It made his business partners in the New York Yankees wealthy.

It made his players wealthy—because he was always willing to pay top dollar to get the best players. He recognized *superstars* were the key to winning. You have to pay big money for *superstars*. Steinbrenner spared no expense. He literally invented free agency— paying unheard-of money to the first-ever free agent, Jim "Catfish" Hunter. He had, by far, the biggest payroll in baseball history. One player (A-Rod) made more money annually than the entire San Diego Padres team!

Steinbrenner was willing to do and pay whatever it took to achieve excellence and greatness. To guarantee excellence. Sound familiar?

Steinbrenner was creative in finding new and unique ways to make zillions of dollars. Sound familiar?

He made his fellow baseball owners rich beyond their wildest imagination. He invented a new kind of revenue stream—his own Yankees TV network called *YES*. Notice the exclamation point in the name? To make money, Steinbrenner knew you have to be a salesman. Sound familiar?

He knew that even if you have an excellent product, it has to be hyped and glorified to get people excited and supportive. Sound familiar?

And Steinbrenner made the other owners rich because he understood the value of self-promotion and celebrity. His New York Yankees always led Major League Baseball in road ticket sales (by a mile). The Yankees packed stadiums across America. Why? He was a great self-promoter. He knew how to produce controversial media headlines. He always wanted his name on the front page of newspapers. He always wanted people talking about him or his antics at the watercooler the next morning. He had a huge ego and was never shy about bragging about his accomplishments. He loved being both loved and hated. He enjoyed stirring up crisis, chaos, and controversy. Sound familiar?

He understood the value of *free media*. You can either spend $100 million on advertising to make yourself famous, or let the media make you famous with $100 million worth of free headlines. He knew nonstop media headlines resulted in ticket sales and record TV ratings. Sound familiar?

Steinbrenner was so good, he even won in death! He managed to die in the calendar year 2010, the only year in history without a *death tax*. His children inherited his multi-billion estate and didn't owe one cent in taxes. Steinbrenner figured out a way to beat the IRS. Now that's my definition of #WINNING with an exclamation point!

Oh, and at the time of Steinbrenner's death, experts estimated the New York Yankees were worth between $2 and $3 billion. Remember he bought them for $8.7 million. Not a bad return on investment!

What exactly was Steinbrenner's life attitude and philosophy? We don't have to guess. As one of my heroes, I've studied his life extensively. I combed through hundreds of media stories and interviews. I'll use Steinbrenner's exact words:

- Winning is <u>everything</u>.
- Being #2 is worthless, meaningless, and anonymous.
- Lead, follow, or get out of the way.
- The reason I get up in the morning is . . . to WIN.
- When I die, what do I want people to remember about me? That I never stopped fighting and trying to win.

Sound familiar?

As if that record of remarkable success wasn't enough, let me give you an exhibit B. As a "hobby," and to prove his philosophy: *winning is everything*, works absolutely anywhere, Steinbrenner agreed to apply his philosophy to American athletes competing in the US Winter Olympic Games.

Steinbrenner took over as the boss after the disastrous 1988 Calgary Olympics. The USA had just suffered our worst performance in history, winning an embarrassing total of six medals, only two gold.

Steinbrenner agreed to become vice chairman of the US Winter Olympic Team. He headed the Steinbrenner Commission—which ripped the team to shreds for the 1988 results and challenged the US Olympic Committee to place an increased emphasis, not just on competing, but on winning. Steinbrenner's message was simple. If you don't aim to win, you won't. If you are going to win, it must be your goal, your focus, your obsession. If our athletes are to win, they need to think about winning 24/7.

There's that concept again—#WINNING.

Steinbrenner brought his trademark discipline, confidence, chutzpah, goal of *winning is everything*, and of course, *no excuses*. He also brought his philosophy of doing and spending whatever it takes to produce a championship winner. His *Steinbrenner Commission* demanded the US Olympic team change the way it did business. A major recommendation was to spend whatever it took to train athletes and produce winners. Steinbrenner argued we could not produce world-class winners unless we treated and trained our athletes in a world-class way.

Steinbrenner personally supported dozens of athletes, providing jobs and funding for their training. He funded the training of thirteen-year-old Michelle Kwan, who went on to become the most decorated figure skater in history. A little known fact is that he even went so far as to pay the medical school tuition for Ron Karnaugh, a US Olympic athlete whose father died of a heart attack during his Olympic opening ceremony. Karnaugh is a doctor today because of Steinbrenner.

Born on the 4th of July, Steinbrenner was an unabashedly "America First" leader at all times. He lived and breathed America, American exceptionalism, and Team USA. America and its representatives always had to lead, win, and be number one. Sound familiar?

Steinbrenner's work culminated with the 2010 Winter Olympics in Vancouver. Team USA won a remarkable 37 medals, the most medals of any country ever in the *history* of the Winter Olympics.

We achieved that remarkable feat in a specific sport (winter sports) where America had never in history competed well. Even Canada, the motivated home country that lives and breathes winter sports collected only twenty-six medals.

Every Olympic leader and executive agreed that this remarkable and unprecedented turnaround happened because of the leadership and winning attitude of George Steinbrenner. From the depths of Olympic despair, this journey started on the day he took over, with the force of his energy and personality. From that day forward, he determined Team USA would focus on winning. Nothing else mattered to George Steinbrenner. Look at the results.

Sound familiar? Steinbrenner's game plan was the playbook for Donald Trump's life . . . business career . . . presidential campaign . . . and certainly his presidency.

Since his election, Democrats have been publicly losing their minds, suffering a complete, hysterical meltdown of epic proportions. Why are the Dems so hysterical, bitter, vicious, and violent? Why have they succumbed to this true mental illness known as "Trump Derangement Syndrome"? Because Democrats have never seen a GOP winner like President Trump in their lives.

Trump is not a traditional or typical politician. He's a business person, a true leader, a doer, a man of action. He's pragmatic and practical. He sees a problem and he fixes it. He knows how to get things done. He knows how to win. Unlike politicians, he accepts no gray area. He doesn't fall short and take credit. He either wins or loses. No one in politics has ever thought this way.

Trump as president has enjoyed so many victories it has left Democrats' heads spinning. This is why they have lost their minds. It isn't fun to lose again and again. It isn't fun to be whacked around like a Whac-A-Mole on a daily basis.

This chapter on winning came directly from a commentary I wrote about Trump's favorite pastime—#Winning. The very week I was busy writing that commentary, Trump enjoyed an unprecedented string of Supreme Court victories—including the Trump Travel Ban, Texas GOP re-districting, the protection of rights for Christians involving bakery owners who refused to bake a specialized cake for a gay wedding, the protection of rights for anti-abortion clinics, and the protection of rights for non-union members who no longer have to pay union dues. Then came Justice Kennedy's retirement—giving Trump a once-in-a-lifetime opportunity to remake the Supreme Court, leaving true constitutional conservatives in control for decades to come.

It was the #WINNING week of a lifetime. Coincidence? Nope. When you make winning your goal . . . when you see it, feel it, smell it, obsess on it 24/7, good things tend to happen.

Add in the booming economy, booming GDP, a tidal wave of high-paying jobs, a manufacturing renaissance that no one saw coming except Trump, record-setting tax cuts, all-time record regulation cuts, Obamacare gutted, new approvals for small businesses to buy health insurance across state lines, dramatically lower welfare and food stamp use, work requirements for welfare, a slew of new rules that brought illegal border crossings to a standstill, progress on funding and building the wall, ISIS all-but-defeated in record time, killing the Paris Climate Change Accord . . . and the TPP (Trans Pacific Partnership) . . . and the terrible Iran deal, winning the first round of the trade war with China, moving our US-Israeli Embassy to Jerusalem, and it's quite the list. Those were all achieved in just Trump's first three years on the job. Before COVID-19 hit and changed everything.

Winning came in waves. But I can assure you none of Trump's supporters ever got bored of winning.

At this same moment in time, we learned Trump's approval ratings were far higher than Obama's at the same point in his presidency (at Rasmussen, the most accurate pollster). We have learned Trump's approval ratings were above ninety percent among Republicans—the second highest in history, and higher among members of his own party than Obama, Reagan, or JFK ever achieved. Again, all of this was pre COVID-19.

We learned that approval for the direction of our country was the highest in twelve years and among the highest in history. And Trump's approval ratings from both small business owners and manufacturers were both the highest in history. And corporate money was flowing back into America like never before in history— over $300 billion in just the first quarter of 2018. Again, all of these remarkable achievements were pre COVID-19.

And President Trump formed *Space Force* as our sixth branch of the military, aiming NASA for future Moon and Mars trips. Isn't this exactly what you'd expect from someone who aims high and expects to always be number one?

Those of us who truly love America and believe in making it great again, will tell you those first three years of Trump's first term were the greatest experience of our lives. And Trump achieved all that while under a nonstop media barrage of negativity and unprecedented vicious attacks, and while facing impeachment. The man is super human. He certainly defines #Winning.

It should be noted that at the end of 2017, *before* most of this winning took place, the Heritage Foundation rated Trump as the most successful first-year conservative president ever—better even than my hero Ronald Reagan. In his first year, Trump trounced Reagan by achieving 62% of his conservative goals versus 48% for Reagan. And, that was before most of the winning mentioned above started to roll in. The next two years were even better.

Then came COVID-19. Will COVID-19 destroy Trump? The jury is out. But it's clear to me, nothing can stop or slow Trump. Not impeachment, not Russian Collusion, not the Mueller witch hunt, not the Ukrainian phone call, and no, not COVID-19. As I write this book, Trump has enjoyed one of the greatest economic comebacks of all time, following the COVID-19 lockdown. We are in the midst of the greatest stock market rebound, the greatest jobs explosion, and the greatest GDP explosion in history. While COVID-19 is still raging. To paraphrase Don King, *Only in Trump's America!*

Trump was *fundamentally changing America* until the COVID-19 pandemic came along. Obama spoke about it . . . dreamed about it . . . but Trump delivered. Yes, COVID-19 got in the way. Yes, COVID-19 was the greatest roadblock in modern history. Yes, COVID-19 set back Trump's timetable to make America great again. But I have no doubt Trump will finish everything he set out to achieve, post COVID-19. One thing I've learned—never bet against Trump (or America).

Trump proves an extraordinary obsession with excellence matters. An obsession with winning matters. An obsession with *first place is all that matters and second place is for losers*. He proves excellence is achieved only through an obsession with winning and by defining, naming, and focusing on specific goals. And as president, Trump has proven those goals are not just any goals, they should be lofty goals that no one else imagined possible.

As the proud author of the book *The Power of RELENTLESS*, I cannot fail to add that Trump's obsession with excellence is only matched by his RELENTLESS attack until each goal is achieved. Then boasting about each success and using each success as a springboard to win over critics and naysayers, to instill confidence, to expand the team of believers and supporters, and to then gain another victory . . . and another . . . and another.

Two great New Yorkers prove it works. George Steinbrenner may have been first. But Donald J. Trump perfected it like no one else in history.

#WINNING

★ ★ ★ ★ ★ ★

──────── CHAPTER FIVE ────────

TRUMP RULE #2
Failing Your Way to the Top

I've just spent a chapter telling you a crucial key to Trump's success is #WINNING. Yes, that mindset is a vital part. But perhaps even more critical is your ability to learn from failure and rise from the ashes. I call it, "Failing your way to the top!" This is Donald Trump's special talent in life. You see, Trump has failed. A LOT.

While #WINNING is the goal, the foundation of success is often failure. I learned this lesson from watching Trump fail and rebound again and again. He is amazing. He is a real-life "Phoenix from the ashes." A modern-day Houdini. Liberal critics often portray Trump as a "loser," "failure," or "fraud" because they say he is not actually a success. They point to his many failures. This only proves their ignorance. This is the reason they have never succeeded at all—except to become critics. And no statue has ever been built to honor a critic. Trump has in fact failed a lot. But that's simply a by-product of how often he has succeeded. Twenty failures could be meaningful, if it's all you've done. But twenty failures versus hundreds of successes is called . . . *#WINNING*

Failure doesn't embarrass Trump. He just learns from it and comes back bigger than ever. But Trump is not alone. All super achievers gamble and fail. A LOT. But what makes them super achievers is that they are relentless enough to turn those failures into #WINNING. Following are a few examples of overcoming failure (some might call it *turning lemons into lemonade*) that I've spent my life compiling. After that, we'll get to the "King of Failure" Donald J. Trump. Trust me, after you're done reading this, you're going to want to *fail your way to the top*, too!

> *"I have not failed, I have just found*
> *10,000 ways that won't work."*
> **-Thomas Edison**

There are many valuable lessons and TRUMP RULES in this book. But none are more important than this one.

The fact is . . .

TO BECOME SUCCESSFUL, YOU MUST BE RELENTLESS IN THE FACE OF FAILURE.

In my experience and observations from a lifetime of meeting with, doing business with, partnering with, and interviewing super achievers, it is obvious that successful people fail far more often than unsuccessful ones. Does that surprise you? It shouldn't. Let me tell you why.

First, successful people are more relentless. They view their failures not as *Failures* with a capital "F," but as *failures* with a lowercase "f." As positive learning experiences.

Second, failing repeatedly is simply an offshoot of how often you are out there trying and fighting for success. For most people, failure happens with a capital "F" because they never try—the worst failure of all. Others might try once or twice, but after they get their head

★ ★ ★

handed to them, they quit and settle for a safe paycheck. They never try again.

But the super achievers never give up. They are the ones swinging for the fences . . . again . . . and again . . . and again. They know it's a numbers game and only a matter of time before they hit a solid double or triple, or a life-changing grand-slam home run. At my speeches and seminars in front of thousands of business people, there is a question I always ask, and to which I provide the answer:

"What do you call someone who starts ten restaurants . . . and nine of them fail? The answer: A millionaire. It only takes one to succeed."

A billion-dollar venture capitalist fund CEO told me recently he always looks for entrepreneurs who have just had a major failure, because experience has shown they are the most likely to produce a success the next time.

A personal friend of mine, Danny Tarkanian, wrote of his dad Jerry Tarkanian, one of the greatest college basketball coaches of all time, that he liked to hire assistant coaches who had just been fired. Why? Because they appreciate a second chance and work harder.

Let's look behind the scenes at the failures and relentless comebacks of a sampling of very successful people. These are relentless celebrities and business superstars who used failure as a stepping stone to achieve great success. I'll save the best for last—Donald J. Trump.

Those of you who have already read my books *The Joy of Failure* (my very first book in 1997), and my business bestseller, *The Power of RELENTLESS* (my first book translated into Japanese), will have already heard a few of these never-ever-ever-give-up success stories. It never hurts to hear them again. They just might provide the spark and inspiration to put your own failures behind you, and step to the plate one more time. Here are a group of superstars who all failed their way to the top!

ENTERTAINMENT "FAILURES"

George Clooney

We all know George Clooney is one of the most famous actors of our time. But did you know:

His first love was baseball. He tried out for the Cincinnati Reds and failed.

In 1982, he got in his car and drove to Hollywood. For a year he slept in a friend's closet and borrowed $200 to get headshot photos.

Over the next twelve years he appeared in fifteen failed TV pilots, a record six in one year alone. His first role was in a movie with Charlie Sheen that was never released. He auditioned for *Thelma and Louise*, losing the part to Brad Pitt who became a superstar. In 1988, he finally landed a part in . . . drumroll please, *Return of the Killer Tomatoes!*.

Did twelve years of failures dishearten him? Probably, but they certainly didn't destroy his confidence or stop him. He kept risking, ignoring the NOs, and in 1994 landed a part in the TV series *ER*. The rest was history. Today Clooney is worth half a billion dollars.[20]

Sylvester Stallone

Here is another movie and TV star we all know for his performances in the *Rocky* and *Rambo* movies, and now, *The Expendables*.

But, what about *Rhinestone . . . Lock Up . . . Oscar . . . Stop! Or My Mom Will Shoot . . . F.I.S.T . . . Driven . . . Assassins . . . The Specialist . . . Get Carter . . . Over the Top . . . Judge Dredd . . . Nighthawks . . . Victory . . .* and, my favorite . . . *Bullet to the Head*?

It will take a real movie buff to remember any of these. They were all total bombs. *Bullet to the Head* had the lowest opening week of Stallone's entire career, $4.5 million. Even *Stop or My Mom Will*

★ ★ ★

Shoot opened to $7.4 million. Sly must have wanted to put a bullet to his head!

But, out of all those failures came three blockbuster winners—the *Rocky* and *Rambo* movie series, and now, *The Expendables*. His career box office total as an actor, director, and screenwriter is well over $7 billion (adjusted for inflation).[21]

His personal net worth is $400 million.[22]

So...who cares about the flops? What does it matter? Sly Stallone will go down in history as a Hollywood film legend and pure box office gold. The lesson? Focus on the winners, ignore the failures— they don't matter.

Oprah Winfrey

We all know Oprah as a television talk show host, actress, producer, and businesswoman. But few know her long struggle. Oprah was born into poverty, dysfunction, and abuse. Born to a teenage mother, she was abused from the age of nine, ran away from home, and got pregnant at age fourteen. But she turned her life around, graduated from college, and entered the TV news business. At age twenty-two, she was fired from her job as a television reporter. Her bosses deemed her "unsuitable for television."

But that wasn't the end of her failures. Winfrey was later terminated from her post as co-anchor of the six o'clock weekday news on Baltimore's WJZ-TV after the show received low ratings.[23]

That led to her hosting a TV talk show, *People Are Talking*. That was considered a huge demotion in the television news world. But, Oprah turned lemons into lemonade. *People Are Talking* may have been another failure, but it led to Oprah being noticed by top network TV executives. She was hired for the *The Oprah Winfrey Show*, and the rest is history.

Her never-give-up attitude led Oprah to the greatest success in TV talk show history. Today, she is a self-made billionaire, the *only* African American female billionaire in the world, and one of the most powerful women on the planet. She owns her own TV network called OWN. Her net worth is $3.5 billion with a salary of $300 million annually.[24]

BUSINESS "FAILURES"

Steve Jobs

Does anyone remember that before the *Mac* there was the *Lisa*? Or that Apple was close to bankruptcy?

As an entrepreneur who has started several different businesses myself, I understand only too well the innumerable obstacles and failures that Steve Jobs encountered in making Apple a success. In the early days of Apple, the joke in the business world was, "What would you call the company if Apple and IBM merged?" The answer: IBM.

But, Jobs persevered and made Apple a success. Then, in 1985 when hard times hit, Jobs was forced out of Apple, called a *has been*. His time as a high-tech star was considered over. Finished. Kaput.

So, what did Steve Jobs do? He started the corporation, NeXT, and a year later, bought an animation company. Both successes from the get-go, right? Well, not exactly. Jobs, ever the risk-taking visionary, invested over $50 million of his own money into the animation company, naming it Pixar. Over the next years, Pixar netted over $4 billion with animated movies including *Finding Nemo* and *Toy Story*. In 2006, Pixar merged with Disney, making Steve Jobs Disney's largest shareholder.

NeXT did not have the same success. Over the following years, the company floundered, losing $100 million as it laid off workers. Finally, facing bankruptcy, Jobs sold NeXT to Apple.

What did Apple get when they purchased NeXT? They got the software that later became the operating system of the iPhone, iPod, iPad, and iTunes. But, perhaps more importantly, they got back never-give-up Steve Jobs. That's why Apple is today among the most valuable companies in the world!

Upon his death, Steve Jobs was worth $10.2 billion.[25]

Jack Welch

For all my middle-aged and older readers, Jack Welch is a well-known name. As the CEO of General Electric, he became known as an icon for his management and leadership of that company.

But for Welch, as it is for most of us, he didn't start at the top, and had more than his share of failures to overcome. He started as a $10,500 per year Junior Chemical Engineer. One of his first management jobs was at a chemical plant. The plant blew up. Welch was held accountable for design flaws. He came very close to being fired.[26]

But, Welch persevered and became GE's youngest chairman and CEO. He was known for his management style of rewarding success and punishing failure. Every year he rewarded the top 20% of managers with bonuses and stock options. The bottom 10% were fired, regardless of circumstance.[27]

Welch died with a net worth of $750 million.[28]

Anyone who becomes CEO of a company after blowing up a plant in his first job understands the concept of *failing your way to the top.*

Charles Schwab

Charles Schwab struggled through school, flunking English twice, not realizing until he was in his forties that he suffered from dyslexia. But as do all of us with a desire to succeed, he found a way, including having friends and classmates take notes and study with him. To this day, he says he struggles to read and write.[29]

His early business career was checkered with the failure of a mutual fund he was managing, and significant debt. But his RELENTLESS attitude led to the founding, and now success, of Charles Schwab & Company. Today his company is the largest discount stock broker in the United States. It manages over $1.65 trillion in assets for 7.9 million clients. Schwab's net worth upon his death was $7.5 billion.[30]

Jack Bogle

Jack founded Vanguard Group, the first mutual fund ever created to help investors and consumers cut the costs of stock investing. Bogle's relentless pursuit of cost cutting was his mantra and lifelong goal. This led to him creating the first index fund available for the general public in 1976. He planned to sell $150 million in shares. It was a massive bust, selling only a miserable $11 million in shares. A Wall Street Journal story reported Bogle's creation was ridiculed as, "Bogle's folly," "guaranteed mediocrity," and even "un-American."

Bogle's index fund languished for years. It remained small and of little interest to investors. But Bogle stayed positive and enthusiastic. Eventually, word spread that the returns were actually very good, but with much lower expenses than your typical mutual fund. Soon, Bogle created index funds for every category of US and international stocks and bonds.

Studies prove index funds outperform 90% of mutual funds. Warren Buffet said of Bogle, "[He] did more for American investors . . . than any individual I've known."

Bogle's belief in index funds during those initial dark days was called "evangelical." Today, index funds manage trillions of dollars. They represent almost 50% of all mutual fund assets.

Walt Disney

Walt Disney failed multiple times on his way to success. He was fired from his first job as a newspaper editor. His boss said he was not creative enough and lacked imagination. He was fired from an ad agency, where his boss told him, "you can't draw."

But those were the easy failures.[31]

Believing in himself, he formed his first animation company in Kansas City. He made a deal with a distribution company in New York in which he would ship them his cartoons and get paid six months down the road. The deal never worked out and he was forced to dissolve his company. It was reported he survived by eating dog food.

Later, following a press conference, a newspaper editor remarked that Disney had, "no good ideas for film production." When Walt first tried to get MGM studios to distribute Mickey Mouse in 1927, he was told the idea would never work because a giant mouse on the screen would terrify women.[32]

Undaunted, Disney began making animated feature films: *Snow White*, *Pinocchio*, *Fantasia*, *Dumbo*, and *Bambi*. Clearly these were all huge successes, right? Hardly. Of the five, only *Snow White* and *Dumbo* made money. It wasn't until eight relentless years later that Disney made another feature-length film.

But Disney went on to be nominated for fifty-nine Academy Awards, winning thirty-two. That's the all time record for the most Oscars won by an individual.[33]

The corporation, now known as The Walt Disney Company produces average revenue of $30 billion annually.[34]

Colonel Harland Sanders

Colonel Sanders was the famous Southern gentleman who founded Kentucky Fried Chicken (KFC). His story reads like a disaster from beginning to almost the end. Yet, his last act was amazing, proving the important thing is to *stay* relentless until the bitter end, or in Colonel Sanders' case, the *amazing success*.

When Harland was just five, his father died. His mom was forced to work, so he learned to cook for his siblings. One of the things he learned to cook was . . . fried chicken. That would come in handy some sixty years later. Talk about turning lemons to lemonade.

More bad turns. Harland dropped out of school and took a series of odd jobs: farmhand, railroad worker, blacksmith's helper. He married and had a son. The boy died. He studied law while working as a fireman. But his law career ended when he had a fistfight in the courtroom with his own client. This guy was going nowhere . . . fast.

He started a lamp manufacturing company. It failed. He became a tire salesman. He lost his job when the plant closed. He managed a gas station, until it closed due to the Great Depression.

He opened a motel. It burned to the ground. He rebuilt it, bigger than ever. After re-opening, it went bust. He was soon divorced.

But he still had that old recipe for "Kentucky Fried Chicken." He franchised it to a Salt Lake City restaurant. Sales tripled! So, at age sixty-five, Sanders traveled the nation selling franchises in his restaurant concept.

Soon he had six hundred locations. In 1964, he sold his restaurant chain for two million dollars. But, he kept his Canadian rights. He spent the rest of his life traveling the world as a spokesman for Kentucky Fried Chicken, as well as running his Canadian locations.

He became famous back home in Kentucky. His buddy, the Governor of Kentucky, commissioned him as a "Kentucky Colonel." At first, his friends laughed at the title. But Sanders got the idea to dress the part. During the last twenty years of his life, he would only be called "Colonel," and never wore anything in public other than a white suit and string tie to match his white mustache and goatee. Colonel Sanders understood branding!

Sanders died at age ninety in 1980. His body lay in the rotunda of the Kentucky State Capital. By then, Kentucky Fried Chicken had over six thousand locations in forty-eight countries, with sales of over $2 billion annually. All the failures of his first sixty-five years of life didn't matter, because he kept fighting, stayed committed, and stayed in the game.[35]

POLITICAL "FAILURES"

Bill Clinton

We all know Bill Clinton as the forty-second president of the United States. But, did you know he lost his first bid for public office when he ran for the House of Representatives? And then, after being elected the youngest Governor in the country, he was defeated in his re-election campaign. Clinton is quoted as joking that he was "the youngest *ex-Governor* in the country."

Considered an up-and-coming future Democratic candidate, Clinton was honored to be asked to give the nominating speech for Michael Dukakis at the 1988 Democratic Convention. The speech was so longwinded and boring that he was booed and forced to ask the audience for quiet. He received the most applause when he said, "In conclusion . . . ."

The normally Democrat-fawning media savaged him. The Washington Post called his speech "Numb & Restless." Johnny Carson called him a "windbag." And, perhaps worst of all, John Chancellor said, "A young man's political career ended tonight."[36]

He faced the media, went on *The Tonight Show* and made fun of himself. Four years later, the "Comeback Kid" was elected president of the United States.

Ronald Reagan

Reagan is known for starting his career as a movie star. But, did you know at best he was a mediocre B-movie actor? In 1954, with his movie career dead, he tried his luck doing a song and dance routine in a Las Vegas lounge act. The show was a bomb and closed in one week.

Looking to improve his image in Hollywood, he auditioned for the part of president in the United Artists 1964 movie *Doesn't He Look Presidential*. The top executives at United Artists decided he didn't look "presidential" and *rejected* him for the part.

Two years later, he was elected Governor of California, and in 1980 was elected president of the United States in a landslide—then re-elected in an even bigger landslide.

Abe Lincoln

A picture of Abraham Lincoln, one of America's most important and famous presidents, could rightly be posted in the dictionary alongside the word *failure*. Allow me to list just a few of Lincoln's setbacks. I'm sure "Honest Abe" thought of them as stepping stones.

- Rejected for law school, he eventually became a lawyer by reading books and observing court sessions.
- His business failed, 1831
- Lost his job and was defeated for legislature, 1832
- Failed in business again after borrowing money from a friend, 1833
- Spent next seventeen years paying off the debt
- Sweetheart, Ann Rutledge, died, 1835
- Had a nervous breakdown, 1836
- Defeated for Speaker, 1838
- Sought to become elector . . . defeated, 1840

★ ★ ★

- Defeated for nomination for Congress, 1843
- Elected to Congress, 1846, Lost re-election, 1848
- Defeated for Senate, 1854
- Defeated for nomination for vice president, 1856
- Again defeated for Senate, 1858
- Then . . .
- Elected president, 1860, led one of the most significant wars in world history, freed the slaves, and saved the union.[37]

WOW! Abe may or may not have been "honest," but he was undoubtedly tenacious and relentless.

HISTORICAL "FAILURES"

Christopher Columbus

Christopher Columbus had a dream of reaching the East Indies by sailing westward. In 1485, needing financial support, Columbus presented his plans to John II, King of Portugal. The king submitted Columbus' proposal to his experts, who rejected it. In 1488, Columbus appealed to the court of Portugal once again, and once again was rejected.

Columbus traveled from Portugal to both Genoa and Venice, but he was rejected by both. Columbus had also dispatched his brother Bartholomew to the court of Henry VII of England, where he was rejected again.

On May 1, 1486, Columbus presented his plans to King Ferdinand and Queen Isabella of Spain, who, in turn, referred it to a committee. Like their counterparts in Portugal, they pronounced the idea impractical and advised their Royal Highnesses to pass on the proposed venture.

But all that rejection didn't stop Columbus. After two more years of continually lobbying at the Spanish court, he finally got his YES and sailed westward in 1492. His miseries were only just beginning. Each of his voyages was met with adversity as he faced and overcame mutiny, vicious and violent storms, starvation, and Indian attacks. But he persevered. The rest is history. Columbus changed the world as we know it by discovering the Americas.[38]

George Washington and the Revolutionary War

Perhaps the most courageous risk takers of all time were the founding fathers of our great country, led by George Washington. These were the richest, most successful men in the colonies. They risked not just their fortunes, but their very lives and the lives of their families.

For seven long years, the Continental army, led by George Washington, lost battle after battle. The British captured New York and the then-capital city of Philadelphia. Over twenty-five thousand Continental soldiers were killed, many by disease, cold, and starvation. Many in Congress wanted to give up, refusing to authorize funds for needed supplies and even threatening to fire General Washington.

Bickering, petty jealousy, starvation, disease and even mutiny by one of the colony's top generals, Benedict Arnold, appeared to doom the revolution. But George Washington refused to give up, or give in. He also had a remarkably relentless supporting cast, that included each of the founding fathers who signed the Declaration of Independence. They had nothing to gain and everything to lose. Yet they put their fortunes, reputations, lives, and families at risk. They never wavered, despite seven long years of defeat and the near bankruptcy of their new country.[39]

Winston Churchill

Churchill is a personal hero of mine. I regard him as one of history's greatest leaders. But he was also one of history's biggest failures.

★ ★ ★

Churchill suffered from clinical depression, drank and smoked too much, and was a lousy father. He failed the exam to get into the Royal Military College Sandhurst (now called the Sandhurst Military Academy) three times.

In his first run for Parliament, he lost. He later won as a Conservative, only to be disowned by his own party. Not to be deterred, he ran as a Liberal, and won. He not only lost the next election, he came in fourth. Was this kind of a defeat going to stop him? Not Churchill. He ran again . . . and lost. So, what did he do? He ran as an Independent and won. When he then rejoined the Conservative Party he commented to the media, "Anyone can rat, but it takes a certain amount of ingenuity to re-rat."

History buffs will recall that in 1915, with 140,000 casualties, the British suffered one of the worst military defeats in history at Gallipoli while trying to capture Istanbul. Churchill was blamed for this defeat, effectively ending his career as an elected politician.

In 1924, with England facing deflation, unemployment, strikes, and a worldwide depression, he was appointed to a cabinet position by the Conservative government to oversee the economy. When the Conservatives lost power in 1929, that career also ended.

The thirties are often referred to as Churchill's "wilderness years," when he was out of power, dishonored, ignored, and laughed at. Then, as Hitler began to come to power in the late thirties, Churchill became a fierce critic of the UK's policies of appeasement. Churchill's demands to rearm and prepare for war were largely ignored.

As it became increasingly clear that Churchill was right and war was inevitable, in 1940, Neville Chamberlain (the great appeaser) resigned. Churchill became Prime Minister of the UK.

The US didn't join the battle versus Hitler and Nazi Germany until December 1941. Until then, the British essentially stood alone after Germany conquered most of Europe, including France. During this time, what did Churchill, the leader of this relatively small island nation do? He single-handedly saved the world from Hitler.

How did he accomplish this? He did it with his relentless, never, ever, ever give up inspiration of the English people. His critics laughed at him. They called him a pompous ass, wildly exaggerative, and said he loved himself more than his country.

But, his leadership inspired not only the British, it also inspired people around the world to heed his call, resist, and remain steadfast and relentless in fighting this unthinkable tyranny.

Following are a few excerpts from some of his more famous speeches:

As the Battle of Britain raged with daily German bombing raids of London and other major cities and the people preparing for an invasion from mainland Europe, Churchill said:

"If the British Empire . . . lasts for a thousand years, men will still say, 'this was their finest hour.'"

". . . we shall fight on the seas and oceans, we shall fight with growing confidence and growing strength in the air, we shall defend our Island, whatever the cost may be, we shall fight on the beaches, we shall fight on the landing ground, we shall fight in the fields and in the streets, we shall fight in the hills; we shall never surrender . . ."

In the battle for air supremacy, the British were greatly outnumbered, outgunned, and inexperienced. Yet brave, young Royal Air Force (RAF) flyers standing tall and battling the Germans toe-to-toe to stop the bombing raids is considered a turning point in the war. Speaking of these young men, Churchill said:

"Never in the field of human conflict was so much owed by so many to so few."

Hero Royal Air Force Pilots became known as "The Few."

★ ★ ★

England, inspired by Churchill standing firm against German aggression, undoubtedly swayed US public opinion that Hitler could and must be defeated, and paved the way for the US to join the allies in Hitler's defeat.

You could say, "Churchill saved the day." That may be true, but even in victory, he experienced failure. When the war ended in 1945, he was considered a national hero, but a political liability. The people may have thought he had the perfect skills for a war-time leader, but they didn't think the same of his peace-time skills. In 1945, his party lost the national elections and he was thrown out of office. Still . . .

- *Time Magazine* called him "The Greatest Person of the 20th Century."
- He is widely considered the greatest wartime leader ever.
- A 2002 BBC poll called him "the greatest British citizen of all time."
- He is one of few people ever named "honorary citizen of the USA."

But, his political career was not yet over. In 1950, his party won the national elections and he was again named Prime Minister, the oldest in UK history, serving until 1955.[40]

Upon his death in 1965, Churchill was given the largest state funeral in world history.[41]

My favorite Churchill saying, and one I strongly suggest you not only memorize but adopt as part of your personal life philosophy:

"Success is the ability to go from one failure to another with no loss of enthusiasm."

Now it's time for the best story of all . . .

DONALD J. TRUMP: THE KING OF FAILING YOUR WAY TO THE TOP!

When liberals attack Donald Trump, taunting and making fun of him, it is almost always about his failures. And, it is true, Trump has failed many times. For a billionaire business mogul whose brand is success and #WINNING, Trump has failed a lot.

But that, my friends and readers, is the major premise of this chapter and this book. Relentlessly overcoming failure is one of the essential TRUMP RULES. Enduring and overcoming failure, is certainly the most critical component to success.

Success doesn't come without taking chances. Show me someone who always *plays it safe* and I'll show you someone who, at best, is mediocre. The biggest losers of all are those who never try. If you play it safe your whole life, you'll never fail, but your whole life will be a failure. If you don't try, you are guaranteed to lose.

But if you try, if you gamble, if you take risks, yes you will very likely experience failure, probably more than once—but, you will also give yourself the opportunity to achieve glorious victory.

That's the Trump story. That's perhaps the most important Trump Rule. As the lottery says, "Ya gotta be in it to win it." And if you're in it, you may fail along the way, but you also stand a good chance of *failing your way to the top!*

Let's take a look at Donald Trump's record of failure. He's right up there with the biggest failures of all time. Those failures are also what have made him one of the biggest success stories of all time. If you want to taste glorious, magical, remarkable, phenomenal success, you must be a combination risk-taker, riverboat gambler, and gunslinger. You must be fearless in the face of failure.

Trump is the poster boy for learning from each failure and rising from the ashes like a Phoenix. Let me put it another way: Donald J.

Trump, "The King of Failure," is also billionaire business mogul . . . Television superstar . . . the world's most famous celebrity . . . and now is also known as president of the United States, commander of the US Military, and leader of the free world!

Ask Trump. Failure ain't so bad!

Here is a sampling of Trump's failed business ventures:

- Trump Vodka—FAILED (Five years in business, finally went out of production.)
- Trump University—FAILED (Six years in business, bogged down in class action lawsuit, business closed.)
- Trump Ice (bottled water)—FAILED (Less than one year in business.)
- Trump Airlines—FAILED (Four years in business, defaulted, turned over to creditors.)
- Trump Fire, Trump Power, Trump's American Pale Ale (carbonated beverages)—FAILED (All trademark applications abandoned or canceled.)
- Trump the Game—FAILED (One year in business, then out of production.)
- Trump Mortgage—FAILED (Eighteen months in business, then closed.)
- GoTrump.com (search engine)—FAILED (One year in business.)
- Tour de Trump (pro bike race)—FAILED (Two years in business, financial distress, sold, name changed.)
- Trump Steaks by Sharper Image—FAILED (One year in business.)
- Trump Magazine—FAILED (Two years in business.)
- Trump Office for Staples—FAILED

- Donald Trump: The Fragrance—FAILED (Discontinued soon after release.)
- Trump Tower Tampa, Trump Atlanta, Trump Philadelphia, Trump Plaza Tower, Israel—ALL FAILED
- Trump on the Ocean (Restaurant and catering hall)—FAILED (Never opened.)
- The Trump Network (vitamins)—FAILED (Two years in business, then closed.)
- Trump New Media (High Speed Internet)—FAILED (Never opened.)
- Trumpnet (corporate telephone communications systems)—FAILED (Never opened.)
- Trump the Animated TV series—FAILED
- Trumped! (two-minute daily radio segment with business and personal advice)—FAILED (Four years in business, then ended.)
- Trump Tycoon Mobile APP—FAILED
- The New Jersey Generals Football Team of the USFL—FAILED (Two years in business, then team and USFL both folded.)
- Trump Hotels & Casino Resorts, Trump Entertainment Resorts (Trump-owned casinos)—FAILED (Multiple bankruptcies, reorganization, Trump stepped down as Chairman.)
- Trump business deals lost after his infamous 2015 presidential announcement—Trump lost deals with NBC, Univision, Macy's, Serta, and many more.
- And, of course, the biggest Trump failure of all time: His entire business and real estate empire was *underwater* and close to bankruptcy in the 1980s. He owed banks billions. Trump is said to have told his wife-to-be Marla Maples, upon seeing a bum on Fifth Avenue:

"See that homeless man? He's worth more than me."

Marla replied, "What do you mean?"

Trump replied, "He's worth zero, I'm worth negative $2 billion."

What is my point in listing my hero Donald Trump's failures, business disasters, and disappointments? To me, this many failures and comebacks is impressive, a sign of being a relentless #WINNER. Any media organization listing these same *Trump Hall of Shame* stories is trying to put Trump down, trying to paint a picture of a failure, a BS artist, and scammer.

But that couldn't be further from the truth.

First, any man who fails this much and comes out ahead is a one-in-a-billion winner . . . a magician . . . a financial version of Houdini. To fail this often, while compiling a multi-billion fortune, is not only a testament to Trump's financial acumen and wizardry, it is also a testament to his relentless risk-taking and never-give-up, Winston Churchill-like and Abe Lincoln-like attitude.

Second, it's time we stop calling it *failing*. It's all part of a philosophy and strategy to become a winner. It's called rolling the dice. Remember my wisdom when presenting business success speeches: "What do you call a guy that opens ten restaurants and nine of them fail? A MILLIONAIRE. You only need one to succeed!"

Third, success is about being relentless. Of all the books I've written, *The Power of RELENTLESS* is my favorite. It's about *stick-to-it-ive-ness*. It's about never giving up. Business is tough. Business startups are the hardest undertaking of all. Seven out of ten business startups fail.

In baseball, a .300 hitter earns millions for getting three hits out of every ten at-bats. Just ask Trump. He understands that three winners and seven losers/failures/bankruptcies equal the life of your dreams! *Business Insider* studied Trump's career. They found sixty-one major business deals. They rated all sixty-one. They concluded

Trump failed with 40% of them. Twenty-four of the sixty-one were outright losers, bombs, disasters, total losses. Of the remaining 60%, sixteen were somewhat successful, but still problematic. That left twenty-one *yuge* Trump winners.

In the limited minds of liberal journalists who know nothing about business or economics, and have never done anything but collect a safe paycheck, that's a terrible record of failure. They don't realize what an amazing record Trump has achieved by hitting 60% winners versus 40% losers. And twenty-one of those were over-the-top home runs. Remember, *you only need one.*

Trump has twenty-one home runs. Very few human beings achieve one in a lifetime. That's why he's a billionaire!

Just as the critics don't matter, neither do the failures. Ignore the failures. Don't let them define you. They are just *blips* on your long successful career. Be relentless. Stay positive and enthusiastic. Keep fighting for that one winner that changes your life. If you're lucky, you might get one or two home runs in a lifetime.

A billionaire might get twenty-one. Bravo. That's why they're filthy rich. But remember, it took Trump sixty-one times at bat to hit those twenty-one home runs.

And the failures? Just like the critics themselves, they are meaningless, anonymous, and forgotten. All anyone will remember is that you are wealthy and successful. Except, as you use them as learning experiences, the failures just fade away.

I learned from the best—Donald J. Trump. Remember, I studied Trump and modeled what I did after him: my attitude, mindset, risk-taking riverboat gambler, and gunslinger philosophy. I've even followed his healthy lifestyle, avoiding both smoking and drinking. In many ways, my career has been a replica of Trump's. Up and down. The high of victory and the agony of defeat. Plenty of failures. My first business book was about my many early failures. It was called

The Joy of Failure. I failed at twenty different careers and businesses, bankruptcy, and divorce.

Since then, I've failed a few dozen more times. But I also hit a triple or two, quite a few doubles, and a whole lot of singles. And, as I write this book, I believe I'm getting real close to multiple *out-of-the-park* home runs.

What I do know is that when a life is up, when it's time to leave this earth and rise to heaven, you want to be one of those that can say, *I got up to bat and was fearless. I may have struck out a few times, but stayed relentless, got a few sweet swings, a few base hits, and hopefully one or two home runs.* It all adds up to being remembered as a #WINNER.

Ask Babe Ruth. The strikeouts don't matter. They aren't remembered. All that's left at the end is your hits, especially your home runs. Babe Ruth, by the way, when he retired was not only the all-time home run leader, but also the all-time strikeout leader. Unless you're a real baseball fan, you probably didn't know that. But Babe understood you can't hit home runs if you don't swing for the fences.

Like Trump, he understood that the glory, celebrity, legend, and wealth comes from the long ball. *Chicks dig the long ball!*

The only way to live the life of your dreams and enjoy incredible levels of success is to learn to *fail your way to the top.* There is no way to hit the home runs without also striking out a lot. There is absolutely nothing worse in life than being too afraid of failure to ever swing in the first place.

And that, my friends, describes the liberal critics, DC swamp bureaucrats, deep state rats, and media detractors of Donald J. Trump. They've never failed like Trump, simply because they never had the balls to get up to bat and swing. That's why Trump is the ultimate champion. That's why TRUMP RULES.

★ ★ ★ ★ ★ ★

──────── CHAPTER SIX ────────

TRUMP RULE #3
Screw The Critics

This could be the most important TRUMP RULE after #WINNING and *Failing Your Way to the Top*. Actually, every TRUMP RULE is important, and they all work synergistically together. Telling critics to, *Go screw yourself!* is right at the top. I do it every day. No surprise—I learned it from Trump.

We all know the foundation of Trump's success is his win-at-all-costs mindset and the fact that he doesn't let failures or setbacks slow him down.

He is relentless!

We also know there is no doubt critics have played, and continue to play, a significant role in Trump's success. He certainly has enough of them. But, to Trump's credit they've never slowed him, discouraged him, or stopped him. To the contrary, they have *inspired* him every step of the way!

Trump has had to deal with critics his entire life. He proves the adages, *The closer you are to the target, the more flak you start attracting* and *If you're not attracting critics, you're doing something wrong.*

As a high-profile billionaire business mogul and reality TV star, Trump attracted plenty of critics, haters, and naysayers. He proved them all wrong—time and time again.

As president, Trump has faced withering attacks, hate, and criticism from . . . EVERYONE. From the left, from the right, from the DC swamp establishment, from the deep state (CIA, FBI, DOJ, and every other government agency), from the media, from virtually every world leader—in short, the entire world.

Every word Trump utters is scrutinized and criticized under a microscope, then exaggerated, or taken out of context. Every action he takes is condemned by someone, or everyone.

If critics bothered Trump, he'd have given up long ago. He'd have retired, resigned, or walked away. Instead, he has spent his life and career ignoring them all. That's precisely why he has achieved greatness on a scale never seen in world history. Perhaps the most important lesson I learned from all my years studying Trump: *Screw the critics.*

Like Trump, I have faced withering criticism in the media, too. But, because of the lessons learned from him, I have enjoyed unimagined success, specifically because I've ignored the critics. And in some cases, used their mean-spirited words to motivate me, drive me, push me to places I would not have gone without their vicious words ringing in my ears.

99% of the time, critics and naysayers criticize out of bitterness or envy. They criticize because they could not achieve what you have achieved, or they simply don't have your vision and therefore they can't see what you see.

99% of the time, they are dead wrong. There is no point listening to them, they can only discourage you from taking action and doing what you know in your gut and heart is right. In many or even most cases, that's their objective. They hope to put a damper on

★ ★ ★

your success, or even stop you altogether. Why? Because they weren't smart enough, or bold enough, or courageous enough to pull off what you are about to pull off. Because they didn't have the vision, foresight, talent, or balls you have.

Or, in Trump's case as President, it is purely political . . . *Resist . . . resist . . . resist . . . at all cost.*

Sadly, critics are responsible for stopping so many people dead in their tracks before they could make their dreams come true. Critics have ruined far more lives than even the most famous evil despots in world history.

Keep in mind critics don't create jobs. Critics don't build businesses. Critics don't invent products that change the world. Critics don't change lives for the better. All they do is discourage others from doing all those great things!

Remember, no statue has ever been built to honor a critic. Only those who take action get statues. Since the moment Donald J. Trump came down that Trump Tower escalator and declared his run for the presidency, he has achieved great things very few people imagined possible. Thank God I wasn't one of those critics. I was on "Team Trump" from that first moment. I took a big gamble and look what happened to my career. As Sarah Blaskey, the author of *The Grifter's Club*, wrote in her book:

> "Root is happy to admit he built his career on the coattails of a giant. He is proud of that."[42]

Meanwhile, what have his millions of vicious, deranged, big-mouthed Trump critics achieved? Absolutely nothing. Zero. Zip. Nada. This chapter is dedicated to freedom. The freedom to free yourself from your critics . . . ALL OF THEM! First, let me convey a few quotes by supposed "experts" and "professionals" who were proven not just wrong, but dead wrong. I mean bigger-than-life wrong. Wrong by proportions as big as the Great State of Texas. I share these quotes with audiences attending my business speeches and seminars across the globe. I share them to prove you should never listen to so-called "experts" or critics. As these quotes prove, those experts and critics are often idiots, fools, and are usually wrong. They are only "experts" at pontificating and ruining other people's dreams, including your own.

Hearing these stories has changed lives by inspiring people in my audiences to go after their dreams with abandon, energy, and enthusiasm known to few, without allowing others to discourage or depress them. How do I know? You should read the emails of thanks I receive.

Second, I'll just list a small sampling of the critics (i.e. idiots) who predicted Trump would never become president. As usual, they weren't just wrong . . . they were dead wrong.

LET'S START WITH "THE EXPERTS" OF HISTORY:

1774

> **"Four or five frigates will do the job without any military force necessary to put down the rebellion."**
>
> Who said it? British Prime Minister Lord North, on dealing with the "pesky" rebellious American colonies. Guess what? The rebellion WORKED!
>
> **Screw the critics. Critics are idiots.**

1859

- **"Drill for oil? You mean drill into the ground to try and find oil? You're absolutely crazy."**

- Who said it? It's recorded that this was the response of geology experts when Edwin L. Drake tried to enlist them to work on his project to drill for oil.

- **Screw the critics. Critics are idiots.**

1876:

- **[This device] has too many shortcomings to be seriously considered as a means of communication. The device is inherently of no value to us."**

- Who said it? Unnamed executives at Western Union talking about the telephone! These guys are unnamed . . . but we all remember Alexander Graham Bell!

- **Screw the critics. Critics are idiots.**

1899

- **"Everything that can be invented has already been invented."**

- Who said it? It's a widely popular belief that the United States Commissioner of Patents in 1899 said it. I saved the best for last! This must be the single dumbest thing ever said by anyone *ever*. Like most of us know, governments are stocked full of idiots who couldn't hold down a job for a week in the private sector.

Screw the critics. Critics are idiots.

1905

"Sensible and responsible women do not want to vote."

Who said it? Grover Cleveland, president of the United States. Not exactly a proud moment in the history of the presidency.

Screw the critics. Critics are idiots. Even the President.

1911

"Airplanes are interesting toys but of no military value."

Who said it? Marshal Ferdinand Foch, commander of French military forces in WWI. Unfortunately, through the years, it has been French military forces that have proven to be of no military value!

Screw the critics. Critics are idiots.

1928

"There will never again be a Negro boxing champion— certainly not in our lifetimes."

Who said it? A boxing "expert" immediately after heavyweight champ Jack Johnson was beaten by a white challenger. I won't say another word.

Screw the critics. Critics are idiots.

1929

"Stock prices have reached what looks like a permanently high plateau."

Who said it? Irving Fischer, America's leading economist only thirteen days before the great stock market crash of 1929! Irving was the first in a long line of economists whose predictions never fail to make us laugh (and broke).

Screw the critics. Critics are idiots.

1940

"The United States will not be a threat to us for decades, at the earliest 1970 or 1980."

Who said it in 1940? Adolph Hitler. Thank God for the human race, this madman was off by three to four decades. Or we might all be speaking German. And this author might not be alive.

Screw the critics. Critics are idiots.

1949

Any baseball fans here? Does the name Cleveland Indians strike fear in anyone's heart? Do the Cleveland Indians inspire greatness? Well, they had one chance . . . Cleveland signed the first black player, Larry Doby. He went to the Cleveland GM to recommend three other African American League players. He said, "They'll all be stars." The Cleveland GM sent scouts to check them out. The scouts said: **"The first one has a hitch in his swing and will never hit major league pitching. The second one is too slow and doesn't have the range as a fielder to play in the major leagues. The third one can't hit a curveball."** Cleveland turned them all down.

Who were they? Hank Aaron, Willie Mays, and Ernie Banks—three Hall of Famers, and three of the greatest players in baseball history.

Screw the critics. Critics are idiots.

1954

"The Japanese don't make the things [the people in the US] want. Japan must find markets elsewhere for the goods they export."

Who said it? United States Secretary of State John Foster Dulles. How dumb is that? I guarantee you, some "expert" said the same thing about the Chinese a few years ago.

Screw the critics. Critics are idiots.

1955

"TV can never become truly popular. Who would stare at that *boob tube* for hours on end?"

Who said it? A high-profile radio executive dismissing any chance for TV to overtake radio. See a pattern emerging here?

Screw the critics. Critics are idiots.

1957

"Man will never reach the moon . . . regardless of all future scientific advances."

Who said it? Dr. Lee de Forest, a famous and respected scientist. Note the date of 1957. Man landed on the moon only twelve years later, on July 20, 1969 (my birthday, incidentally).

Screw the critics. Critics are idiots.

1964

"Ronald Reagan doesn't have that presidential look."

Who said it? A United Artists movie executive, rejecting Ronald Reagan as an ACTOR to play the part of the president of the United States in a 1964 film. Two years later, Reagan was Governor of California . . . sixteen years later, he was elected the real president of the United States.

- Screw the critics. Critics are idiots.

1965

- "This concept is interesting . . . but in order to earn better than a 'C,' the idea must be feasible."

- Who said it? A Yale economics professor commenting on college student Fred Smith's idea for an overnight delivery service to compete with the US Postal Service. Fred went on to found Federal Express. Today, the US Postal Service cannot compete with FedEx!

- Screw the critics. Critics are idiots.

1968

- "The battle to feed all of humanity is over. In the 1970s hundreds of millions of people will starve to death in spite of any crash programs embarked upon now. There will only be 30 million people left in America—if it survives."

- Who said it? Paul Ehrlich, Biologist, scientist, and noted mentor to Al Gore, the man who has screamed like a hysterical madman about global warming for two decades now.

- Screw the critics. Critics are idiots.

1972

"The current craze for bottled water is 'lunatic asylum thinking.' It will fade away as quickly as it came."

Who said it? Dr. Abel Wolman, Professor at John Hopkins University, known as America's leading authority on water! After selling the stocks of Evian and Perrier short; my guess is poor Professor Wolman didn't have enough money left to buy a bottle of spring water!

Screw the critics. Critics are idiots.

1977

"There is no reason why anyone would want a computer in their home."

Who said it? Ken Olsen, Founder of The Digital Equipment Corporation, at a meeting of The World Future Society. See what I mean about "experts?" The World Future Society? I wonder if Mr. Olsen also missed the value of indoor plumbing.

Screw the critics. Critics are idiots.

That ends my historical replay of some of the dumbest predictions ever by the (supposed) smartest and sharpest so-called "experts" and critics of their time.

But, they all pale in comparison to the most spectacular failed predictions by experts EVER assembled in one place at one time. Read and laugh at these predictions about Donald Trump's presidential run.

Here is just a small sampling . . .

Acclaimed expert and political guru Nate Silver said,

"*. . . Donald Trump isn't a real candidate.*" He wrote the following about Trump's chances of winning the GOP nomination:

June 16, 2015

"Taking into account name recognition, Trump's net favorability rating (favorable minus unfavorable) of -32 percentage points stands out for its pure terribleness at this point in the campaign. Like his unfavorable rating, it is by far the worst of the 106 presidential candidates since 1980 who are in our database.

For this reason alone, Trump has a better chance of cameoing in another "Home Alone" movie with Macaulay Culkin — or playing in the NBA Finals — than winning the Republican nomination."[43]

By August, Silver's and other critics' opinions had gotten even worse (if that's possible):

Nate Silver predicted that Donald Trump had a two percent chance of winning the nomination. Katherine Miller of BuzzFeed put it at zero percent. And *FiveThirtyEight's* Harry Enten put Trump's chances at *negative* ten percent. That was for winning the GOP nomination, not the actual presidency.

Politico ended 2016 with an article about all the critics who blew the election prediction by a mile with this story on December 28th, just after the election.[44]

In June, the *Washington Post's* Greg Sargent called the possibility of Trump winning "a fantasy."[45]

In July, *Moody's Analytics* suggested that the electoral outcome would be an easy Hillary Clinton victory.[46]

In August, one of *The POLITICO* Caucus's GOP insiders declared Trump's chances of winning were literally less than zero. He said for Trump to win, "it would take video evidence of a smiling Hillary

★ ★ ★

drowning a litter of puppies while terrorists surrounded her with chants of 'Death to America.'"[47]

In September, Obama campaign manager David Plouffe outlined why he believed Hillary Clinton had a one-hundred percent chance of winning.[48]

The professional pollsters weighed in too:

The day before the election, Larry Sabato's Crystal Ball prophesied 322 electoral votes for Clinton and 216 for Trump.[49]

The Princeton Election Consortium gave Clinton a 99% percent chance of winning.[50]

The *Huffington Post's* forecast gave Clinton a 98% percent chance of winning.[51]

PredictWise gave Hillary an 89% percent chance of winning.[52]

The *New York Times's* The Upshot gave Hillary an 85% percent chance of winning.[53]

FiveThirtyEight gave Clinton over a 71% percent chance of winning.[54]

More from Politico's end-of-year summation of the futility of political experts . . .

Dana Milbank in the *Washington Post*, October 2, 2015: "I'm so certain Trump won't win the nomination that I'll eat my words if he does. Literally: The day Trump clinches the nomination I will eat the page on which this column is printed in Sunday's Post."[55]

FiveThirtyEight's Nate Silver reported in October, "Women are defeating Trump."[56]

After the third and final presidential debate, political expert Bob Beckel declared on CNN that the presidential race was "over."[57]

Philip Bump wrote in the *Washington Post*, "Donald Trump is facing an apocalyptic election scenario, thanks to women voters."[58]

The respected Cook Political Report reported Democrats would pick up five to seven Senate seats, and Clinton would likely turn at least a couple of red states blue in the presidential race.[59]

A few more wildly bad predictions by media "experts" were provided by the Washington Post:[60]

June 17, 2016:

"Over the last two decades, American presidential elections have all been relatively close. But with Donald Trump at the helm, the Republican Party faces the prospect of a historic landslide closer to the creamings received by Barry Goldwater in 1964 (who lost by 23.6 points), George McGovern in 1972 (24.2 percentage points), and Walter Mondale in 1984 (19.4 percentage points). At this point, the only real question appears to be how huge (or beautiful — pick your Trumpian adjective) the margin will be." (Jeet Heer, New Republic)[61]

July 13, 2015:

"The chance of his winning [the] nomination and election is exactly zero." (James Fallows, the Atlantic)[62]

July 17, 2015:

"Donald Trump is not going to be the next president of the United States. This reporter is already on record pledging to eat a bag of rusty nails if the real estate tycoon with the high hair manages to snag the GOP nomination, much less takes down likely Democratic nominee Hillary Clinton next fall." (Ben White, CNBC)[63]

August 26, 2015:

"Donald Trump is going to lose because he is crazy." (Jonathan Chait, New York Magazine)[64]

August 15, 2016:

"That's a guy who knows he is going to lose. That's a guy who knows he is going to lose. You start talking that way and, again, I don't know that he's ever wanted to win. It's sad. It's sad and pathetic what's going on out there." (Joe Scarborough, MSNBC)[65]

October 18, 2016:

"The good news: He will lose this election badly, by which I mean poorly. Exceedingly poorly . . . He will lose the popular vote, and he will lose the electoral vote." (Jim Nelson, GQ)[66]

November 6, 2016:

"I tweeted about this yesterday, but I'm gonna put the take here because maybe you're already freaking out about Tuesday and starting to drink heavily. Here's the deal: Donald Trump is going to get his a-- kicked. Anyone who says otherwise is either a) afraid of jinxing it and/or making Hillary Clinton voters complacent (understandable); b) afraid of being wrong (Nate Silver); c) supporting Trump; or d) interested in making this a "horse race" for the sake of maintaining public interest (most of the television media, along with grotesque s---bags like Mark Halperin). But this isn't close, and never was." (Drew Magary, Deadspin)[67]

What's more telling is that these same clueless, bitter, hateful liberal pundits became even more bitter critics of Trump after his victory. After all this remarkable "wrongness." Before the election was won by Trump, these same media experts made, and continue to make, the same hysterical predictions about "the end of Trump," over Russian collusion . . . over the Stormy Daniels affair . . . over the separation of illegal alien parents from children at the border . . . over the Trump-Putin Summit in Helsinki . . . over the Ukrainian phone call . . . over the China trade war . . . over the COVID-19 pandemic . . . over the post-COVID-19 economic collapse . . . and on and on.

These liberal critics and media have become so deranged they went totally off the rails after Trump's Summit with Putin . . . calling Trump "a traitor," claiming he either "betrayed America" or "gave the worst performance with a world leader in the history of America," or claimed "Putin has compromising pictures of Trump with Russian prostitutes."

After days of nonstop media hysteria hammering away at "Trump the traitor," a new NBC News and Wall Street Journal poll came out showing:

1) Trump's popularity had *improved*. His approval rating was the *highest* of his presidency.
2) His approval rating among voters from his own party was among the highest in *history*.

Then, in quick succession, came polls from Gallop and American Barometer both showing Trump's approval at the highest level of his presidency and just about the highest in history among voters from his own party. Three respected polls were showing the exact same results.

Once again, Trump's critics weren't just wrong, but spectacularly wrong.

The takeaway of this chapter?

Screw the critics because . . .

A) Critics are idiots . . .
B) Critics are bitter and jealous . . .
C) Critics want you to fail, so they are just pouring out wishful thinking . . .
D) Critics are usually dead wrong about everything. That's why they're critics. They can't accomplish anything themselves, so they guess for a living.

President Trump has made a career from ignoring critics, using their cannon fodder to inspire him to achieve greatness while proving

them hysterical, ridiculous, and almost always spectacularly wrong.
So can you!

Stop listening to critics, naysayers, negative nincompoops, time
wasters, emotional leeches, and vampires . . . and most importantly . . .
so-called "experts." Most dreams are killed by listening to people
who have no clue what they are talking about! Their only goal is
to discourage you from achieving your goals and to destroy your
confidence. Or, it may not be an agenda against you personally. The
critic's ego is just so small, he or she is rooting for anyone or everyone
to fail, in order to make themselves look brilliant by comparison.

From now on . . .

Listen to your gut . . . Listen to your heart . . . Believe in YOU . . .
Trust in you . . . Believe in your dreams . . . Never, Never, Never, EVER,
Ever Give up. And in the immortal words of Donald J. Trump . . .

"Screw the critics."

★ ★ ★ ★ ★ ★

CHAPTER SEVEN

TRUMP RULE #4
The EGO Rules

We can't ignore what is undoubtedly Trump's most controversial personality trait and perhaps the single most important Trump Rule—EGO.

Many people think Trump's ego and his willingness to fight back, standing up for who he is and what he believes, is why he is so hated by the establishment. Not true. The reason Trump is so hated and vilified is because for the first time since Ronald Reagan was president, the DC establishment (i.e., "swamp") doesn't have either one of their own, or a weak puppet they can control as President.

Trump beat their establishment candidate and is now threatening their gravy train. With a community organizer like Obama as President, the powerful DC swamp establishment insiders, super-wealthy, and billionaire globalists (think George Soros) had the perfect puppet whose strings they could pull with impunity.

Hillary, as President, would have been a little different, but just as good. As an establishment DC swamp creature herself, Hillary was one of them—a string puller herself pocketing hundreds of millions from corrupt cronyism, willing to sell out America to the highest bidder.

Trump is exactly the opposite. He cares first and foremost about hard-working American citizens and taxpayers, which means "draining the swamp," and taking power away from the establishment globalist elites and giving power back to the people. And, as an experienced businessman, he knows exactly how to do it. Trump has the ego to trust himself and, most importantly, the ego to not only ignore the critics, but to fight back and take them head-on. This explains why he is so despised by the establishment. Trump (and his large ego) roll over for no one.

Donald Trump is all ego. And I mean that in a positive way. Who says ego is bad? Ego is critical for success. This entire chapter is devoted to *The Trump Ego Rules*. Trump proves ego is a valuable part of your tool box. If you don't believe in you, why should anyone else? Ego is so important, it permeates most, if not all, the other TRUMP RULES.

Here are the five *Trump Ego Rules* you'll need to learn from Trump to succeed. Plus, a bonus story at the end that I know you'll enjoy. I call it, *THROW GRANDPA FROM THE PLANE*. If you didn't understand the importance of ego, chutzpah, and self-promotion before, I guarantee you will after you're done studying this chapter!

TRUMP EGO RULE #1: IF IT'S TO BE IT'S UP TO ME:

One of the things I learned by watching Donald J. Trump do his thing is this simple: *Ego is good.*

Even as a young college graduate, just starting my career in the business world, I intuitively understood what Trump was about—ego. Trump proved again and again that the guy with the biggest ego "rules"—rules the business world and rules the country. The person with the biggest ego gets the most beautiful spouses, gets the biggest buildings, and builds the biggest brand.

It was clear Trump was always the boss. He made his own decisions. He trusted his own gut. Sure, he hired lawyers and consultants and experts to advise, but in the end, only *the Donald* made the final decision. In the end, it was up to Trump to promote Trump, to market Trump, to sell Trump. Trump was the CEO of the law firm of *Me, Myself, and I*.

I quickly realized we could all learn a few things from Trump. Things I'd never been taught in high school, or at Columbia University.

Other than reading, writing, and arithmetic, public school teachers and college professors often teach the wrong things. They should stick to those three. But as far as success in business, or a competitive career goes, teachers know essentially nothing. They know nothing because most have never lived and competed in the real world. They've lived a sheltered, cared-for life in academia. Even worse, they know little or nothing about money, since they have always had a secure job and safe paycheck (plus pension). That's why, sadly, almost every lesson taught in school and college leads to failure in the business world.

As a result, young impressionable students are taught that ego is bad. That couldn't be further from the truth. I've been fortunate enough to meet many billionaires, business moguls and political legends. They all have that same quality as Trump—loads of ego. People who have no clue about what it takes to succeed think it's a character flaw. *It's not*.

As a matter of fact, based on all the big-ego business superstars I've met, it's a prerequisite. All super-achievers have a huge ego. Every business owner I've ever met has a huge ego. Every legendary politician I've ever met has a huge ego. Every superstar entertainer and athlete I've met has a huge ego. Virtually everyone that makes big bucks has a huge ego. Being humble is greatly overrated.

Students at school are also taught that "there is no 'i' in teamwork." That's correct, but there's also only limited money or fame in it. The key to success is not being humble, or playing nicely with others. Spend your lifetime playing nicely and you know what you'll get? A cheap gold watch and a cheap retirement cake. If you don't spend your life promoting and selling your talents, no one will ever notice.

What can you learn from Trump about ego? Perhaps the most important lesson is that you, and only you, are in control of your destiny. America was made great through personal responsibility, self-reliance, and rugged individualism. Today our country is badly divided. Just about half the nation depends on the government for virtually everything. Like baby birds with their mouths open, they wait for their mother to drop food in their mouths. But it's not just big government they depend on—it's big corporations to provide jobs, big media to translate the news, big education unions to educate their kids, and Big Pharma to keep them healthy. Worst of all, they listen to so-called "experts" and authority figures to tell them how to think.

The other half of America (63 million Trump voters) wants little to do with the government, big corporations, or big media. That's why they love Trump's independent thinking, contrarian attitude, and maverick, in-your-face style.

Trump doesn't always play by the rules; Trump doesn't take orders; Trump doesn't give a damn what others think. As my great friend Corey Lewandowski says, "You gotta let Trump, be Trump." Trump's ego, personality, and energy are so big, his name is a noun, verb, and adjective. He's even his own zip code!

But there's a smaller subset of those Trump voters, the 28 million small business owners in America. That number includes independent contractors and professionals (lawyers, doctors, dentists, accountants, etc.). I'm in that crowd. This group is populated by independent thinkers, contrarians, mavericks. They don't rely on "experts" to tell them what to do. They rely first and foremost on their own brains, brawn, wits, balls, hustle, and ego to survive. They would rather apologize later than ask permission now. They have a keen understanding that . . .

If it's to be, it's up to me.

Trump and "the Trump Army" understands the answer always lies within you. This is what we learned from Trump. We don't wait for government to save us, or protect us, or make us wealthy. We put on our big-boy pants and make it happen. My success has come from *my* hustle, *my* hard work, *my* vision, *my* faith, *my* action, *my* energy, *my* enthusiasm, *my* tenacity, and *my* relentless spirit. I am the managing partner in the Law Firm of *Me, Myself, and I.*

Remember when Obama said, "You didn't build that"?

Let me say, *"Bull sh—t."* I have been the architect, contractor, and interior designer of every inch of my life. I built it. I didn't sit around waiting for anyone or anything to give me a break. My mouth wasn't open, waiting for Big Government or Big Daddy to throw food my way. I went out and hunted my own prey. I owe thanks to a number of people who have helped me along the way, but I owe nothing to government.

One of those people is Donald J. Trump. I scored the goal, but he gets an assist.

I've accomplished miracles with the TRUMP RULES. You'll read more about that later. But what's interesting is, like Trump and so many other entrepreneurs, I did it by myself. I didn't rely on others to sell me. I sold myself. The simple fact is no one can sell me as well as I can sell me.

Early in my career as chief salesman, rainmaker, and human Energizer Bunny, when I tried desperately to find an established agent to represent me in my quest to become my generation's Jimmy "The Greek" (the legendary Vegas odds maker, famous for his role on CBS's NFL pregame show), I was rejected by every agent I contacted. So, I did the job myself. With an assist from my mentor, Doug Miller, who portrayed my agent in a few key phone calls, I acted as my own agent.

The result? I may be the only national TV anchor and host in the history of American television to land a job at a major TV network without one day's experience on television at any level.

And I'm probably also the only guy to ever land a major TV host job with myself as my agent. Not just the first time at CNBC (then known as Financial News Network), but the second time around with my football pregame show, *Wayne Allyn Root's WinningEDGE*. And the third time, too—with *The Wayne Allyn Root Show* on Newsmax TV.

I landed all three gigs through the law firm of *Me, Myself, and I*. I pitched and pitched and pitched some more. I was the pitcher and the cleanup hitter. I depended only on me. And I pulled off three miracles. No agent or manager involved. If I can do it, so can you. The key is EGO. Believe in yourself and you can make it happen.

Over the years, I've retained a number of agents to sell my reality television show ideas. They never sold one. All my television hits were sold by one guy—*me*. Although my great friend and sometimes TV partner Michael Yudin gets an assist.

I hired several literary agents. But all my biggest book deals were successfully sold by one agent—*me!*

In the business world, deals rarely come your way by luck, or coincidence. In my case, not one ever did. Every deal was created by my relentless pursuit ... my contacts ... my energy ... and my enthusiasm. No one else closed those deals. It was always the law firm of *Me, Myself, and I*.

In the speaking world, I've hired multiple speakers' agents and speakers' bureaus to represent me. Yet, over 90% of my speech bookings have come from one guy's efforts—*me!*

Now I'm a nationally-syndicated conservative talk radio host. I hired big-time radio agents for years to represent me. Yet none ever landed even a local radio show for me. Guess who finally sold me successfully? *Me.* Big surprise.

I personally sold my talents to Edward Stolz, owner of KBET 790 AM Talk in Las Vegas. Thank you, Ed, for believing in me, even though I'd never hosted one minute of radio in my life. Within one year, I sold my talents to national radio syndicators Floyd Brown and Fred Weinberg of USA Radio Network. No agents involved. Once again, I relied on me. I sold me. Another big victory. No agent ever did it. I did. Surprise.

The moral of the story is . . . stop waiting for someone or anyone to save you. You'll be waiting a long time—*Eternity.* To sum it up, there are three laws at work:

A) *If it's to be, it's up to me.* Your action, energy, and motion will create openings and opportunities. Sitting still waiting for someone else to save you will lead to . . . *nothing.*
B) No one can ever sell you as well as you can sell yourself.
C) No one will ever believe in you with the same level of passion as you believe in yourself.

Where did I learn all this? Three guesses. From studying, watching, and modeling Donald Trump. Surprise.

In the end, it's up to you. Don't be shy. The famous old saying is: *Opportunity only knocks once.* Not true. The raw truth is . . . *it never knocks at all.* You have to create opportunity. You have to make it happen. You have to grab opportunity like a caveman, club it over the head, and drag it home to your cave.

Get off your butt, stop complaining, stop protesting, stop sitting around waiting for handouts, or luck, or government, or an agent, or a sugar daddy, or a lawsuit to change your life. You are your own best agent. Your success depends on you. Your success depends on you relentlessly selling *you*. Your success depends on pitching, not bitching. Your success depends on the law firm of *Me, Myself, and I.*

I learned this all from Trump. Yes, he toots his own horn. Yes, he's his own best salesman. Yes, Trump relies on Trump to sell Trump. Yes, Trump is his own best promoter and publicist. It's worked out pretty well, hasn't it?

It worked out pretty well for me, too. I promise, it will work out well for you, too. Only you can sell you with the kind of passion, conviction, and energy necessary to change your life!

And remember, being humble is greatly overrated. Whether you like it or not, in this world, TRUMP RULES. Thanks President Trump for showing the way.

TRUMP EGO RULE #2: SELF-PROMOTION

I also learned this one from Trump at an early age—right out of college. There is nothing wrong with self-promotion. As a matter of fact, if you won't or can't sell you, no one else will. Not only is it necessary for you to sing your own praises, it is the best and perhaps the only way to get ahead. People are busy. Bosses and decision-makers are busy. Wealthy business owners are busy. They might have 100 or 500 or 1000 employees. Jack Welch of GE used to have 200,000. Trust me, if you don't sell them loudly on your talents and accomplishments, the CEO or decision-makers will never notice. The quiet ones never get noticed. The truth is, *the squeaky wheel gets the grease.*

You'll read it more than once in this book . . . Mohammed Ali's famous quote fits perfectly here: "It ain't bragging if you can back it up." Ali transcended boxing. He became a world-class legend because of his big mouth, big ego, taunts, nonstop bragging, and funny rhymes. I doubt he would have become *the greatest* without screaming, to anyone who would listen, "I'm the greatest."

But even Ali takes a backseat to the greatest self-promoter of all time: P.T. Barnum.

P.T. was the ultimate showman. He made millions in the late 1800s (when a million dollars really meant something) showing off "oddities" around the globe.

He then invested those millions in real estate, particularly around Bridgeport, Connecticut, where he tried to encourage industrial development. In 1855, the real estate market crashed. P.T. Barnum was bankrupt. He owed his creditors nearly half a million dollars, the equivalent of over $10 million today. P.T. endured years of lawsuits and public humiliation.

But Barnum never gave up. The ultimate showman, he gave lectures around England about showmanship and making money. That's a lesson in chutzpah and ego: A bankrupt man, heavily in debt, gives speeches about wealth and success.

It worked, as chutzpah usually does. He was able to pay off all his debts. Soon, he regained control of his main attraction, *The American Museum* in New York City, filled with those "oddities." P.T. added America's first aquarium. Then, at the ripe old age of sixty-one, he entered the circus business. *Barnum's Grand Traveling Museum* raked in over $400,000 in its first year. It eventually became *P.T. Barnum's Greatest Show on Earth.*

P.T. became a living business legend, a marketing and promotion expert, and a household name worldwide! His circus business eventually became *Ringling Bros. and Barnum & Bailey Circus.*

By 1899, P.T.'s autobiography was second in America in copies in print, topped only by the Bible. Just one of his many huge mansions later became the University of Bridgeport. He became a philanthropist, giving away millions of dollars. He founded Bridgeport Hospital. Later in life, he was elected to the Connecticut legislature and then was elected Mayor of Bridgeport, Connecticut, the scene of his earlier disastrous downfall and real estate collapse.

At his death, P.T. Barnum was the most famous American in the world. But his true success did not start until he was in his sixties.[68]

Are you still not convinced about the value and importance of self-promotion? Let's take a look at the life story of another great self-promoter: Mother Teresa. I'll bet you didn't expect *that* name!

Mother Teresa is perhaps the most famous Catholic in modern history. She was known for her relentless devotion to the poor, starving, sick, diseased, disabled, and downtrodden. Her work, opening 517 missions in 133 countries, won her the 1979 Nobel Peace Prize and inspired millions of fans around the world to get involved in charity. In 2003, she was beatified by the Catholic Church, one miracle away from sainthood.[69]

The words that come to mind when thinking of the work of Mother Teresa are *loving, humble, charitable, saintly*. But not self-promoter, right? Wrong.

There was another successful trait of Mother Teresa's that received much less attention. She was one of the most relentless, shameless, in-your-face promoters, hustlers, and charity fundraisers in history. And as far as humble, she may have said humble things, but Mother Teresa could have taught P.T. Barnum a thing or two about self-promotion!

Mother Teresa understood that celebrity leads to millions of dollars in donations. Celebrity comes from one place—the media. So, Mother Teresa courted the media relentlessly. Irish rocker Bob Geldof said of Mother Teresa, "The way she spoke to journalists showed her to be as deft a manipulator as any high-powered American public relations expert."[70]

★ ★ ★

If your goal is helping the poor, sick, disabled, and dying, and you understand that building a celebrity brand will allow you to raise hundreds of millions of dollars to alleviate suffering, and the way to build a celebrity brand is to promote, promote, promote, and court media 24/7, then it's smart to court the media and build a celebrity brand as the most kind, humble, religious, devoted-to-charity Nun in the world. And that's exactly what Mother Teresa did. It was a purposeful, calculated campaign to put her charity on the map—to do good by promoting herself 24/7.

Mother Teresa's good deeds received high-profile media attention, which in turn attracted donations from all over the globe. Checks and cash poured in in envelopes by the thousands every day, amounts in the millions per day. Offices were set up by the Catholic Church just to open all the envelopes and count all the cash.

But her courting of the super-wealthy was even more relentless. Legend has it that Mother Teresa had a unique technique for prying large checks from wealthy men. She achieved great success by relentlessly pitting the egos of wealthy men against each other. There's that concept again—all wealthy and successful men have outsized egos.

Mother Teresa was a brilliant promoter and manipulator. I mean that only as high praise. She understood the power of her own brand name. She would invite the richest men in the world to a charity fundraiser for her mission. No one could possibly turn down a personal invitation from the world-famous Mother Teresa.

Then, at the event, she would put them on the spot publicly, asking *one* billionaire, in front of the entire crowd, how big a check he could write to her charity. The embarrassed and ultra-competitive billionaire would, of course, offer a million dollar check to avoid looking cheap. Mother Teresa would then publicly ask the billionaire standing next to him if he could top that donation. She'd go around the room asking the same question until she was satisfied she'd squeezed, embarrassed, and *guilt-ed* every dollar possible out of these wealthy men. Hilarious. Brilliant. And wonderfully effective. What a promoter!

This future Saint understood that *all is fair* and *anything goes* when raising money for a great charitable cause. Millions of poor and diseased people around the world benefited from her relentless fundraising. Her missions treated the poorest of the poor and the sickest of the sick—with diseases such as AIDS, Leprosy, and TB.

Mother Teresa is, today, officially called the "Blessed Teresa of Calcutta." A former nun in her employ reported that just one of her order's bank accounts in the Bronx, New York had over $50 million it in. She kept bank accounts all over the world. It is quite likely that Mother Teresa was running a billion dollar business upon her death.[71]

Mother Teresa proves self-promotion and *The Trump Ego Rules* work, even if your goal is saving the poor and sick, or even if your goal is Sainthood! Yes, Mother Teresa was a self-promoter, but used it for good.

> *I choose the poverty of our poor people. But I am grateful to receive it [the Nobel Prize] in the name of the hungry, of the naked, of the homeless, of the crippled, of the blind, of the leprous, of all those people who feel unwanted, unloved, uncared, thrown away of the society, people who have become a burden to the society and are ashamed by everybody.*
>
> —Mother Teresa accepting the Nobel Peace Prize in 1979

Trump obviously listened and learned from great self-promoters like Mohammed Ali, P.T. Barnum, Mother Teresa (and don't forget the ultimate New York promoter George Steinbrenner). And like all great students, Trump studied and learned well. Then he by-passed *the Masters*. He took self-promotion to the next level. Even P.T., Mohammed Ali, and Mother Teresa never came close to becoming president of the United States, commander-in-chief of the greatest military in world history and leader of the free world. That *Triple Crown* certainly makes Trump the greatest self-promoter of all time.

Trump listened and learned. I listened and learned from Trump. Just as I hope you will now listen and learn from the **TRUMP RULES**.

TRUMP EGO RULE #3: BRAGGING

Liberal critics call Trump a braggart. Well, as Mohammed Ali said, "It ain't bragging if you can back it up." Trump is a billionaire, a luxury brand, a reality TV mogul, and president of the United States all rolled into one. I think it's clear he's not bragging, he's *doing!*

I also believe there is method to Trump's madness. Bragging serves a purpose. It sets the bar high. He puts tremendous pressure on himself and those around him to perform at the highest levels. Each time Trump "brags" he is setting up a lofty goal to aim for. And what a motivational tool. He is burning the bridge behind him—either succeed, or look like a loser. Once Trump brags about some great future achievement, he has no choice but to make it happen. What is truly sad is that no matter how much the achievement will help America and the world, his detractors (especially the lying "fake media") will do everything in their power to oppose it.

Bragging also serves a second purpose. That purpose is *Positive Thinking*. You must first see it and feel it and taste it before you can achieve it. By bragging, Trump is seeing and feeling his future success, as if it has already happened. Trump is brilliant. This is how you manifest success in your subconscious. This is how you make something most people think is impossible, possible.

Others laugh at Trump, scoff at him, call him a braggart, even call him a conceited fool. Trump is no one's fool. He's playing chess while everyone around him is playing checkers. In his mind's eye, Trump has already achieved the thing he is bragging about, which in turn helps him to see a clear path to his goal, which puts tremendous stress and pressure on him to deliver, which is what helps him to actually turn his wild, unimaginable dreams into reality.

TRUMP EGO RULE #4: CAJONES

Here's a real-life story from Civil War days that says it all. I can't explain this remarkable Trump-like quality any better. So, I'm going to use a story directly from the pages of my hit political book, *The Murder of the Middle Class*.

This guy is a American Civil War version of Trump, circa 1863. This is one of the great *cajones* stories of all time.

I'm a war buff. And there is no greater story of victory than that of Colonel Joshua Chamberlain during the Civil War Battle of Gettysburg in May 1863. What makes this story so remarkable was that Chamberlain was just a college professor from Maine, with no military experience. Yet, he led a regiment into battle at Gettysburg. He was ordered to defend a small hill named Little Round Top. What he did that day helped turn the tide for the Union. His efforts led to the victory at Gettysburg, which in turn changed the course of history. The North won the Civil War and his actions were the catalyst.

With Union forces under heavy attack and about to falter . . . with his men outnumbered, in disarray, running out of ammo and about to retreat, Chamberlain ordered a counter attack with only bayonets. He was surrounded and outnumbered, yet rather than retreat, he attacked! This crazy bold move emboldened his own troops, while it shocked and confused the Confederate forces. The small unit under Chamberlain's command charged right at the larger force—without guns. With just bayonets, down to their last men, this small force turned the tide. The shocked Confederates were caught off guard and captured.

The Union went on to win Gettysburg. Chamberlain received the Medal of Honor, the highest award for bravery in the United States military. He was promoted to commander, then General. Chamberlain served in twenty battles and numerous skirmishes, was cited for bravery four times, had six horses shot from under him, and was wounded six times, even given up for dead by surgeons.

Chamberlain's heroism, bravery, and tenacity was recognized by General Grant. He was given the honor of commanding the Union troops at the surrender ceremony for the infantry of Robert E. Lee's Army at Appomattox Court House, Virginia. He then went onto a successful political career as the four-term Republican Governor of Maine.[72]

What the GOP needs today is 535 Joshua Chamberlains in the United States Congress. 535 leaders with the spirit, boldness, bravery, tenacity, and heroism of that Maine college professor.

I wrote that section in my hit political book *The Murder of the Middle Class* in 2014—one year *before* the Trump phenomenon appeared on the scene. It's clear I was describing Donald J. Trump. He is the only Republican leader today with the spirit, boldness, and *cajones* of Joshua Chamberlain. That spirit won back the White House for the GOP, against all odds. That spirit beat the "unbeatable" Hillary Clinton. That spirit has allowed Trump to fight the entire Washington DC swamp. It has been one man charging, without weapons, up a steep hill against a force of thousands. And he made them retreat and surrender! That's Trump in a nutshell.

Except he's not unarmed. Trump's ego is a nuclear weapon!

TRUMP EGO RULE #5: REINVENTION

Reinvention is another priceless TRUMP RULE. Have you ever seen anyone who reinvents themselves more than Donald J. Trump? He constantly reinvents his career. He constantly reinvents his businesses. He even reinvents his wives. Trump has reinvented himself a thousand times. He has risen from the ashes of defeat and death like a phoenix.

Trump's success in real estate and casinos started to fade. So, he became a licensor of a brand to others—the Donald Trump brand. When that success started to fade, he became a reality TV show producer and star. When that got boring, he decided to reinvent himself as president of the United States.

I watched, listened, and *modeled* my life after Trump. How many times have I reinvented myself? I've lost count. Much of my success has come from my ability to reinvent myself on what sometimes seems like a weekly basis. Any guy that goes from living in a bedroom in his parents' home to "King of Vegas Sports Gambling" (as the media dubbed me)—and then goes into politics and wins a vice presidential nomination, is pretty good at reinvention. When the success of my political career started to fade, I reinvented myself as a conservative radio and TV talk show host. Just as I finished this book, I began a new journey in the sports gaming business.

Who knows what will come next for me—after all, I'm just getting warmed up at fifty-nine years old!

In today's competitive world, it's important to showcase different talents and be, not only open to, but also prepared to change course at a moment's notice. This is true whether your goal is to keep your current job against brutal competition, or thrive in a new career.

Finally, I end this chapter with the greatest story of self-promotion ever inspired by the TRUMP RULES. I call it . . .

THROW GRANDPA FROM THE PLANE

His real name was Norm Johnson. We weren't blood related. I first met "Grandpa Norm" when I married into his family. But we hit it off instantly like grandpa and grandson, so he insisted I call him *Grandpa Norm.* Just like that, he became my adopted grandfather. It was love at first sight. We shared a love of God, family, sports, sports cars, and most importantly, fitness.

Most importantly, we were both workout fanatics. In those days I lived in Malibu, California and had a world-class home gym in my home. I worked out two hours a day. Norm LIVED in the Pasadena Athletic Club. Yes, Grandpa Norm *lived* in an apartment above the gym. Just like me, this ninety-plus-year-old worked out two hours a day. Our relationship was meant to be.

But there was a big difference between the way we had led our lives. I was already a celebrity and television star at the age of thirty, while Grandpa Norm had lived an *everyday-Joe,* blue-collar life. Norm was a retired print shop worker. He had been an anonymous, working-class guy his entire life. After getting to know him, I found out this was one of his life's regrets. Grandpa Norm wanted to be *someone.* He wanted people to know his name before he left this earth.

Six months before his ninety-second birthday, Norm came to me with a birthday wish. He said, "Grandson, I love you and am going to ask you for a huge gift. I'll be ninety-two on my next birthday. As a special gift, can you make me famous? I've been a *nobody* my entire life, but before I die I want to be famous. I want to live your life, even if only for a few days. I want my *fifteen minutes of fame.* Can you do that for me?"

How's that for pressure? A nice, humble guy has walked the earth for ninety-one and a half years, completely anonymous. Now he wants me to change that, out of the blue, with the snap of my fingers, and make him magically famous on his ninety-second birthday.

Impossible? Of course not. Especially not if you've spent your life studying the greatest showman and self-promoter ever—Donald J. Trump!

As you'll read, later in this book, I had used the techniques of self-promotion, chutzpah, and *the Trump Ego Rules* to promote myself from a small bedroom in my butcher father's home to national TV anchorman and host of five shows on CNB—without ever being on TV one day of my life beforehand. So why couldn't I self-promote Grandpa Norm to fame?

I dreamed up one heck of an idea. I came back to Grandpa Norm and told him, "I have the idea that will turn your dream into reality, Grandpa. Are you ready to be famous? You'll need to take a leap of faith with me. Literally. Are you ready? We're going to celebrate your ninety-second birthday with a Grandfather and Grandson skydive! You do that with me and I'll make you famous. Are you willing to jump out of a perfectly good airplane from thirty thousand feet up, then dive down to earth at over 120 mph?"

Grandpa never hesitated, "Grandson, I'm in. Let's take that leap of faith! And why not? I'm going to be ninety-second years old. What do I have to lose? If I miss, I'll already be halfway to heaven!" How's that for a great attitude?

So, now I did what came naturally. I morphed into a combination of Donald Trump and P.T. Barnum. I became grandpa's PR man extraordinaire. I did for grandpa what I'd done for myself. I went on offense. I attacked the media with abandon for the next five months. I bombarded them with press releases, phone calls, and FedExs with my invitation to the event. Remember, there was no Internet invented yet.

I learned from Trump to never wait for the media to reply. I hounded them with follow-up calls. I wouldn't take NO for an answer. Trump taught me to always play on offense. Don't wait for them—you make it happen, you force them. I would not rest until I made Grandpa Norm famous.

One other thing Trump's life and exploits taught me. Never leave it to chance. Always come up with an angle the media can't ignore. An old man about to turn ninety-two years old jumping out of an airplane is one hell of an unusual angle. I played that angle up for all it's worth.

One other thing Trump taught me. Never just tell anyone, make them see it and feel it. Put it on video. So, I sat grandpa in front of a video camera and interviewed him. I took the best parts of the interview and put them on a videotape (I think a VHS in those days). Then I sent the tape to hundreds of media. On the cover of the VHS it said: *THROW GRANDPA FROM THE PLANE.*

Then came the big day. I held my breath. Would the media show up? When Grandpa and I landed safely, we had over thirty news organizations from all over America waiting for us. Every news station in LA was waiting for an interview. Local NBC TV News opened the 5 p.m. newscast in the second largest city in America with our skydive, live, and with an interview with Grandpa Norm! All of Los Angeles watched. Grandpa was a star for the first time in his ninety-two years. Grandpa made the most of the opportunity, asking the beautiful anchorwoman, Colleen Williams, for a date, live with the whole LA watching. She reported she was married. He said, "That's okay, you can still be my friend." Hearts melted all over LA. This story suddenly went national.

Remember, it's all about promotion . . . and energy . . . and personality . . . and ego . . . and getting lots of free media . . . and getting the right "hook" or angle once you're in the media. Sound familiar? This is vintage Donald Trump.

Soon, Rosie O'Donnell came calling. At the time, she had one of the biggest talk shows in America. I sent the video to Rosie's producers. I knew they could never resist a sweet ninety-two-year-old jumping from an airplane. Rosie sent first class tickets to New York, where her show was filmed daily, and a limo to take us to the airport. This was Grandpa Norm's first-ever limo ride and first-ever first class flight of his life.

When we got to New York, Grandpa informed me it was his first ever trip to Manhattan, too. It was certainly his first time on national TV. Are you getting the picture? Something special was happening here. Like Mother Teresa, I used self-promotion to do good, to change a sweet old man's life.

Rosie had Grandpa Norm OPEN THE SHOW by introducing Rosie. Next, she interviewed him on national TV about his life. Then, she showed her thirty-five million television viewers the video of the skydive. She asked Grandpa, "Why did you do it?" Grandpa Norm pointed to me and said, "There's the guy who MADE me do it. My grandson, Wayne, pushed me out of the plane!" The audience roared with laughter. Grandpa was famous, for the first time in his ninety-two years.

To end the interview, Rosie's producers rolled out a cake with ninety-two candles and the entire studio audience sang *Happy Birthday* to Norm. With thirty-five million people watching, Rosie and Grandpa blew out the ninety-two candles and hugged each other to wild applause.

But wait. We were not quite done. Waiting backstage to appear on Rosie's show that day were Drew Barrymore and Estelle Getty, the star of *Golden Girls*. They were two of grandpa's favorite actresses. Drew hugged grandpa and asked for *his* autograph. Estelle told grandpa he was *her hero*.

Next, the pilot for American Airlines announced over the intercom what an honor it was to be flying "the most famous ninety-two-year-old in America." Then he asked the entire crew and all the passengers to join him in singing *Happy Birthday* to Norm. For the rest of the flight, Norm was asked for autographs by dozens of passengers. The flight attendants had to ask passengers to stop walking up to the first-class cabin because they were creating a mob scene.

When Grandpa Norm got home, he was awarded the key to the city of Pasadena. Blue Cross Blue Shield awarded him their "Ageless Wonder" award and featured a story on Grandpa Norm in their nationwide newsletter. All over America, the media featured stories about Grandpa's skydive. Other elderly Americans were inspired by Grandpa to skydive. And Norm got fan mail by the duffel bag from the US Postal Service. Thousands of letters—including about fifty marriage proposals!

Are you starting to see the value of self-promotion? Being humble and "nice" got Norm ninety-two years of a boring, anonymous life. One day of thinking and acting like Trump made him a legend. How's that for powerful?

Norm died a happy man, but only after going race-car driving with his adopted grandson Wayne (that's me) at 150 mph at the California Speedway in Fontana, California in front of a crowd of reporters for his ninety-third birthday. We were busy planning his ninety-fourth birthday when Norm passed away from the flu. But he left this earth happy and fulfilled. We packed more in his last two years than the first ninety-two years. Self-promotion, chutzpah, and ego made all the difference.

I think President Trump would be proud of this story. It shows we all can benefit from just a little injection of Trump.

Now go out and produce your own story—inspired by *The Trump Ego Rules*.

Remember: *If it's to be, it's up to me . . . the squeaky wheel gets the grease . . .* and "It ain't bragging, if you can back it up."

──────── CHAPTER EIGHT ────────

TRUMP RULE #5
Always Pitching, Never Bitching

Here is perhaps the single most important lesson I learned from Donald J. Trump. Not from President Trump. This one was from the very early days of real estate guru and business mogul Trump. The *Art of the Deal* Trump. And of course, it has continued with President of the United States Trump. I've spoken again and again about Trump out-working and out-hustling every competitor. It's why he is who he is, and where he is.

But . . . what exactly is Trump doing when he works and hustles so hard? He is pitching, pitching, pitching and pitching some more. He never rests. He's never satisfied. He always has a new deal to pitch and every pitch comes with twenty different sales angles.

Thanks to Trump, my favorite saying for thirty years now has been: *Always pitching, never bitching.* Just watch Trump and you'll understand. He's the *King of Pitching.* He never wastes his time complaining or protesting. The moral of the story is: If you spend every spare minute pitching new deals, you'll never need to complain or protest.

Trump's book should have been called, *The Art of the Pitch*. Here's my favorite Trump pitch of all time. And it hasn't even succeeded (as of this moment). But it's *that* good that I felt compelled to include it as exhibit A for the *Pitching Hall of Fame*!

Even as president of the United States, Trump is pitching 24/7. And he understands that to pitch and close the deal, you need a unique sales angle. Something that stands out from the crowd and captures your potential customer's attention. Trump created one of the greatest and most creative pitches of all time for North Korean Dictator Kim Jong-un. It had multiple angles. It was a *Hall of Fame Pitch*.

The first sales angle was: *celebrity*. Kim loves celebrity. Kim loves celebrity so much, he is fascinated by Dennis Rodman, a D-list celebrity in the United States. I'm sure Kim has watched *Celebrity Apprentice* dozens of times. Actually, I'm guessing he's watched every episode that's ever aired.

People will buy anything from a celebrity they idolize. That's why celebrities are hired to sell products all over the world. Trump understands that. Trump used his celebrity to his advantage. Kim stated, "Standing next to Donald Trump didn't seem real. It was a fantasy." From that point on, the advantage was all Trump. *Trump the celebrity* could sell something to Kim that no average politician could.

The second angle was *the pitch* itself. Trump sold Kim on the Trump brand of world class luxury and prosperity. Trump painted a picture of a bright, sunny, prosperous future for North Korea—involving million dollar condos like Trump Tower on the beach, next to a yacht club with yachts and speedboats. Trump painted a picture of North Korea looking like Palm Beach or La Jolla. Trump sold Kim just like he sold thousands of millionaire real estate investors on many of his condo projects.

The third angle was the *vehicle* he used. No other world leader would even think of it. Only a real-estate developer and lifelong salesman and pitchman would. It was a vehicle right out of my business bestseller *The Power of RELENTLESS*. In my book, I recommended selling anything, anywhere with the power of VIDEO. I know Trump understood this concept. Because A) He read and endorsed my book. His enthusiastic endorsement is featured on the back cover. And, B) All real-estate developers sell their condos or estates with the power of a first-class video. You can tell someone about a dream or goal until you're blue in the face, but a video *shows* them. It paints a picture like Picasso.

Trump created a Hollywood-movie quality video that he watched with Kim. This video painted the picture of a wealthy North Korea. Trump didn't just tell Kim how beautiful and prosperous he could make North Korea by pursuing peace, he showed his vision to him on video. The movie could have been called, *Making North Korea Great Again*. The real-estate developer-turned-president used this video to close the sale, just like selling a condo at Trump Tower.

Hilarious. But brilliant. Who but Trump would have ever thought of such a thing? The jury is out if it worked or not. Time will tell. But to me, it's the greatest pitch of all time by any world leader negotiating with a madman dictator. Only Trump.

I learned from Trump to spend my days hustling and pitching. I start each day pitching deals and I end each day pitching deals. Yes, that includes Sundays, holidays, and my birthday. I'll rest when I'm dead.

What's the importance of pitching? What exactly do I mean by "pitching?" Trump taught me to disdain a "job." I don't need no stinkin' job. I don't want a "safe paycheck." Forget "tenure." I don't want a guaranteed job for life. I don't want a "safety net." There is no wealth in any of that. No upside. No opportunity to change the world.

No celebrity. No hero. No legends are created. You can never become special with a safe paycheck and tenure.

My life is based on performance. On commission. On deals. I'm a world-class pitcher. The more deals I pitch, the better the odds I can close one or two. So, I'm always pitching as many deals at once, as humanely possible. The more deals I pitch, the better chance I hit on at least one or two home runs that brand me as a winner and super-achiever, and change my life (and hopefully, my kids' lives and my grandkids' lives, too).

From the moment I wake up until the moment my head hits the pillow at night, I'm pitching *me, myself, and I*—my brand, my companies, my products, my talents. I have no time for complaining or protest marches. I'm too busy hustling and pitching. If only more people spent less time bitching and more time pitching, they'd have nothing to bitch about!

Trump is exhibit A. No matter how filthy rich Trump got, he was always hustling and pitching. He always had a hundred different careers, businesses, and sales pitches going at once. Why? First, because he loves the chase, he loves to pitch, he loves to close the deal, and he loves the *Art of the Deal* (designing and carrying out the plan that allows you to close the deal).

Second, because it takes twenty pitches to hit one home run. People with safe jobs and safe paychecks don't understand this life . . . this mindset . . . this way of thinking. They see twenty Trump failures and they call him a "fraud" and "loser." I find that hilarious. He's a billionaire and the most famous brand name in the world, but he's a "failure"? How absurd. How ignorant.

Guys like Trump (and me—because I learned from Trump) are always juggling fifty balls in the air at once. If forty-eight fail, that's okay. Because we know one will be a moderate success and one other will be a home run. That's precisely why we pitch so many deals at all times. It's all a numbers game. And we're enthusiastic about all fifty pitches—simply because you have to be to have any chance to close the deal.

Like Trump, I'm no longer just a human being. I'm more a combination human Energizer Bunny, mafia hit man, and *heat-seeking missile.* The phrase "pitching" simply denotes taking aggressive, nonstop action to search for new clients, new customers, new investors, new business partners and backers, new deals, new businesses to build, new careers, and new opportunities.

Here's my daily agenda. First, I make a list of my targets of opportunity like a mafia hitman. Then I go after them like a heat-seeking missile. I go down the list each morning and start attacking. I'm always on offense. I don't wait for opportunity, I chase it. I don't wait for the phone to ring, I make it ring. I go after my targets of opportunity a hundred times a day.

I email them . . . I call them . . . I text them. I meet them for lunch, dinner, or both. And by the way, I try to always pay. Whoever reaches for the check holds the upper hand. The guy who pays the bill is the winner. He has the energy, balls, and confidence to succeed. People want to do business with that guy!

If I don't reach my targets, I move them to tomorrow's list. I call until I get them. Once I get them, I call or email or meet until the deal is done. I don't care how long it takes. I am relentless. I never give up. I always get my man.

I only cross them off the list once I get a resolution. Even if I get a "NO" I treat that as a "maybe." I keep pitching. Trump taught me to never let go—to become a pitbull.

Once I cross someone off my hit list, it's time to find new targets of opportunity, or as I call it, "refill the pipeline." You can never count on one opportunity, or one career, or one investor. You have to always have at least fifty balls juggling in the air. And, as soon as you lose one, you must start pitching to refill and replace that *hole* in your pipeline.

Think of Trump with twenty Trump real estate projects at all times, Trump television shows, the Trump licensing business, Trump books, Trump-branded products. I learned well. I have a dozen different careers at this moment. I'm working on so many deals, I need a chart on my wall to remind me of all the deals and the names of each person attached to each deal I'm pitching.

I have a local radio show, national radio show, multiple podcasts, reality TV shows, a sports gaming business, a political web site, a business speaking career, a political speaking career, weekly newspaper columns, books, and spokesman career. All the while managing 25 to 30 clients at all times who advertise on my shows.

Thanks President Trump. You taught me well. I'm always pitching, never bitching. I'm far too busy to even think of a reason to complain (other than paying too many taxes and fighting too many regulations). But then that's why I helped elect Donald J. Trump as president—to solve that problem.

We need smaller government, dramatically lower taxes, and far fewer regulations so guys like me and Trump can pitch, pitch, pitch, and make the economy grow. Taxes get in the way of pitches. A high-tax system is tailor-made to hurt people who pitch and produce . . . and redistribute our hard-earned money to people who bitch (and never produce).

But the people who pitch create all the jobs, pay all the taxes, and therefore fund almost the entire government. So, my pitch is to leave us alone and let us pitch to our heart's content. The more we pitch, the more society benefits—including the bitchers.

Now, how I pitch is my own personal system that I developed over many years. This baby isn't Trump's invention. It's my personal gift to you. Read on.

THE PIPELINE

You must keep your pipeline filled at all times. If you're wondering, *What's a pipeline?*, it's your potential deals, jobs, careers, investors, and opportunities. Like a talented circus juggler who keeps a lot of balls in the air, you need a full pipeline that you are always juggling and pitching.

The average person juggles just one ball at a time. They depend on one job, or one career, or one paycheck, or one working spouse, or one sugar daddy, or perhaps government checks to "save" them. A few people have two *balls in the air*. Both scenarios are tragic mistakes.

If that describes you, it is time to fill your pipeline. You need options and backup options . . . and backups for your backups. Not just with one, two, or three balls . . . but a bare minimum of twenty to thirty balls. I personally prefer to juggle fifty balls at all times. That's how you fill your pipeline.

As an example, I might be raising money for a new business idea. Let's say I need to raise $500,000. I would never rely on one investor to write that check. If he says "no" I am left with nothing. I'll most likely be speaking to fifty investors who are each capable of writing the check I need. And I'll have fifty more in the pipeline as backups in case the first fifty fall through.

If you're a cop or fireman or teacher, why not use your free time to build a small business or open a retail store . . . or build a MLM/home-based business . . . or become a salesman . . . or make commission by "dialing for dollars"—raising money on the phone for a charity. Better yet, do all of them! *Always* keep your pipeline filled.

If you're an actor, don't read one screenplay or script. Read twenty-five scripts. And while you're working on your acting career, start writing, producing, and directing too. Or sell ten-million-dollar-homes in Beverly Hills and Malibu while you're acting. *Always* keep your pipeline filled.

If you're a stockbroker and have two hundred clients, congratulations! But never rest on your laurels. Be sure you set aside a couple of hours per day to find another hundred. Or write a book about stock picking. It will give you instant credibility. Or, make speeches in the community to find more clients. Better yet, do it all. *Always* keep your pipeline filled.

If you're a realtor and have fifty listings, congratulations! But you still need to set aside a couple of hours per day to hunt for new listings. Go get fifty more. Or write a book about real estate. Again, instant credibility. Make speeches in the community to find more clients. Better yet, do it all. *Always* keep your pipeline filled.

Here is the point. Never leave your life in the hands of others. Always have backups, and make sure your backups have backups, and those backups are backed up by more backups. *Always* keep your pipeline filled.

Now that I've laid out what it is you have to do, here's my gift. Actually, two gifts; two creative ideas to keep you motivated.

EARLY MORNING PIPELINE

First, always do your pitching in the early morning, before you start your day at your regular job or career. *The early bird catches the worm* does not mean the worm should have stayed in bed longer. It means the early bird eats! You're at your freshest and most positive early in the morning. As the day wears on, you get more negative, or worn down by your day job or life's troubles and challenges. Set aside an hour each morning—including weekends—to identify targets of opportunity, draw up your "hit list," and start pitching.

In that hour, pitch at least three new people or opportunities each day. Hopefully you'll pitch even more. But at least three. I try to pitch five per day. This is all *before* starting your regular workday.

At one of my seminars, I spoke to a young man just starting out as an insurance salesman. He told me he was taught to make five unsolicited sales pitches every day. Unsolicited didn't mean calling friends or neighbors. It meant literally stopping people on the street, or in the bar, store, or at church and pitching insurance. You know what I told him? "Good start, but you need to up your pitch rate to at least ten a day."

Over a lifetime, think of the deals you'll create. Think of the new opportunities. Think of the fortune you'll earn. That one hour each morning is your pipeline to riches, your pipeline to changing your life. It's your one big advantage over the competition. While they're still sleeping or eating breakfast, you're building a foundation to super-charge your life. That one hour each day is pure gold.

Remember, you can catch up on sleep when you die. You are put on this earth to do something special. Is one extra hour a day of work really asking a lot if it changes your life? Put in an hour and I guarantee great things will come; your life will change. Pitching, pitching, pitching with your morning pipeline is how you turn dreams into reality.

And of course, your pipeline is expandable. Do one hour. Or do two hours. Or set aside three hours. Why not three hours of pitching from 5 a.m. to 8 a.m.? Then off to your regular job that pays the bills. Think of the seeds that will be planted. Think of the fruit your pipeline will bear down the road.

Or, at the very least how about one hour a day, plus three hours on Saturday and Sunday. That's eleven hours a week of P&P— pipeline and pitching. Move five *steps* forward for each hour. That's fifty-five steps per week to change your life. That's 2,640 steps per year towards changing and improving your life. That's 26,640 steps forward over the next decade. Think how that adds up over a lifetime. Bravo!

Pipeline Rewards

Train and motivate yourself with rewards. Make up a list of what you like to do and want to buy. Assign points to each item on your list. I call it my "Joy List." Each time I do what I'm supposed to do in my morning pipeline session, I give myself reward points (just like airline miles). I keep track on a chart. Once I accumulate enough reward points, I give myself a gift from my Joy List. Make it FUN to pitch. Every time you pitch, you are closer to buying a gift that gives you joy.

This is how I live my life. This is how I build my career. This is how I multiply my wealth. Thank you, President Trump, for inspiring my life of hustling, pitching, juggling, and filling my pipeline.

─────────── CHAPTER NINE ───────────

TRUMP RULE #6
It's All About the Story

S torytelling—another *TRUMP RULE* where Trump sets the standard. He may be the best storyteller of our generation.

Let me open this chapter with my personal storytelling experiences. In my own career, I've sold hundreds of millions of dollars of diverse products on TV, radio, and online. As I'm writing this chapter, I have recently been the face and voice of the following products on my TV and radio shows: Precious metals, rare coins, rare color diamonds, health insurance, life insurance, IRS tax resolution, financial advice, financial newsletters, age management clinics, law firms, offshore homes for US citizens, firearms, ammo, target practice APP, long-term food storage products, medical clinics for men, nutritional supplements, sunglasses, books, bulletproof clothing for school children, prostate pills, plastic surgeons, business products, healthy alkaline-infused water, men's hair replacement surgery, new automobiles, real estate brokers, small business loans, personal loans, restaurants, political candidates, pain clinics, doctors, dentists, orthodontists, home security, and drug and alcohol rehab clinics, among others. Many others.

How can I possibly successfully sell all these different products? How do I attract enough calls to keep these diverse advertisers happy?

The key is I'm a talented storyteller. My advertisers ask me to write the ads and I am more than willing to do so. As a matter of fact, I believe there are few people who can write ads as fresh and compelling as I can. Why? Because I learned from Trump.

I'm a great storyteller. Facts and stats bore people. I have a keen understanding that no one wants to listen to facts or stats. Let me enlighten you as to what they do want to hear:

1) Endorsements of the company or product by someone they trust, and . . .

2) Emotional stories that move them to feel something special deep down inside. To evoke those emotions, stories must resonate with their own lives. If you can make that happen, you can sell anything, to anyone.

I create a personal story for every product. I do that whether I'm the spokesman for the company, or if I'm just the face or voice in the advertisement on my TV or radio shows. I will relate a story about how I've used the product and it's improved my life, or tell the story of other clients whose lives were changed. As the saying goes, "Facts tell, stories always sell."

It's the exact same reason my business and political speaking careers are successful. I seldom simply recite facts or stats. In my speeches, I tell stories. I might tell as many as a dozen personal stories in each speech. That's how a speaker connects with their audience.

As a matter of fact, I often tell the story of how I first met President Trump, and the story of joining him for dinner at Mar-a-Lago. Those are stories that interest most people. Facts don't. I do the same thing on my radio and TV shows. Each show is filled with emotional story after emotional story. Three hours a day of emotional, personal, and always colorful, passionate stories. Plus, I take dozens of calls from my listeners with their personal stories.

Let me repeat . . . as the saying goes: *Facts tell, stories always sell.*

But I've saved the best for last. Politics, if done right, is all about personal and emotional stories. It's about connecting one-on-one with voters. Bill Clinton was great at it. Ronald Reagan was great at it. Obama was great at it. Do you notice a pattern? All three were elected president by wide margins—*twice!*

But who is the best at storytelling in modern history? President Donald J. Trump.

Here is what I wrote back in 2015 in my national bestselling book, *The Power of RELENTLESS*, about the art of politics:

"Politics is all about storytelling. The winning candidates are the ones who not only have the most compelling personal stories, but who are also able to tell them in a way that connects with the emotions of the voter. The losing candidates are usually the ones with loads of facts on their side, but are boring storytellers. No one remembers, and unfortunately, no one cares. But a great story—voters remember those forever!

Stories are memorable, facts are not. After I've given any of my speeches (business or political), not one person in the room ever quotes a single fact I've told. But they're all quick to tell me how much they enjoyed certain stories I told . . . my journey to become Jimmy "The Greek" . . . my presidential run . . . my home-schooled daughter graduating from Harvard . . . Grandpa Norm jumping out of a plane . . . my nonstop stories of overcoming failure to enjoy success. Those they remember with ease! *Facts tell, stories sell.* Remember that and you'll be a star at whatever you choose to do in life."

Keep in mind, my book, *The Power of RELENTLESS* was written in early 2015 when Donald Trump had not yet given a single political speech. I knew back then what the GOP needed to win the 2016 election—a storyteller.

Trump soon appeared right out of Hollywood central casting. He is the best storyteller in modern political history. Maybe ever. Liberal critics complain and denigrate him for not telling facts. I think they're just mad because Trump adopted their long-time strategy of telling emotional stories . . . and he does it _better_ than they do!

Democrats want GOP candidates to keep quoting stats and facts. Why? Because they know it doesn't work. They want us to nominate boring speakers who are unable to make an emotional connection with voters . . . speakers who quote facts.

Trump may quote a few facts, but he does it with colorful, memorable stories. That's why he's president of the United States.

Have you ever attended or watched a Trump rally on TV? It's story after story. Emotional and personal stories. Few stats. Few facts. _Just the story ma'am._

These rallies are the most entertaining events in the lives of most of the attendees! Trump fans come from hundreds of miles away to experience a Trump event. They bring their kids. They wait for six, eight, ten, sometimes twelve hours to get into these events. Then Trump enthralls them with the equivalent of an old-time _Christian revival_. It's story after story from the life of a wild, high-energy, engaging, charismatic, billionaire storyteller. Many are stories only a billionaire business mogul and TV celebrity could tell.

It's entertaining as heck! I've listened and watched dozens of his rallies. During his first presidential campaign, I was opening speaker and Master of Ceremonies at many Trump events in Las Vegas. What makes Trump so amazing is that he can tell the same story over and over again, and each time it's a little different. Because there are no scripts or teleprompters (unheard of in politics). No one writes campaign speeches for Trump. He just goes out and starts talking.

It's a *stream of consciousness.* He'll add a twist or change the emotion level, such that audiences never get tired of hearing him.

Trump connects. Trump resonates. People leave and they feel like they just became a part of Donald Trump's life. He connects with them like family. They feel like he is the father out to protect them and their loved ones. They feel as if Trump is honoring them, unlike the so-called political and social elites who take them for granted and even look down on them. Finally, someone cares about *them.* Finally, someone appreciates them. For the first time, they aren't invisible!

Now, add in the fact that they've been thoroughly entertained for sixty to ninety rollicking minutes. A Trump event is a Christian revival combined with a rock concert. Other politicians need to bring celebrities along to get an audience revved up. Not Trump. He is the biggest celebrity in the world!

Because of Trump, politics is no longer boring, it's exciting and emotional. It's all about stories. How do I know? I'm a witness. At various times back in 2015 and 2016, there were other GOP candidates for president in Las Vegas at the same time as Trump. One of these candidates attracted one hundred people to his rally. Another attracted two hundred. A third attracted fifty. A fourth had a cocktail party at a private home . . . twenty well-heeled donors showed up. I opened for Trump in front of well over seven thousand. It was like opening for the Rolling Stones!

Yes, Trump is the greatest storyteller of our time. It works. Need proof? He's president of the United States.

It wasn't a short-term phenomenon. Up until COVID-19 struck, Trump's rallies attracted tens of thousands, wherever he went. He filled basketball and football stadiums. *Facts tell, stories always sell.*

A handful of people might force themselves to drive fifteen minutes to hear facts from a traditional politician, but that's only if there isn't a football game on TV. Trump is a football game mixed with a rock concert. Trump is a folk hero. Trump is a religious experience. Trump is a once-in-a-lifetime experience. That's why thousands of people come from hundreds of miles away and wait hours in the hot sun to hear President Trump speak.

What is the lesson here? Business, like politics, is all about sales. And sales is all about stories. To connect with your clients and customers (just like connecting with voters), you must tell powerful, personal, emotional and entertaining stories that move them emotionally. A person who can do that will make millions, or as Trump proves, even billions of dollars.

And since I believe EVERYTHING is sales, I urge you all to learn to tell more compelling stories and less facts, regardless of your field of endeavor. If you can do that, unimagined success and a fortune awaits. As the saying goes, *Facts tell, stories always sell.*

★ ★ ★ ★ ★ ★

CHAPTER TEN ———

TRUMP RULE #7
Celebrity

Trump understands the value of *celebrity* like no one else in the business world *ever*. Like it or not, celebrity sells. Celebrity attracts attention. Celebrity adds credibility. People buy things from celebrities they'd never buy from an average person. People believe what celebrities say, even if they'd never believe the exact same sales pitch from anyone else.

Trump has always understood the value of *the limelight*. He always made sure to be photographed with the biggest celebrities, the most beautiful models and actresses, at the hottest restaurants, nightclubs, events. He always made sure to place himself in the most flattering way on "Page Six" of the *New York Post* and every other gossip column in the media world. For Trump, it is always about *star power*. He knew that celebrity is the ultimate brand builder.

Why do you think the top brands all hire famous models, actors, actresses, and personalities to pitch their products? Why do new restaurants, bars, and nightclubs throw parties and invite top celebrities for free? Why do clothing brands send their products to celebrities for free in the hopes they'll be photographed wearing

155

them? Why do top brands fight to give their products away free in *gift bags* at major Hollywood events? Why do you think those same top brands hire $20,000 per month PR firms to place articles about them in the media? Because celebrity sells. Celebrity literally can make or break any brand.

Trump took it a step further. Not only was he surrounded by celebrities, he created *Celebrity Apprentice*. It became one of the biggest TV hits in Hollywood history. Then, by being elected president, Trump solidified his status as the biggest celebrity of all.

What exactly does all this glitz, glamour, and celebrity get you? What's the point of it all? FREE MEDIA. Celebrity attracts media because famous names and faces sell newspapers and create higher ratings. So, the media is desperate to cover celebrities and celebrity news all day long. It makes them rich. And when they give you free media . . .

IT MAKES YOU FILTHY RICH!

This is Trump's secret weapon. This is why celebrity is worth its weight in gold. Trump parlayed his celebrity and his friendship with celebrities into a billion-dollar luxury brand. Celebrity literally made Trump's brand. It gave Trump name recognition, media coverage, credibility, and billions in sales. The Trump name screamed "celebrity" and millions of people across the globe wanted to associate with Trump to feel like a celebrity themselves.

It's a vicious cycle . . . Trump hangs out with celebrities . . . Trump sells his products based on celebrity . . . Trump gets billions of dollars in free media because the media makes billions of dollars covering Trump's celebrity and his outrageous, controversial statements . . . millions of people across the globe want to say they own Trump products, or live in a Trump property, or read his books, or watch his TV shows so his celebrity can rub off on them. That makes Trump even richer and more famous.

The ultimate example, though, is Trump running for President. Without celebrity, he would never have won the nomination, or the general election. But his celebrity and "star power" commanded the media to follow his every move.

Understanding the value of *free media*, Trump would say something outrageous, colorful, or controversial (usually a mix of all three). Understanding how Trump's controversial statements would raise their ratings and make them billions of dollars, the media would make every Trump utterance a screaming headline. They fed off each other.

Eventually Trump received billions of dollars in free media during the campaign. Hillary may have outspent him 2 to 1 or more, but Trump got billions of dollars in free media. So, Trump never needed to spend billions of dollars on TV ads. The media provided all his promotion and advertising for free. THANK YOU VERY MUCH!

It's one heck of a love-hate relationship. The media hates Trump, but they can't live without him. He single-handedly creates their high ratings. And Trump hates the media, but he can't live without their *free media*.

To Trump, the old saying is pure gold, *There is no such thing as bad media, as long as they spell your name right*. Good or bad, he's always in the headlines. For over three years now, when anyone turns to the news, it's Trump, Trump, Trump, and more Trump. Other people occasionally make the headlines, too—but only by talking about Trump, or attacking Trump, or charging Trump with something.

The media is all Trump, all the time. It's no longer 24-hour news. It's *24-hour Trump news*. If the media could fit 36 hours of Trump-talk in a day, they would.

If the topic is politics, it's about Trump. If the topic is business, it's about Trump's brand, his children's business brand, Trump's economic policies, or Trump's economy. If the topic is sports, it's Trump and the kneeling NFL players, or Trump and LeBron James. If the topic is the COVID-19 pandemic, then it's Trump's response to the pandemic. If the topic is celebrity gossip, it's what each celebrity thinks about Trump. If the topic is global, it's what world leaders think about Trump. If the topic is weather, it's about how Trump's policies on climate change affect the globe, or how Trump is handling a hurricane or other weather disaster. Name the topic, Trump is involved, blamed or credited.

The media may hate Trump, but he is the only thing they cover 24/7. And they made him president with their nonstop coverage and billions in *free media*. Liberals may hate Trump, but he is living rent-free in their minds, 24/7. Celebrities may hate Trump, but they've made him the biggest celebrity of all time.

Trump's understanding of celebrity and the value of free media have combined to make him a billionaire brand, president of the United States, leader of the free world, commander-in-chief, one of the most famous human beings in history, and certainly the most talked about celebrity in world history.

─── CHAPTER ELEVEN ───

TRUMP RULE #8
Everyone Needs a Brand

Donald Trump is one of the greatest branding experts of all time. That's how he made his billion-dollar fortune. He knows the four rules of branding . . .

- KISS: Keep It Simple, Stupid.
- Make sure it's memorable.
- People have to hear it and instantly say, "WOW. I want that."
- Attach it to celebrity.

The Trump brand is one of the greatest brands in the history of real estate worldwide. The brand has all the right elements. First, the name is memorable. It's easy to remember because it's built around a household name and *the celebrity of Trump*. The second part of the brand is *luxury* and *exclusivity*. When you buy a Trump condo, you know you will be experiencing the finest luxury in the world. The third part is the WOW factor. Everyone instantly upon hearing that brand name wants to *be like Trump*. They want the Trump brand to rub off on them. They want to feel like celebrities themselves. How simple is all of that? Trump wins with all four rules of branding.

Apprentice and *Celebrity Apprentice* were no different. The names are simple. The concept was easy to remember. For *Apprentice,* you win it and you get a dream job working for Donald Trump. For *Celebrity Apprentice,* you get to watch celebrities perform tasks, up close and personal. The winner gets to donate a big reward to a great charity. In both cases, you get to be *branded* by Donald Trump.

Both concepts were built around Donald Trump—the biggest celebrity on the show, along with his bigger-than-life personality. It is that same celebrity status and prickly personality that won him the presidency. While Trump's understanding of branding served him well in business, it was when he ran for president that he perfected the art. It was there he put to use everything he had ever learned about branding to make himself president of the United States.

To politicians, whether liberals or conservatives, it all seemed absurd and juvenile. What presidential candidate would call their opponents and critics silly, even insulting names: "Crooked Hillary" (for Hillary Clinton), "Slow Joe and Phony Kamala" (for Joe Biden and Kamala Harris in 2020), "Cheatin' Obama" (for former President Barack Obama), "Little Marco" (for Marco Rubio), "Lyin' Ted" (for Ted Cruz), "Low Energy Jeb" (for Jeb Bush), "Pocahantas" (for Senator Elizabeth Warren), "Crazy Bernie" (for Bernie Sanders), "Low IQ Maxine" (for Congresswomen Maxine Waters), "Cryin' Chuck (for US Senate Minority Leader Chuck Schumer), "High Tax Nancy" (for US Congress Minority Leader Nancy Pelosi).

What president would do that? Only someone who understood branding and was truly brilliant. Only the greatest branding expert of our time. And, it worked. Let's study the method to Trump's madness.

First, Trump didn't bother to nickname anyone who didn't pose a threat to his winning the Presidency. Why waste time on people who are meaningless? And why give them free publicity? Just let them wither in anonymity. Brilliant.

On the left, Trump branded only Hillary and Bernie Sanders during his first presidential run. On the right, only Jeb Bush, Marco Rubio, and Ted Cruz were branded. Notice that no other candidate posed a serious threat. Trump destroyed his only real competition by mocking them. It worked to perfection.

Let's look at the priceless one a little closer: "Crooked Hillary." Simple. It can't get any simpler. Anyone with a sixth grade education can remember and understand it. It conveyed exactly what he wanted voters to remember about her: Hillary is a crook. Hillary is corrupt. Hillary is robbing taxpayers blind. For a brand to stick there has to be some truth in it. Most voters know that over the years both Bill and Hillary Clinton have been caught, or rumored to have been involved in many corrupt acts.

Trump branded and destroyed Hillary with a two-word brand— "Crooked Hillary." She can't be trusted." BOOM. Everyone could understand and remember that. "Crooked Hillary" is branding at its finest.

"Slow Joe Biden" is also brilliant branding in its simplicity. Joe is old and slow. Time has caught up to him. Simple. Bernie Sanders is "crazy extreme" in his far-left views. Jeb Bush is certainly low energy. Marco is short in stature. That is first-class branding. Truth in advertising. Make up a slight to cast doubt on your competition, but be sure there is some truth in it. Be sure it's simple and easy for everyone to remember. Be sure they see the logic—that's what makes it memorable.

By entering politics at the highest levels, Trump put on a four-year, nonstop branding clinic for every business owner and entrepreneur in the world. It just doesn't get any better than that!

The other key to branding is repetition. You need to say it again and again in order to remind your customers, or in this case, voters. So, Trump called her "Crooked Hillary" thousands of times—in tweets, in speeches, at campaign rallies, in ads, in TV interviews. In the end, no one could forget Hillary was crooked. That's branding.

I learned well. I'm not Wayne Allyn Root. I'm a brand. On my national radio and TV shows, I'm "WAR." Those were my initials at birth. Who can forget a TV host named W.A.R.? My fans call my TV and radio shows and say, "Hello WAR." When they see me in a restaurant they yell "WAR!" It works. Simple. Easy to remember. Memorable.

In every business speech, I'm the SOB (Son of a Butcher). At the end of my speeches, fans stand in line for an hour for a picture and for me to sign my books. What do they say? "I want a photo with my favorite S.O.B!" It works. Simple. Easy to remember. Memorable.

And in my other career as a sports prognosticator, I was once dubbed, "the King of Vegas Sports Gambling" by the media. I think it was an article read by five people maximum, including my mother. Yet I loved that brand the minute I heard it. I knew there was gold in that brand name. I've since used that name to identify myself in thousands of TV ads, TV shows, and radio shows. I'm not Wayne Allyn Root, I'm "the King of Vegas," Wayne Allyn Root. Again, simple and memorable. I've attracted millions of calls from potential customers because of that brand. I've earned millions of dollars with that brand. When I was awarded a granite star on the *Las Vegas Walk of Stars*, what did my star say?

Wayne Allyn Root "The King of Vegas."

That's branding. I learned it from studying Donald J. Trump. Thank you, President Trump.

Everyone needs a brand. What's your brand? Create it. Make it simple and memorable. It will change your life.

──────── CHAPTER TWELVE ────────

TRUMP RULE #9
The Power of Relentless

Yes, I wrote the book on this one. Literally. Back in 2015. And guess whose endorsement was on the back cover? Donald J. Trump.

I may have written it, but Trump defines it. What is Donald J. Trump, if not relentless? His middle name is relentless. It should be Donald R. Trump.

Do I really need to say much more about this topic? Yes, I do. No matter how much some people hate President Trump, they have to admit, he is relentless! All of his success—at business, real estate, entrepreneurship, sales, promotion, branding, television, publishing, and of course politics, relates in one way or another to being relentless.

The man has beaten back the entire world—from the DC swamp . . . to the political establishment of both parties . . . to the entire GOP Congress . . . to deep state agencies: CIA, FBI, and DOJ . . . to selfish, self-centered CEOs who couldn't care less about giving jobs to American citizens . . . and to the UN and other globalist organizations, even NATO and some of America's allies. He has been savagely slandered, libeled, humiliated and threatened. Fortunately, he has been under-estimated every step of the way. I always say "NBAT: Never Bet Against Trump." Why? In a word, because Trump is . . .

RELENTLESS.

I'm proud and honored that my book about becoming more relentless became a #1 national bestseller in August of 2015, according to CEO-READ. It is 243 pages defining how to become more relentless, and how it can be harnessed to achieve your dreams.

Trump rarely endorses anything that isn't his exclusive property. This wasn't Trump's book. It was mine. I was honored and thrilled he made an exception for my book. He must have recognized his own dominant trait when reading through my book. I'm guessing it was so obvious, it hit him in the face. Trump is relentless? Duh. Trump had to make an exception and endorse my book—because it was that clear this trait defined him.

But right here, let me simplify things. After a lifetime of studying Trump, I came to the conclusion that "relentless" is the foundation of everything that makes Trump *Trump*. And it's almost always the foundation of any super achiever you'll meet. They're all smart . . . creative . . . passionate . . . driven . . . ambitious . . . they all have world-class work ethic . . . they're all great salesmen and women . . . most of them graduated from elite universities. But the one thing that separates them from the pack is *the power of relentless*.

The really great business superstars never, ever, ever give up. They're like a pitbull with a bone in his mouth. They're like a bull in a china shop. They just won't let go. They won't stay down on the canvas. The odds don't bother them. Tell them it's impossible, it just drives them harder. They always find a way to get back up, keep fighting, and eventually get what they want. They're tenacious and relentless. Trump defines relentless. He is the most relentless person to ever walk this earth. He literally willed himself—as a one-man army—to win the presidential election against enormous odds.

You want to win big? Achieve greatness? Beat the odds? Forget brains, your college pedigree, money, or looks. They all help. But willing yourself to become relentless and unstoppable is where it's at. Refuse to give up, no matter what, or who stands in your way. That mindset alone will change your life.

If you want to learn in detail about this integral and foundational *Trump Rule*, go to Amazon and order a copy of **The Power of RELENTLESS.**

It's a great companion book to this one. Study both books. Own them. Make them part of your game plan. Between those two books, anything is possible. You too can become a "mini Trump."

* * * * * *

──── CHAPTER THIRTEEN ────

TRUMP RULE #10
Chutzpah (a.k.a. Becoming More Jewish)

This is the last of the Big Ten TRUMP RULES because it sums up and repeats pretty much everything that I've already talked about. This one is the essence of Trump. This one defines synergy.

You may think I'm kidding with the subtitle of this TRUMP RULE. I'm not. This Jewish boy is dead serious. Columbia University might be the most radical liberal (i.e., socialist), politically-correct university in America. Yet, even when I attended Columbia back in 1979 through 1983 where everyone was ultra-liberal, ultra-guilty about "white privilege," and deathly afraid of being called a "racist" or "politically incorrect," they offered a class in *Ethnicity in America*. I know because I took the class. The conclusion of this class was that the most successful group and race of people to ever come to America was, and is, the Jewish people. *It's not even close.*

Even politically-correct Columbia could not deny the over-the-top success of the Jewish people.

As you read this chapter, you'll find out that the people of China are well along the path to "becoming more Jewish." They, too, want to copy the Jewish people. They are studying the Jewish people every day, in every way, to learn "The Jewish Way."

Trust me, Trump understood this *way before* the Chinese!

Donald Trump has been surrounded by successful Jewish businessmen his whole life. He grew up in Queens, NY . . . a pretty *Jewish place*. He did business in New York City . . . a very *Jewish place*. Specifically, his career was built in the real estate industry in New York . . . literally almost 100% *Jewish*.

The young Donald Trump watched, listened, and learned like a sponge. I've been around Jewish people my entire life and I can say, without doubt, Donald Trump is the most Jewish non-Jew I've ever met in my entire life. He could be my older brother. He could be my Uncle. He could be my Godfather. He could be any of the Jewish friends or relatives I grew up with on the streets of New York. He's *that* Jewish in every way.

I want to tell you a *Jewish story*. My lifelong friend and mentor, Doug Miller grew up as a Presbyterian Christian on a Nebraska farm. But he learned the most important lesson of his life from a New York City ultra-religious Jew. Here is Doug's story. It applies perfectly to Donald Trump.

> *"After earning my MBA at Stanford, I moved to New York for adventure and opportunity. I had an office in the Empire State building doing business deals with a group headed by Ali Dayan. Ali was Orthodox Jewish and about twenty years older than me. We soon developed a close, almost father-son relationship.*
>
> *One year, during the Jewish high holy days, Ali was headed to Temple. I told him, 'Ali, say a prayer*

for me.' He looked at me, came over, and put an arm around my shoulder. Then he said, 'Doug, I'm going to do something much better than that. I'm going to teach you to be more Jewish . . . in other words, how to look out a little more for yourself, and a little less for the other guy!'"

Doug looks back on his life and says, "as a Midwestern farm boy, Ali had me pegged. That one simple statement changed my life. It not only made me a more successful businessman, it made me a better husband and father, being more aware of my family's needs and looking out for them first, as opposed to strangers, or everyone else equally (as I had been taught growing up). Everyone isn't equal. Your family, your country, and God come first, and then worry about everyone else."

I'm sure that's a lesson Donald Trump learned very early in his life. You can see it in the way he runs the country. President of the United States Donald Trump views his job as looking out for you and me as American citizens first and above all else. I for one certainly appreciate (and prefer) President Trump looking out a little bit more for you and me and 330 million other Americans, before he worries about *the other guys and gals.* The world is not equal, certainly not for a US president. The president's job is to always look out for US interests and US workers first. Then, after that, he can worry about the rest of the world. Thank you, Mr. President for looking out for us like a Jewish father!

But what exactly does it mean to "become more Jewish"? The following section comes directly from my best-selling book: *The Power of RELENTLESS.* Up until this one, it is the favorite book I've written. Not surprisingly, that book was enthusiastically endorsed by none other than . . . **Donald J. Trump.**

Quite frankly, this excerpt is too perfect not to feature here in the TRUMP RULES. It describes and defines traits that made the Jewish people so over-the-top successful . . . and traits that have made Donald Trump so over-the-top successful. And, lo and behold, they pretty much match to a T (as in Trump).

The *Jewish Rules of Success* **are** the TRUMP RULES. No coincidence. The word synergy could have been created to describe the similarities between Donald Trump and the Jewish people. Trump may not be Jewish by birth, but he has modeled *the Jewish Way* like no one else.

This entire excerpt and ***The Nine Super Rules of the Jewish People*** make for valuable **TRUMP RULES**. Enjoy.

THE RELENTLESS TRIBE

"The Jews who wish for a State will have it. We shall live at last as free men on our own soil, and die peacefully in our own homes. The world will be freed by our liberty, enriched by our wealth, magnified by our greatness. And whatever we attempt there to accomplish for our own welfare, will react powerfully and beneficially to the good of all mankind."

— Theodor Herzl, from his book *Der Judenstaat*, 1896

Now that I've related a few great relentless stories and introduced you to some of the most relentless individuals in world history, it's time to meet the most relentless group. This small tribe is the definition of relentless. This tribe literally invented relentless. This tribe has survived and thrived against incredible odds for over six thousand years with **the power of relentless.** You could say they are the *model* for this book. They are the Jewish people, and even more specifically, the Jews of Israel.

Israel is a nation of some six million Jews. It is one of the smallest nations in the world. Its size is about eight thousand square miles, two and half times the size of Rhode Island, and only slightly larger than the Canary Islands. It is only two hundred sixty miles at its longest, sixty miles at its widest, and between three and nine miles at its narrowest.

Would you be surprised to learn the three countries that lead the world in venture capital dollars are America, China and . . . *Israel?* Yes, Israel. This tiny country attracts venture capital investment thirty times higher, per capita, than all Europe combined.

Let's look at a few more remarkable facts about the amazing people of Israel[73]:

- Israel has the third highest rate of entrepreneurship in the world, the highest rate among women and people over fifty-five.
- Israel has more high-tech startups, per capita, than any nation in the world.
- Israel has more biotech startups, per capita, than any nation in the world.
- Israel has more business startups, per capita, than any nation in the world.
- In pure numbers, Israel has the second most business startups of any country in the world, behind only the United States.
- Israel has more companies listed on the NASDAQ stock exchange than any other country in the world, other than the

United States and Canada. More than Europe, India, China, and Japan *combined.*

- Relative to its population, Israel is the largest immigrant-absorbing nation on earth.

- Israel leads the world, per capita, in patents for medical equipment.

- Israel's citizens have the highest ratio of computers in the world.

- Israel's citizens have the highest ratio of university degrees in the world.

- Israel leads the world in the number of scientists and technicians in the workforce, with 145 per 10,000, as opposed to eighty-five in the US, over seventy in Japan, and less than sixty in Germany. With over 25% of its work force employed in technical professions, Israel places first in this category as well.

- Israel has the highest number of Nobel Prizes, per capita, in the world.

- Wikipedia reports the Israeli economy is ranked as the world's most durable economy in the face of crisis. The Bank of Israel is ranked first among central banks for its efficient functioning. Israel is also ranked first in the world in its supply of skilled manpower.

- With only seven million citizens, the Israeli economy is bigger than her twenty-two Muslim Arab neighbors *combined* with a population of over three hundred million.

- Israel is the "Hong Kong of the Middle East" with a booming economy, even in the middle of a global economic collapse. Israel's GDP growth was 4.7% last year.

So, the question becomes WHY? What accounts for all this outrageous economic success by such a small tribe as the Jewish people?

The answer is simple: the Jewish people lead the world in being relentless. Throw anything at them: hatred, persecution, steal their property, enslave them, torture them, murder them, yet they survive. More than survive, they move on, and thrive. That's **the power of relentless**.

I recommend to Israel's enemies, you are far better off studying the Jewish people and emulating them than fighting with them . . . because you'll never win. No one in history has ever defeated the Jewish people . . . and no one ever will. That's **the power of relentless!** If you can't beat them, why not learn from them? Wouldn't it be ironic if Israeli's enemies greatly improved their people's lives by becoming more Jewish?

My many Jewish friends and relatives often lament that God did not bless the Jewish people. They say history shows a pattern of unmatched pain, prejudice, adversity, and tragedy suffered by this tribe. Yet, I would argue that all that pain has been a blessing. It has created the most unstoppable, unbeatable, and most relentless people in world history. One could argue that was God's plan all along. Perhaps God was playing the role of Marine drill sergeant. Those "hard asses" embarrass, humiliate, exhaust, starve, and often torture their rookie soldiers. But there's a reason. It toughens them and keeps them alive when the battle begins.

Soldiers survive, then go on to thrive because of their *hard-ass* Marine drill sergeant. Later in life, long after they've left the Marines, gotten married, had kids, and lived their lives, soldiers think back fondly on the lessons they learned from the torture dished out by that drill sergeant.

Jews too were forged from God's tough love.

The Jews, and in particular, the Jews of Israel, are exhibit A for the famous saying, "Anything that doesn't kill you, makes you stronger." Fire turns iron into steel. The Jewish people were mentally forged as steel.

Once you've been discriminated against, persecuted, robbed, hunted, enslaved, tortured, and murdered, something as simple as asking an investor to write a check or refusing to accept NO in a business transaction doesn't seem like such a big deal.

What did generations, actually centuries of pain, persecution, and tragedy teach the Jews? *Basically, every rule you're about to learn in this book!*

So, before we go any further, let me give you nine *Super Rules* learned from the world's most relentless tribe:

First and foremost: You must be relentless to survive. If you set your mind to be relentless, to never give up or give in, no matter what . . . no one can defeat you.

> **The fact that I am relentless is why I wrote this book. Hopefully, the fact that you want to be relentless and are willing to do whatever it takes to be so is why you are reading it.**

Second: It's good to have a chip on your shoulder. Jews are always the underdog. They are always either ignored or treated with disdain. That's a big advantage. It drives you, it makes you perform at your best, and it makes you over-perform.

> **I've lived my life with a chip on my shoulder. I've gone into every business deal with a chip on my shoulder. I'm always motivated to shove that smirk off my opponent's face and make him eat crow. That's my winning edge in business and life. Please disrespect me and underestimate me.**

Third: Stop complaining. Complaining gets you nowhere. Take action. Do something about your lot in life. Take the time you might have wasted complaining and use that time to take action. You'll find what a waste of time it was to even consider complaining in the first place.

> **I don't waste my time complaining. I always take action, and although at times that action is complaining, I only do it if I believe the complaint will result in action and resolution. Taking action is your best revenge!**

Fourth: Life is short, so take action N-O-W. Don't wait for tomorrow, or next week, or next month. You never know what tomorrow brings, so do it now. Today is as good a day as any to get started turning your dream into reality. If you put it off until tomorrow, it may never happen.

> **I always take action . . . aggressive action . . . at the earliest possible opportunity.**

Fifth: Turn lemons into lemonade. God never promised to make life easy. Ask the Jews. But, you can turn each challenge and setback in life into a learning experience. When something bad happens, don't give up. Learn from your mistake, get back up, use that failure as motivation and new-found wisdom to succeed the next time.

> **As you already know from my personal stories, I specialize in turning lemons into lemonade.**

Sixth: Take control of your life. Jews have experienced what it's like to be under a tyrant's control . . . to be enslaved . . . to feel helpless. It's horrible. So, Jews learned to control their own destiny by taking personal responsibility and being self-reliant. The only people you can depend on is you and your own family. Never, ever, ever think you can depend on government. Government's first concern, and that includes every elected official as well as every government employee's first concern, is not you . . . it is their own job and well-being.

How do you take control of your own life? You educate yourself to control of your mind; you find a job you love and, if need be, create your own business; you own your own home; you invest wisely so you are in control of your own retirement. Let me reiterate . . . If you can't find a job you love, stop complaining and create your own. NEVER depend on government or the kindness of a stranger to save you. "If it's to be, it's up to me."

> **I've only had a job with a boss a couple of times early in my life. I learned what I needed to learn, then quickly left to start my own business. I love working for the most generous boss in the world—*me!***

Seventh: If owning your own business is your goal, what should that business be?

Answer: Do what no one else wants or is willing to do. Do what others consider "low class" and beneath them: SELL! SELL! SELL!

Sell homes, stocks, cars, clothing, mortgages, insurance, precious metals, diamonds, jewelry, entire companies, or money (banking). Sell yourself. The product doesn't matter. You get rich in this world only by selling *something.*

People who work at Ford Motor Company may think they work for a company that manufactures cars. WRONG! They work for a company that *sells* cars. You only have the right to make it if you can sell it. Otherwise, you become that worst-of-all-possible companies—a company with a lot of expensive and worthless inventory. Then you go out of business.

Far more Americans got rich selling picks, shovels, food, and clothing to the miners of the famous Gold Rush than got rich working the mines. Who are the wealthiest people in every society? **The business owners and salesmen.**

Guess who got the last laugh? The Jewish people—the tribe doing that "low class" thing that few want to do, or that most are afraid to do, or that so many think is "low class"—selling anything and everything!

> **Like Donald Trump, I'm a proud salesman. I've been selling things my entire adult life. But in each case the number one commodity that I'm selling has always been *me!* Selling isn't "low class." It's the best way (and some might say the only way) to make enough money to live a life that is First Class.**

Eighth: What's the worst thing that can happen to your tribe? It's hard to get any worse than the infamous Holocaust. Over six million Jews were wiped from the earth, after first having their property, homes, businesses, jewelry, and even their gold teeth stolen.

After having something like that in your history, it's tough to scare you. After torture and death, everything else seems like a walk in the park. Little things no longer bother you. You become fearless. And that's the key to success in almost every field, but especially in business: NO FEAR. Few people have that trait. Those that do can achieve anything. Those that are fearless can make the impossible *POSSIBLE.*

> **I'm fearless. But I've been fearful about *physical* challenges my entire life. I don't like heights. I'm not big on swimming in deep water. I don't climb mountains. I don't ride motorcycles. But I'm fearless**

177

when it comes to financial challenges. I risk my money on a moment's notice. That's precisely the thing you must be fearless about to live the life of your dreams!

Ninth: The final lesson learned by the Jews from centuries of pain is a tolerance for risk. To be successful in life and earn serious money you need to be a gunslinger and riverboat gambler. You don't get rich from a safe weekly paycheck. You don't get rich by settling. You don't get rich off a "job." To be successful, you need to risk your own money. I consider riding motorcycles and jumping out of airplanes stupid risks. That's risking your life and your health for what, a momentary thrill? A smart risk is putting your money into a business. A smart risk is investing in yourself.

I've been a risk taker my entire adult life. But I'm only a daredevil risk-taker with money, not my life!

So, there you have it, nine *Super Rules* by which to lead your life. The business world may be brutal, but not compared to the lifetime experiences of the Jewish people. The business world may sometime seem like war, may sometimes seem bloody, but not when compared to what Jews have lived through.

That is why the Jewish people, particularly the Jews of Israel, are the most RELENTLESS people in the world. They never stop fighting for their goals, never let a challenge or setback slow them down, never give up or give in. They never stop starting businesses, no matter how many times they have already failed. They never stop asking customers or clients to buy their products, no matter how many have already said "NO." That is how they have managed to produce a stunning record of financial success.

And for good measure, throw in the world's highest percentage of immigrants. Anyone who chooses to immigrate to Israel, a country under continual threat of war and annihilation, is mentally tough, comfortable with risk, and has certainly already learned well *the power of relentless.*

I am very proud of my Jewish heritage. I am also bursting with pride for the people of Israel. But the question becomes, "Can anyone learn to think like the Jewish people?"

The answer is a resounding *YES.* The Chinese are obsessed with learning how to succeed and obtain wealth. Over one third of the books sold in China are about financial success. And a large portion of those books are about *Jewish success.*[74]

Some of the best-selling business book titles in China in recent years:

- *The Eight Most Valuable Business Secrets of Jewish Wealth*
- *The Legend of Jewish Wealth*
- *Jewish People and Business: The Bible of How to Live Their Lives*

In a recent year, six of the best-selling books in China were about the financial success of the Jewish people. The Chinese people aren't interested in being Jewish. They are interested in what they can learn from the Jews. Learn how to think like they think. Learn their mindset. Learn the traits that made Jews so remarkably successful. Learn to harness *the power of relentless.*

As Steve Jobs of Apple once said, "Good artists copy, but great artists steal." The success secret that the Chinese are so desperate to steal is: *becoming more Jewish.*

Now it's your turn.

That section was from my bestselling book, *The Power of RELENTLESS.* As I re-read this chapter from my own book, I realize I left out a very important trait of the Jewish people. It is the foundation of the TRUMP RULES. It's also the foundation of Trump himself. That trait is CHUTZPAH.

This really is the most important Jewish trait. The Jewish people have chutzpah like no other group in world history. But Trump obviously watched, listened, learned, and modeled what he witnessed growing up in New York real estate. Trump has mastered chutzpah better than his teachers and mentors, the Jewish people. It's clear to me Trump has more chutzpah than anyone in world history.

Chutzpah is a Yiddish word for being so confident in yourself, you have the nerve to dream big dreams that no one else believes possible. While others laugh at your nerve, perhaps even calling you a braggart, you make it happen. That's chutzpah. Trump has it in spades!

After my book *The Power of RELENTLESS* was published, a Japanese publisher approached my publisher to re-publish my book in Japan. It became my first book published outside the United States, in a foreign language. The Japanese publisher chose the new subtitle (without consulting me):

"By Las Vegas Jewish billionaire Wayne Allyn Root."

I was flabbergasted when I heard that subtitle. I immediately contacted the Japanese publisher, "You can't call me a billionaire. I'm not Donald Trump. I'm *not* a billionaire. And why on earth would you list me as 'Jewish' on the cover of the book?"

He replied, "First of all, are you worth at least nine million US dollars. So, you are a billionaire in Japanese yen. Secondly, Jews are revered in Japan. We believe you are the most special people on earth. You are the best at making money and achieving remarkable success. It is very important to list you as Jewish on the cover of the book."

Point made. I learned, at that moment, the Japanese have plenty of chutzpah too!

★ ★ ★

Just like in China, the Japanese people recognize that much can be learned from studying the wisdom of the most successful race of people to ever walk the planet earth. Like the Chinese and Japanese, Trump clearly sees the Jews of Israel as special and blessed by God. And, it's equally clear he has modeled himself after them.

So, now you see why these Jewish traits are a foundation of the TRUMP RULES. Every single Jewish trait is a Trump trait. It's an exact match. I'd argue it's no coincidence.

Look closely. Trump is relentless and fearless. He lives life with a chip on his shoulder. He doesn't complain, he does something about it. He takes nonstop action. He doesn't let grass grow under his feet—he takes action in "a New York Minute." He doesn't let failures slow him, or stop him. He turns lemons into lemonade—he learns from each failure and finds a way to turn it into a future victory. He always owns his own businesses and works for no one. He is a fearless financial risk-taker and salesman extraordinaire. And Trump clearly has that Jewish trait of chutzpah—always aiming higher than anyone imagines possible.

Perhaps most importantly, and the really good news for the American people, is that unlike most previous presidents, and virtually all politicians, Trump is beholden to no one. So, unlike any other politician of my lifetime, he does what he thinks is right. He ignores the critics. He doesn't care who is angry or offended. Trump is his own man, with supreme confidence in his wisdom, talents, and vision. That's true chutzpah.

One more key takeaway . . .

Donald Trump's chutzpah is all about having the audacity to dream big dreams and always expect to win. He built his personal success by building and branding bigger than anyone ever . . . and by winning.

It's all about being number one. But now Trump is applying that mindset to America and the American people. Now he's dreaming big and winning for <u>YOU</u>.

President Trump has clearly shown that he measures success in his position as president of the United States by how much he is improving the lives of American citizens. His statements "Make America Great Again," "Make America Safe Again," and "America First" aren't just empty political slogans. They are how he measures his performance. He wants to win for Americans, just as he won for himself. These big goals truly guide every decision he makes and every action he takes.

I'll share a story that proves even people halfway around the world (with no axe to grind) understand Trump's mindset. I was in a limo back to the airport—provided by the business conference I had just spoken at in Johannesburg, South Africa. This was in 2015—just after Trump declared his run for president. The driver was listening to BBC Radio. The radio host was talking about American politics. Trump (as usual) was the topic. I asked the Black South African driver what he thought of Donald Trump. I didn't think he'd even know who he was.

The Black South African limo driver, 10,000 miles away from America, proceeded to tell me Trump's entire life story during the long ride to the airport. Then he told me how blessed we were in America that Trump would be our next president.

I was shocked. I asked how he knew so much about Donald Trump? He replied, "Sir, I have watched every episode of *The Apprentice*. I want to be rich. Mr. Trump inspires me. He makes me want to be great. Just like he does for every contestant of *The Apprentice*. Average people are turned into superstars by Mr. Trump. He makes each one of them better. That's what he will do for America."

Smart and ambitious people the world over know that Trump represents winning, success, and chutzpah.

But Donald Trump had to start somewhere, too. He had to study, watch and listen. It's clear who Trump modeled his business career after: the Jewish people. Smart and ambitious people the world over should also study the Jewish people—watch, listen, and learn. Just as Donald J. Trump did.

Trump's remarkable success proves, we all need a little more chutzpah. And we can all stand to become a little more Jewish.

SECTION III

Trump Squared

─────── CHAPTER FOURTEEN ───────

More Valuable
TRUMP RULES

N ow that I've gotten the priceless BIG 10 out of the way, this section of the book will review all the other valuable TRUMP RULES. There is so much synergy and overlap in the TRUMP RULES that some of this will be a review, addition to, or even a repeat of some of the BIG 10. These TRUMP RULES are so important that they simply cannot be repeated or pounded home too often.

ACTION—TURNING DREAMS INTO REALITY

Remember the Trump Rule about branding? Trump's brand is action. President Donald J. Trump is certainly a man of action. Only action turns dreams into reality.

Shortly after graduating from Columbia University, I was asked by my mentor, Doug Miller, to share with him my dreams of what I wanted to do and who I wanted to be in the future.

"That's easy," I told him. "It's a goal I've been pursuing since I was sixteen. I love sports, I like to pick pointspread winners, and I'm great on television. I want to be 'the King of Vegas Sports Gambling.' I want to be my generation's Jimmy 'The Greek.'"

For those younger readers who might not know, Jimmy "The Greek" Snyder was a TV personality who was the *go-to* expert on Vegas gambling odds, not only on sports, but on everything from presidential elections to what the English Royals would name their next child.

"Jimmy is old and will probably retire soon," I told my mentor Doug. "Someone will replace him. Why not me?" Doug looked at me (I think a little blown away by such an audacious dream), but then gave me a piece of advice that changed my life.

"OK," he said. "The first thing we need is a plan. A plan is how you change a dream into a goal. You may or may not achieve it, but at least you will have a chance to make your dream a reality. Plans are what make dreams come true, as long as you take action."

And, you know what? Plans were made, goals set, and my dream came true. I became my generation's Jimmy "The Greek" and went on to be awarded a 180-pound granite star on the Las Vegas Walk of Stars. It says: **Wayne Allyn Root; The King of Vegas**. How cool is that? The day of my ceremony was named *Wayne Allyn Root Day* in Las Vegas and in the state of Nevada, by proclamation of the Governor.

I later changed my dream to become involved in politics and, true to form, developed and executed a plan for that. The result? I became the Libertarian Party's vice presidential nominee in 2008 and today I'm a respected political pundit and talk show host listened to and watched by millions of people daily. It wasn't a coincidence or dumb luck. It was a dream . . . a goal . . . a vision . . . that, with a detailed plan, hard work, a relentless mindset, combined with action, that became my reality.

Don't get me wrong . . . there was luck along way. But it wasn't "dumb luck." It was smart luck. The kind of luck that is the residue of a plan designed to keep me in the game and take advantage of opportunities as they presented themselves.

The fact is, my run to be the Presidential candidate for the Libertarian Party was only the first step of a longer term, detailed plan. The goal of that plan was to gain enough celebrity, name recognition (branding), and credibility in the media to land me a national radio and/or TV show. It actually led to both. I love it when a plan comes together.

This media platform also led to a nationally-syndicated newspaper column and many books (six since my presidential run—but who's counting?) and roles as spokesman/rainmaker for products and companies (many dozens).

I think it's safe to say the plan worked.

I repeat—there are few coincidences in life. It's always about a plan and being relentless in carrying out that plan.

It is clear Donald Trump knows all about dreaming big, creating a plan, and then taking action. He is masterful at turning those dreams into reality with a plan. Google it and find online videos of Donald Trump's media appearances from thirty years ago on TV talk shows like "Oprah" where he is talking about . . .

A) Running for president.

B) His belief in how middle-class Americans are being screwed over by the elite and how he wants to change it.

Notice Trump's campaign themes then are almost exactly the same as he used thirty years later to be elected president.

Does Trump dream big? There is no bigger dream than MAGA: "Make America Great Again." Politicians called it corny, unrealistic, a pipe dream, or a con. For traditional politicians who only care about enriching themselves, I guess it seemed like a pipe dream or con.

Not with Donald Trump. He turned his campaign slogan into realistic and doable goals, then reality, with a plan. What was that plan?

- *Cut taxes dramatically. Check.
- *Slash regulations like no president in history. Check.
- *Start building the wall and control illegal immigration. Check.
- *Rebuild US manufacturing. Check.
- *Make the US economy great again. Check (until COVID-19 came along).
- *Create jobs by the millions. Check (until COVID-19 came along).
- *Destroy the ISIS caliphate. Check (in record time).
- *End the terrible Iran deal. Check.
- *End the Paris Climate Change accord. Check.
- *Support Israel like no other president in history. Check.
- *Name multiple Supreme Court judges. Check.
- *Name conservative federal judges—Trump has named over 200 at last count. Check.
- *Make better trade deals for US workers. Check.

Then Trump took action based on that plan. And what has Trump done? During his first term as President he has either accomplished each step of the plan or put into motion the actions needed to *get 'er done*.Actually, the only promise not kept was repealing Obamacare. Trump did kill the Obamacare mandate. But he was a single vote away from accomplishing a total repeal of Obamacare—until the late Senator John McCain famously put his thumb down. McCain prevented a perfect record. Unheard of in the history of the presidency.

Trump doesn't pussy-foot around.

He gets things done.

He takes action.

He makes things happen.

Politicians, on the other hand, see a problem, talk about it, and set up a blue-ribbon commission to study it. Seldom does anything actually happen. As an experienced CEO, Trump sees a problem and takes action to solve it. It is that straightforward and it is a role Trump has been preparing himself for his entire life.

This is also the part where "leading from the front" comes in. By definition, a "real" plan must include specific action steps. Otherwise, it's just day-dreaming with no shot at reality. With action steps, you have no choice but to lead. That is the very essence of Donald Trump.

I initially intended to end this chapter right here, but realized that for all my readers who have not had the opportunity to read my powerful business/self-help book, *The Power of RELENTLESS*, there was a section in that book which needed to be included here.

I want my books to be more than just a historical record of my observations and opinions. I want them to change reader's lives. To that end, since this chapter is about how dreams become goals, and then reality with a detailed plan and then action, the following excerpt from *The Power of RELENTLESS* provides some very powerful tools on how to develop your own personalized step-by-step plan. If you have already read it, please feel free to skip ahead, although it never hurts to read it again. It is my fondest hope it will provide that one gem, or germ of an idea that will change your life.

I know Donald Trump is a master at taking action to turn dreams into reality. I don't know if Trump follows any or all of the specific action steps listed below. But, I'm guessing he has his own version of these steps. Because *truth is truth*. This is how you turn dreams into goals, and goals into reality. I do know the steps below have worked like magic for me and will work for you as well.

Trump is super-human. He is one-in-a-billion. He may or may not need these detailed action steps, but the rest of us mere mortals do. So here goes . . .

So, how do you become a man or woman of action?

I grabbed this entire section from my book, *The Power of RELENTLESS,* because A) Some things you can't say better than the first time. And, B) This is the exact action plan I teach at business seminars around the world.

One of the key lessons of Napolean Hill's famous book, *Think and Grow Rich,* is that you must have detailed, specific goals. You can't *ready, shoot, aim.* We all need to know the target we're aiming at in order to hit it. *Think and Grow Rich* actually used the word *"obsession"* to describe the attitude about your goals necessary to achieve success.

Unfortunately, right here is where so many other books leave the subject. This is where I start. I'm going to take you step by step through the detailed process of how to create your goals and how to then turn them into reality. It's a 12-step process.

1. Find Your Passion and Purpose. It is not possible to set goals until you first identify your passion and purpose. Identifying these together, while applying Positive Addictions, will lead to enthusiasm, commitment, tenacity, energy, relentlessness, and eventually, success.

Positive Addictions are not just needed to achieve a state of mind that leads to success. Before you ever set out on your journey, Positive Addictions will allow you to go deep within yourself and identify your purpose.

As you know from my own story, my personal passions and purpose has changed several times over the years. It will probably be the same for you. If so, more power to you. As we age and change (and accomplish success), our goals change too.

2. Map Out Your Goals. Once step one is out of the way, it is time to map out your goals. This doesn't need to be long. You can

★ ★ ★

do it on the back of a napkin. Lay out your goals for the short term (six months and one year), two years, five years, and ten years. Know that it is natural that these will evolve and change along the way. Just update them as they change.

3. Create a Dream Book or Vision Board. This is a powerful tool used to help clarify, concentrate, and maintain focus on specific life goals. Fill it with images that represent whatever you want to be, do, or have. I prefer both an old fashioned *photo album* where I place photos of my goals and a vision of my future. But I also like to mount a *vision board* on the wall of my office where I see it throughout the day.

Today's youth would no doubt prefer an online vision board kept on your computer. The reason I prefer an old-fashioned photo album is that I place that album on my nightstand. I can't go to sleep without seeing it. That is my reminder to look at it each night before bedtime.

What is the point of a dream book or vision board? Humans are busy and constantly bombarded by distractions. A vision board helps you:

- Identify your vision and give it clarity.
- Reinforce your daily affirmations.
- Keeps your attention and focus on your intentions.

Don't forget to update it as goals are reached and new goals are set.

I've made at least four specific dreams or visions happen as a direct result of my dream book and vision board. For many years I put my dream Las Vegas mansion in my dream book. That vision inspired me to finally take the bold step of moving my family and business from Los Angeles to Las Vegas. And the home I bought in Las Vegas looked eerily like the one I had stared at in my dream book for five years.

Once I moved to Las Vegas, I added a new dream. For years, I hung a photo on my wall of a beautiful home on a ski slope in Park City, Utah. Eventually, I bought my own dream home on a ski slope in Park City. It took about three years of seeing it to make it happen. But the key was I kept it in front of my eyes 24/7. I saw it every day. I couldn't miss it. I wanted it so badly, I could taste it, hear it, feel it. There it was . . . on my wall . . . staring right at me every day. And then . . . *it was mine.*

I also put photos of my dream sports car in my dream book—a black Aston Martin DB9 Volante (convertible). It was right out of the James Bond movie. I stared at it every night before I went to bed. Then, in 2006, I bought it. In black—exactly as I saw it in my dream book.

Once you turn your dream into reality, it's time for a new dream. So I soon set my sights on a white-on-white Maserati Quattroporte. It's basically an exotic race car disguised as a 4-door ultra-luxury car. On the outside it is beautiful. On the inside it is luxurious. But under the hood it's an Indy race car—with a twin-turbo-charged Ferrari engine, capable of 0 to 60 in about four seconds, and a top speed of 190 mph. Last October, I brought my white-on-white Maserati Quattroporte home. Who says dreams don't come true? They most certainly *do* when you have a dream book or vision board!

4. Create a Contract with *Me, Myself, and I.*

This means exactly what it says. Write a contract with yourself, identifying the goals you will attain (not want to, or wish to, but *will* attain). Most importantly, in the written contract, include the specific steps you are committing yourself to take and agree to follow through on to accomplish those goals. Contracts are important. Most normal people don't break contracts. You are legally obligated to keep your word. Your sub-conscious mind sees written words and your signature on a contract and believes you are obligated—just like every other legal contract you've ever signed. This is just one more piece of the puzzle to create a positive, confidant, relentless mindset.

5. Write Your Own Obituary. Yes, you heard me. How do you want to be remembered after you're gone? What are truly the most important things you want to have accomplished? Think about it, then write your obituary as it will appear in the newspaper or online after your death. Now . . . start working in reverse. Live your life that way to make it happen. Talk about clearly seeing your "*end goals.*" This is the end goal of all end goals!

6. Keep a *Black Box*. A black box is the recording device on planes that investigators use to piece together and solve a mystery as to why a plane crashed. The black box saves lives by making sure we learn from tragedies, thereby never repeating the same mistake. Well that's the exact same purpose for your personal *black box.*

Basically, it's a weekly journal where you write about your mistakes, frustrations, rejections, failures, defeats, and, of course, your victories too. I fill it in once a week at bedtime. Then I review it once a week as well. Like a *black box*, this will save you from making the same mistakes again and again. Write your results down for just five minutes, once per week. And review it once a week or so for five to ten minutes. You'll see patterns developing. You'll start to see why the same bad things keep happening to you. And you'll *correct* it.

This journal's sole purpose is to be just like a sports coach making notes on his clipboard, which he studies and then makes halftime adjustments. Its purpose is to record and review what happened during the week and make the adjustments and changes necessary to get the intended results.

I'm sure you've already noticed a number of these Positive Addictions are directly focused at giving you the time, space, and structure to THINK. It is a truism that life gets busy and so many people, once headed in a direction (whether good or bad), simply run on "automatic." They are too distracted to change direction. Don't be one of those. Make the necessary "halftime adjustments." A daily journal gives you the information and tools to do exactly that. Isn't it sad that action plans and life-improving tools like this aren't taught in school?

7. Make a Daily *Hit List*. Just like a mob "hit man." Make a straightforward list of what you want to do each day to make your dreams come true. Make it as specific as possible, so you can check off each line item as you achieve it. Then, on to the next. And the next. Until you've crossed each "hit" off your list. Those you don't complete, add to tomorrow's list. That is how you are forced to follow-up.

8. Choose an *Accountability Partner*. This is a peer, a friend, or co-worker who understands your goals, and is preferably headed in the same direction. They should be a cheerleader—always ready to offer positive reinforcement. This is someone you can always call to go over goals . . . motivate you . . . uplift you . . . stop you from doing negative things . . . hold you to your scheduled Positive Addictions. This is the person to whom you are accountable, forcing you to make the phone calls, go to meetings or job interviews, or take whatever actions are necessary for you to succeed. It is especially powerful if this is a spouse or business partner (so you see them daily). The key is you have to do the same for them.

I've never been to an AA meeting—I thank God that I've never had a problem with drugs or alcohol. But AA does wonderful things for people with addiction issues. The key is they are each assigned a "sponsor." That sponsor is just like an accountability partner. They look out for you. They are always willing to take a call and give you strength or counsel. Well we all need a sponsor in our lives. Not just addicts. Here's your chance. They will help you and you will help them, by holding each other accountable.

You may think I have overdone the importance of accountability and follow-up. That simply isn't possible. All the past tense affirmations in the world will not work without discipline, accountability, personal responsibility, follow-up, and the commitment to do the work.

9. Find a Mentor. Unlike an accountability partner, this is not a peer. This is someone older, wiser, and preferably much more successful than you. Someone who has already achieved great success and or celebrity. This is not someone that has time to talk to you every day, or at all hours of the day and night. This kind of person is too successful to be bothered by nonstop calls from you.

This is a once per month, or once per quarter call for general advice and motivation. Find someone you believe you can learn from. Don't hesitate to ask someone older, higher up in your own organization, or even someone who might be considered famous, or who you might think has no time for someone like you. You'll be amazed how many people love to be needed and are ready to help. Most smart and successful people want to *do good* and give back. You are giving them a chance.

If you handle the relationship properly, a good mentor will also be aware of your goals and where you are in your career and may make introductions or present you with opportunities they come across.

You read earlier about my relationship with my mentor Doug Miller, and how important it has been to my success. Every step of the way, Doug gives me good advice, counsel, and keeps me focused. It wasn't just that he was there to guide me through the hard times, he was also someone to high-five and celebrate my successes.

My relationship with Doug started over thirty years ago and continues to this day. As he recently told me, "Over the years, this has become very much a two-way relationship that has undoubtedly helped me as much as it has you."

Everyone needs a Doug.

10. Find a Business Coach. A business coach is similar to a mentor, but this is a professional coach giving you much more of their time and input—*for a fee*. You can ask them anything, you can bother them whenever you want—because you're paying for it. And you can be sure they're good at keeping you motivated and on track, because this is what they do for a living. A good business coach is there to keep you on track and be brutally honest with you when creating both an overall and daily game plan.

As most of you know, one of my passions in life is sports. It is no secret that the most important "player" on any team is the coach. Quite frankly, coaching is everything—not only in sports, but in business, relationships, and life itself. A good coach can make all the difference in the world. A good coach can take a losing team and, almost overnight, turn them into a winner. When that coach leaves after a decade of nonstop winning, the next coach rarely ever succeeds at the same level. Why? Because coaching is an art. Few have that "it" factor. Find one and hire them to guide you.

A sports writer once said of legendary Alabama football coach Paul "Bear" Bryant, "He can whip you with his players . . . or he'll give you his players . . . take yours . . . and he'll whip you with your players!"

So, find a mentor, or hire a true business or even life coach. This type of coaching has become a big business. Just remember, like all professions, there are only a few good ones, a lot of mediocre ones, and way too many bad ones. Once you find a good one, keep him or her for life!

11. Keep a Progress and Rewards Chart. A common method of training children is to keep a *progress chart* with rewards if they clean their room, mind their manners, do their homework, etc. It works like a charm for kids, but it will work even better for you!

As you check off your daily list of tasks, assign yourself points for each positive achievement. On days you fail, take points away. Decide beforehand how the point system will work and what the rewards are when you reach predetermined levels.

Rewards can range from: An afternoon off . . . day off . . . three-day weekend . . . day spa . . . massage . . . 5-star restaurant . . . going shooting at gun range . . . a new suit, dress, or shoes . . . even a vacation or new car.

And remember—DON'T CHEAT!

The point of this is motivation. As long as you're honest with yourself, this progress and rewards chart will super-charge your motivation. We all want gifts. It started at a young age on Christmas and birthdays. It never went away. It never will. That's why everyone loves Christmas. We all feel like kids on Christmas morning. Getting gifts is a wonderful feeling. So write down all the things you want . . . crave . . . make you happy . . . float your boat, etc. Then assign points for good days, good actions, and good results. As soon as you reach a target, go buy a gift for yourself. Soon you'll train your mind to fight for those gifts . . . to never give up . . . to never accept NO. Because that gift you want is waiting. All the naïve people who claim "greed is bad" don't understand life or human nature. "Greed is good" (as Michael Douglas said in "Wall Street"), *if* it's used in a positive way as motivation for achievement.

And if you are one of the rare people in this world who thinks material things are bad, well then by all means set up your rewards as the chance to give donations to charity, or trips to the hospital to volunteer with sick kids, or days dressed as Santa to ring that bell for The Salvation Army at Christmas, or a day volunteering at an animal shelter.

Maybe your reward is that each time you close a big deal, you rent a big truck, fill it with groceries, and head to a poor neighborhood to hand out turkeys or free groceries. *Great!* I like this idea so much, I think from now on my reward system should include both material rewards and a charitable component each time I hit my target. I just made this decision while writing my own book!

But the fact is, rewards work. Use them as motivation to do great things . . . achieve great things . . . hit targets . . . beat the odds . . . and make the impossible *possible*.

12. Follow-up Your Goals. Rarely does anyone teach you this in school, at the workplace, or in life. But the reality is that the *follow-up* is more important than creating your goals in the first place. Follow-up is more important than taking action on your goals. Success is ALL in *the follow-up*. Without follow-up, it's all wasted. You did all that work for nothing. Because rarely does anything ever work the first or even second time. It takes persistent, dedicated, committed, *relentless* follow-up to achieve any kind of success.

That concludes your RELENTLESS GOALS lesson for today. Now, go set some goals! Then set your rewards in place as you hit your targets. And then, follow-up with relentless abandon!

President Donald J. Trump has his action plan. *Now you have yours*.

ENERGY

Do I need to say much here? Trump's brand is also energy. Trump *is* energy. Trump defines energy. For Trump, it all begins and ends with energy. Trump has more energy than any president or politician *ever*. He certainly has more energy than any seventy-three-year-old in the history of the world (although he may lose that record when I turn seventy-three in about fifteen years). He is simply amazing.

Trump is living proof of the value of energy. The simple fact is people with energy attract the best relationships, both business and personal. People with energy get the best jobs. People with energy build the greatest businesses. People with energy set records. People with energy change the world.

Why? Because people feel your energy and want to plug into your energy source. Energy is contagious. It's like a drug.

Trump ran for president against the sixteen best Republican presidential candidates in history. He beat them all for one main reason: Trump had more energy than all of the others *combined*.

There is a reason why so many people are not successful. There is a reason why so many people are bitter, disappointed, depressed. There is a reason why so many people are jealous, envious, and forever making excuses why they didn't achieve the role, job, title, or position they craved in life. There is a reason so many people didn't get the girl or guy they wanted. There is a reason so many talented people never get the big promotion they desire. There is a reason so many businesses fail.

The answer isn't brains, or IQ, or luck, or coincidence. There is a concrete reason why one person succeeds and others fail. **It's energy.**

Those who have it, breeze into the room and light it up. They make everyone around them feel like a billion dollars. They make everyone feel good, feel hopeful, feel excited. When they walk in, it feels like a tornado or tsunami just hit. It's exciting. It takes your breath away.

In short, people with energy make things happen. Their energy changes the world. That's Trump. Trump has it, most people don't. That's why Trump is so successful. Not only does he have a high level of energy, he has more of it than anyone I've ever met. That explains his over-the-top level of success: billionaire mogul . . . the most famous real estate brand in the world . . . one of the most successful TV shows in the history of Hollywood . . . and president of the United States (to name just a few).

But energy can work for anyone and everyone. As the author of this book, I can testify to the role energy (and enthusiasm) has played in my life. The most famous "signature" part of my speeches goes something like this:

> *"Now that you've all gotten to know me for about an hour or so, please raise your hand if you agree with this statement: Wayne Allyn Root has a ton of energy and enthusiasm . . ."*

At this point, every person in every audience, in every country in which I've spoken, raises their hand and screams "YES!" while smiling and laughing loudly.

I then add, *"Now compare my energy and enthusiasm to an employee of the Department of Motor Vehicles."*

Now, every person in every audience, in every country in the world laughs loudly! Everyone gets the joke. I've tried this line all over the world and I haven't yet found a country where people don't immediately get the point.

Energy is important. Energy sells. Energy creates success. Entrepreneurs like me and Trump have it, government employees generally don't. That's why they are government employees—with a safe job, safe weekly paycheck, and lifelong pension without any care about actual performance, or actual results.

Entrepreneurship isn't easy. It's tough. It's not for average people without super-human energy and drive.

But the great news is everyone can have super-human energy. It isn't something most of us are born with, but it can be taught. It can be produced, created, manufactured. Coming up is one way to manifest energy.

I listed a much more detailed, in-depth system for creating energy in my book, *The Power of RELENTLESS*. That was my book and my personal ideas and advice. This is a TRUMP RULES book. But coming up is a simple quick way to manufacture more energy in your life . . .

RELENTLESS MOTION

Trump is more than just energy. He is MOTION. Not just any motion, but relentless motion. Trump never rests. He never slows down. He is a tornado of activity, almost 24/7/365.

Motion creates energy. You can model Trump and create energy, too. But first you need to understand the concept of motion.

I can't say it any better, so I'm going to take a short section directly from my book, *The Power of RELENTLESS*.

What defeats and destroys success and achievement for most people? Four things:

- Doubt
- Fear
- Stress
- Depression

Not coincidently, those are the same four things that destroy positive thinking. And of course, as we've already hammered home again and again, positive thinking is one of the bricks in the foundation of success and achievement.

Not coincidently, those are the same four things that kill confidence. And of course, as we've already hammered home again and again, confidence (a.k.a. faith) is necessary to produce mega success.

So, what is the antidote to doubt, fear, stress, and depression? MOTION.

And not just any motion, but rather something specific: *RELENTLESS MOTION.*

In a nutshell, that's what my entire book is about. Whether it's:

A) **Mental motion** (prayer, meditation, affirmation, visualization, goals, optimism, etc.) . . .
B) **Physical motion** (morning walk, yoga, fitness training, weight training, etc.) . . . Or,
C) **Financial motion** (hitting, pitching, hooking, hammering, hounding, chopping, juggling, filling the pipeline, following-up, etc.).

The point is, the way to counter stress, negativity, doubt, fear, and depression is to always be in RELENTLESS MOTION. Sometimes it's mental motion, sometimes it's physical motion, sometimes it's financial motion, but the point is . . . *you gotta keep moving to win!*

Each of my Positive Addictions are crucial to your success. It is the synergy of all of them together that is so powerful. I could not subtract any one of them. They each have a crucial role. But this "addiction" is last for a reason. I always save the best for last. In the end, everything I teach comes down to motion. Each of these 18 Positive Addictions comes down to motion. ***The power of relentless*** comes down to motion.

If you're sleeping—*you're losing ground.* Sleep after you're dead. There's plenty of time for that.

If you're sitting, *you're losing ground.*

If you're on the couch watching TV, *you're losing ground.*

If you're wasting time slouching off, *you're losing ground.*

If you're not in action, in motion, risking, attacking, taking the offense, *you're losing ground.*

If you're not up early relentlessly pitching and hitting and hooking, *you're losing ground.*

RELENTLESS MOTION equals confidence. It equals progress. It always results in a step forward, never backward.

You will get tested.

You will get attacked.

You will get smashed in the face.

And when you do . . . Mike Tyson was right . . . for most normal people, their plan goes out the window. The proper response to being punched is RELENTLESS MOTION.

I'm human. Just like everyone else, I have good days and bad days. Other people respond to a bad day with Prozac. I respond with motion. And it works every time (without the side effects of drugs).

One of the best examples of this in my life happened during the writing of this book. Not just the book, but more specifically, during the writing of this section of the book you're now reading. One of the companies I'm a spokesman for called to say they were ending our relationship. Due to the poor economy, they could no longer afford to keep paying me. During the same three-day period, not one . . . not two . . . not three . . . but four deals I was working on . . . deals I thought were done, or as close to done as you can get without signed contracts yet . . . all fell through. I lost important income, plus four potential new deals at the same time. WOW. *Crushing.*

What was my response? Well, as always, I responded with mental and physical motion. I prayed, meditated, affirmed, visualized, practiced yoga, took my morning walks, exercised hard, ate healthy and organic, etc.

But more importantly, I responded with *financial motion.* I tossed and turned all night. I couldn't sleep. So, I got up at 5 a.m. the morning after all of this happened and I got on my computer and phone and started ATTACKING . . . *with an enthusiasm unknown to mankind.*

I contacted new potential clients, and followed-up with people and deals that I had heard nothing about for months, that I had forgotten about, that I had given up for dead. I emailed . . . I called . . . I emailed some more . . . I called some more. Then I followed-up some more. There was no time for depression, doubt, or fear. I just attacked like a cornered wolverine. I took aggressive action. I was a man in motion. I relentlessly made something happen.

In 48 hours, I had four new deals and four new income streams. Outside of magicians David Copperfield or Criss Angel, not too many people can do what I did. I created magic . . . quickly . . . out of nothing. That's what motion does. It creates magic. It creates poetry. It creates beautiful music. It creates positivity. Good things are just attracted to people in motion.

Negativity, complaining, blaming, sitting, or lying around in shock saying "woe is me" are dream killers.

MOTION IS A DREAM FULFILLER.

Motion is a doubt, fear, stress, and depression killer. Tens of millions of Americans live on pills for depression. But it's action and motion that effectively kill depression (without side effects). That's how you respond to a punch in the face or gut . . . or in this case, a flurry of smashes to my face and gut. I didn't retreat. I didn't hide. I didn't rest. I took the offense. I smashed back and won.

RELENTLESS mental, physical and financial motion is the answer to doubt, fear, stress, and depression. Motion is a double "natural born killer," because motion kills more than just your own personal depression (mental sadness). Motion is also the antidote to a national economic depression as well. Motion is a double-edged depression killer.

You know who is always in motion, perhaps more than any other living human being? Donald J. Trump. He's not just in motion, it's always forward motion. He's always on offense, attacking. Not everyone has Trump's level of energy, but everyone needs a little more energy. That should be your goal. In the end, you have to find a way to beat depression, or negativity, or even the seeds of doubt.

Any crack in your confidence can destroy everything you've worked so hard to build. RELENTLESS MOTION is the answer. Never stop moving, never stop fighting, never stop thinking of creative ways to pitch a new deal.

ENTHUSIASM

Energy and enthusiasm go hand in hand. Trump has world ·class quantities of both energy and enthusiasm. This TRUMP RULE of enthusiasm has been both good and bad for Trump.

Let's start with the good. Smart super-achievers understand *the glass is always half full*. Trump approaches each deal with tremendous enthusiasm. That is why he has enjoyed remarkable success. That's why he has perhaps the greatest *closing rate* in the history of business. He doesn't just talk about deals, he *closes* them. He makes things happen.

Critics attack Trump by bringing up his failures. I listed each of them in an earlier chapter. And, the list is long. Trump has failed a lot. But that is simply a by-product of how many times he has been to bat, swinging for the fences.

Most people have one or two failures in their life. That's because they've only tried three things. If they were lucky, they succeeded in one and failed in two. Trump has tried hundreds. He understands it's all a numbers game. And you only have to hit on one to become a millionaire. Hitting two or three out of a hundred gets you to billionaire status.

Trump's enthusiasm and his belief in himself . . . the belief that he can create *the best, the biggest, the greatest, the most amazing*, is why he has such a great success rate, such a great *closing* rate, such a great legacy. In the end, taking everything he's tried and done into account, Trump will go down as one of the great business and political legends in world history. And certainly one of the most famous people to ever walk this earth.

I credit enthusiasm and energy for that.

But enthusiasm has also led to a misperception of Trump by his critics and enemies. They call him a failure and a fraud because he has failed so often. But they don't understand his record may be a thousand successes vs. twenty failures. That record might be the best in history. But since Trump's critics and enemies have neither energy, nor enthusiasm, nor rock-solid faith in themselves, they've never tried to succeed a thousand times. They have no clue how many gambles Trump has taken, how tough the battle is, or how many failures he's had to overcome.

And since they lack enthusiasm, they don't understand Trump's mindset. His enthusiasm is what leads him to believe he can conquer anything, become the best at any undertaking, and make any product into a winner with the Trump brand name. Most of the time, Trump is right. But it all starts with that trademark Trump enthusiasm. It's the only way to turn a product, or role, or opportunity, into a winner. It is the reason for his amazing legacy.

But when he fails, and failure is occasionally inevitable, that initial enthusiasm (*Trump steaks are the best ever, Trump Airlines will be the best ever, Trump wine is the best wine ever*, etc.) comes back to haunt him. It gives critics *ammo* to try to make Trump look exaggerative and even foolish.

In reality, to succeed in the *dog-eat-dog* business world, you must tackle each and every opportunity and challenge with that same level of over-the-top, gung-ho enthusiasm. There is no other way to succeed.

Yes, some people don't exaggerate. They don't claim victory before they achieve it. They don't claim, "I'm the greatest, I've created the best." But that's why they aren't billionaires, don't own Trump Tower on Fifth Avenue in Manhattan, were never the producer and star of *Celebrity Apprentice*, and aren't president of the United States.

It looks like enthusiasm paid off pretty well for Trump. It can for you too. The lesson here is that it is better to be overly enthusiastic and hit it big one out of ten than to lack enthusiasm and never succeed in the first place.

After all, what do you call a businessman who owns ten restaurants and nine of them go bankrupt? MILLIONAIRE. You only need one! To get it, you'd better be enthusiastic.

COCK-EYED OPTIMISM

Like Trump, I've learned to be incredibly positive and to be a cockeyed optimist about my own ideas. I believe in me. To be successful, that's what matters. You need to reserve your energy and enthusiasm for YOU. You need to invest in YOU.

What matters is that you are 110% *all in* for your own plans. You must always believe in you. You must always have faith in your talents, your dreams, and your vision. You are your own best salesman, promoter, manager, and PR agent at all times.

Two studies back me on this. I've quoted them in speeches across the globe and in several of my books. Both studies were compiled at Duke University's Fuqua School of Business. Duke researchers studied three thousand successful CEOs. Their goal was to find common traits the rest of us could learn from. And the number one trait was ... drumroll please ...

Optimism.

Not just simple, run of the mill optimism.[75] These super-achievers were *through the roof optimistic*—at least, about themselves, their companies, their own goals, their own talents.[76]

Because I've studied super successful people my whole life, I'm willing to bet that while they are super positive about themselves and their own success, they are far less positive about others. I'm betting they are actually pretty darn cynical about everyone else's ideas and talents. That's part of what makes successful people successful. They have a critical, cynical nature; they're skeptical about the claims of others and quick to find fault.

But, they are through-the-roof positive and cock-eyed optimists about their own ideas and talents. *I'm number one!* should be their chant. I can count the super successful people I've met in my life on one hand who don't fit this personality trait. My count is 0.

Yes, this is exactly Donald Trump's personality. But this isn't just a TRUMP RULE. Every New York millionaire, billionaire, and zillionaire I've ever met shares this trait. We believe in ourselves with every fiber of our soul, but are cynical and extremely cautious about the ideas and plans of others. We learned this trait the hard way—on the rough and tumble streets of New York. And it serves us all well. Successful people are cynical about others, but they always believe 110% in themselves.

Why does optimism work? Because being positive, optimistic, and confident about yourself allows you to be fearless. Being fearless means you're willing to take risks that the rest of society is not willing to take. It is that risk-taking that produces super-achievers.

"Fearless" describes Trump to a T. He is always confident in himself and his ideas. Trump is, therefore, fearless. He is willing to take big risks. When they payoff, it brings him more fame and fortune.

But it's not just Trump. Once again, this describes every successful millionaire, billionaire, and zillionaire I've ever met. They are all *riverboat gamblers*. They all swing for the fences. They all have huge cajones. But, gigantic risks like this can only be undertaken if you believe 110% in yourself. It goes hand-in-hand. Optimism about yourself and your ideas is what gives you the confidence to take big risks.

Of the thousands of super successful and filthy rich people I've met and studied, I've found only three ways to get rich, other than being born into the lucky sperm club:

- Risk everything you've got to build your own business.
- Sacrifice salary for stock or stock options, based on performance.
- Become a salesman and make the bulk of your income from performance-based commissions, often as an independent contractor with no salary or benefits.

Risky? Yes. Frightening? Yes. A big gamble? Yes. But these are the people who get rich in a capitalist society. No risk, no reward. If you settle for a safe paycheck, you will never get rich.

This same Duke study backed me up. Just like Trump, these optimistic CEOs turned out to be riverboat gamblers. Their boundless optimism and enthusiasm gave them the faith to bet big on themselves, time after time. They all took big gambles. They won some, they lost some. But the winners made them wealthy. Smart, courageous super-achievers are always willing to bet on themselves.

Here's a second study by Duke Business School researchers. Instead of CEOs who have already made a fortune and fought to the top of the corporate ladder, the researchers studied MBA graduates just starting out in their careers.

They found the ones with the most optimism had more success with their careers. They spent less time searching for jobs and received more offers, better offers, higher compensation, and got those offers faster than other MBA grads.[77]

Then the researchers took it even a step further. They studied these recent MBA grads once they started their new jobs. Guess what they found? The more optimistic ones were promoted faster in their first two years. Meaning "cocky" is good. Trump is hated for being "cocky." But there is no other way to succeed.

After a lifetime of studying successful people and lecturing about success, I believe it's clear you need to believe in YOU. You need to be highly optimistic about YOU. But you can and should be highly cynical about everyone else.

I guess you can sum up what I'm trying to say with this: You may not like Trump, but to be successful we need to be a little bit more like him!

CHANGE

There was one more very important trait the Duke researchers isolated. The most optimistic MBA grads were also more willing to accept change. If they were failing, they were more willing to admit it, change course, and come up with a new game plan. That, too, is a Trump trait.

Trump has changed course a thousand times. He's changed battle plans. He's changed branding strategies. He's changed careers. He's found ways over, under, around, and through obstacles. He's smashed through brick walls and glass ceilings. The key to Trump's success is a willingness to change course and change plans as often as some people change socks. That's part of a risk-taking personality. Making changes is risky and scary. It takes balls to rip up your first plan and start over from scratch.

Trump's business plan is to always attack . . . and if not successful, change plans. Then attack again . . . and if not successful, change plans again. Then keep attacking and changing plans until you find one that works.

I have no doubt if Trump is re-elected and gets eight years in the White House, Obamacare will be repealed and a wall with Mexico will be built. He will also find a way to comeback from the COVID-19 pandemic and rebuild the US economy. Trump always finds a way. He built one of the great economies in world history once (after Obama). He will find a way to do it again—even if he has to change course a hundred times.

It may take most of his eight years, and countless fights, countless failures, and countless changes of direction. But in the end, Trump will "Make America Great Again." He will win. He always does. NBAT: *Never Bet Against Trump.*

RIVERBOAT GAMBLER

I'll keep this short and sweet. It's pretty obvious that Trump is a riverboat gambler. Duh. Trump is one of the biggest and greatest gamblers in world history. It's why he flops so often. It's also why he hits grand-slam home runs so often.

As Trump has proven, again and again, without risk, there is no reward. You must take chances, often big chances, to make it big, to see your name in lights. The bigger the risk, the bigger the reward.

Trump has been a riverboat gambler his entire life—from real estate, to casinos, to public companies, to television shows, to his underdog presidential run. Trump has no interest in playing it safe. He rolls the dice on big ideas and big financial risks, time and time again. With Trump, it's always a high-wire act that attracts the world's and media's attention.

When you study my career successes . . . many of them literally miracles . . . you'll see I learned well from the master. Everything I've ever achieved came from taking huge gambles. It's the Trump way. No guts, no glory. No risk, no reward. Trump understands the whole point of gambling. You gotta be in it, to win it. Those words are the famous jingle from the New York State Lottery. New Yorker

Trump must have been listening. Nothing great is ever achieved without taking a risk. Trump has always been a riverboat gambler and gunslinger. Here are just a few ways Trump has applied his gambler's mentality to the presidency (and international diplomacy).

Trump took the ultimate risk by agreeing to the North Korean Summit. If nothing had been achieved, he'd have walked away with egg on his face. But without risk, there is no reward. Trump took a huge gamble, and to the victor go the spoils. If nothing comes of Trump's brilliant pitch to Kim Jung-un, Trump will move on. He'll find his glory elsewhere. But only Trump would have dared meet with Kim. To the victor goes the spoils. If by chance Trump scores a victory, he wins the Nobel Peace Prize.

Trump moved the US Embassy to Jerusalem. Every critic in the world screamed this was a disastrous mistake. They all warned it would lead to terrorism, or worse, war. Trump ignored the critics and moved forward. There was no terrorism, or war. All the experts and intellectuals (as usual) were dead wrong. Trump won a huge victory for himself, America, and Israel. No guts, no glory.

Trump once again ignored all the critics and experts and threats by killing the infamous Iran deal. The result? Iran's economy started a massive collapse from the moment the deal was canceled. Trump understood something very few in the world understood. He understood the Iran deal, negotiated by Obama, was artificially propping up the Iranian entire economy. When Trump took the bold step of canceling the deal, their economy resumed its collapse and the Iranian people lost faith in their government.

Obama had made the ruling mullahs look good, which strengthened their evil grip on power. Brilliant move by the intellectual Ivy League genius Obama, huh? But President Trump, the guy liberals call "dumb," pulled the rug out from under the mullahs and thereby showcased their corrupt weakness. Suddenly the Iranian people took that as a cue to revolt. Amazingly, Iranian people were in the streets with signs that said, "Death to Palestine." Under Obama, every Iranian protest sign said, "Death to Israel." Quite a change of heart because of one man—President Donald J. Trump.

If the evil Iranian government is eventually either overthrown or forced to make major concessions to its people, President Trump deserves the credit. Another diplomatic stroke of genius. The downfall of the Iranian terrorist regime because Trump killed the infamous Iran deal could land Trump a second chance for the Nobel Peace Prize.

And, as I put the finishing touches on this book, Trump announced a peace deal between Israel and the UAE. Peace in the Middle East between Israel and its Arab Muslim neighbors, although predicted by no one, has been a Trump goal since long before he even thought of becoming president. And, if by some miracle it is accomplished, that amazing one-in-a-billion victory would earn Trump a third bite off the apple: The Nobel Peace Prize.

By the way, gamblers understand you don't need to win them all. What if only one of these victories comes through in the end? What if North Korea fails? What if Iran is not overthrown? But Trump gets a peace agreement in the Middle East for Israel. Trump understands all you need is one! Any one of those three makes him a legend. Any one of those three wins him the Nobel Peace Prize. All three make him the G.O.A.T. (the greatest of all time).

We all can learn from riverboat gamblers like Donald Trump. Most of us can't afford, or wouldn't want, to risk everything we have on one idea. But we could all stand to become a little less humble, a little less risk-adverse, and a little more of a riverboat gambler.

THE FOLLOW-UP

Here's another valuable lesson I learned from President Trump. Always follow-up relentlessly for anything you want in life. Whether it's the girl you love, or the job you crave, or your dream career, or the home of your dreams . . .

- **Don't leave it to others.** *If it's to be, it's up to me.*
- **Attack, attack, attack.** Always play on offense.
- **Follow-up.** You'll rarely get it on the first try, or the second, or third. It's about commitment, determination, tenacity.

Success is rarely easy. It takes great effort. Most people give up way too soon. Sometimes they give up just moments before they would have achieved success, moments before they would have achieved the life of their dreams. Their idea was strong, but their resolve was weak.

What I learned from Trump is to keep fighting, never give up, see "NO" as just the start of a negotiation. Success guru Napolean Hill counseled that in sales, success is rarely ever achieved on the first pitch. Much more often it is achieved on the 10th pitch. Find me two salesmen, both pitching the same product. One gives up on the first, second, or third try. The other keeps fighting, keeps coming up with creative new sales pitches, won't give up. He gets the sale on the tenth try. That's Trump.

Trump never gives up. Trump follows up as long as it takes to close the deal successfully. Think of his presidential run. Polls showed him losing by double digits. Polls showed him as the most unpopular candidate in modern history. The media said he had no chance to win, no path to electoral victory. Trump was out-spent two to one by Hillary. Trump had that disastrous *Access Hollywood* "locker-room video" hanging around his neck. Any career politician would have given up. Anyone not immersed in sales their entire life would have given up. But Trump the CEO and salesman extraordinaire had been closing deals no one thought possible for decades. Trump knew it was all about the follow-up. So, Trump the politician doubled down.

Trump just kept coming back at the media. Trump just kept following up with voters. As Yogi Berra would say, "It ain't over till it's over." Trump just kept trying to close the deal with more outrageous tweets, more attacks on Hillary, more rallies all over the country.

Hillary may have out-raised and out-spent Trump by two to one, but Trump out-worked and out-hustled Hillary by ten to one. Trump flew to more rallies in more far-flung states in a day than Hillary did in a week. Only a world-class salesman would understand each of these rallies was a "sales call" and a chance to *follow-up* with customers (i.e. voters). In the end, the most relentless salesman, the one who followed up the most, won.

Following Trump's example, I've been a relentless *follow-upper* for many years now. One of the best examples has to be my local Vegas radio show, national radio show, and from 2017 to 2020, my Newsmax TV show. At various times, I've had a combined twenty-five to thirty advertisers and sponsors on my shows—all of whom I brought to the table. I'm the only TV and radio host in America I know who is the chief salesman for his shows. In each of these cases, it has taken ten, twenty, sometimes even thirty calls, emails, and in-person meetings to close each deal.

If I made one call or held one meeting and accepted "NO," I'd have zero advertisers. I'm successful because I am willing to keep coming back, pitching and asking and hammering and hounding for the sale, again and again. The success, the victory, the close, is always in the follow-up. I wear most people out. I out-last them.

When I finally get that elusive YES, most of my clients become friends for life. They thank me for being willing to hang in there so long. They admit I made their lives or careers better by being so relentless. They are glad I followed up. Then they ask me to come to their office and give a speech to their employees about being relentless, never giving up, never accepting NO, and always following up.

Like the Texas Rangers of the old Wild West, or the Canadian Mounties, or Donald J. Trump, I always get my man.

It sometimes just takes 100 calls, emails, and meetings over many months, years, or sometimes decades. But I'm always optimistic, always positive about my pitch, my angle, the close, and my chances of success. It's always in the follow-up. Ask the salesmen extraordinaire turned president of the United States about that.

WORK ETHIC

Everyone who knows me calls me either "the hardest working man they've ever met" or "the hardest working man in show business." I am proud of those labels. I learned them from all those years of studying Donald Trump.

I credit my success to out-working and out-hustling my competition 24/7. I learned that unmatched work ethic by *modeling* Donald Trump. Trump is always working, always hustling.

President Trump is no different than TV mogul Trump, or real-estate titan Trump, or billionaire brander Trump. He is a human dynamo, always working, always hustling, always pitching.

Trump out-worked and out-hustled Hillary by a mile. Hillary complained about Russia. She should have worked harder, then she wouldn't have had to worry about Russia. But, she never came close to Trump's work ethic.

Trump, a 69-year old man at the time, traveled to three or four rallies a day, across multiple states. He'd start the day in Pittsburg, fly to Mississippi, onto Texas, then end up at a rally in Michigan.

Trump is amazing. He has the stamina of an enthusiastic 21-year-old college student.

How can anyone out-work or out-hustle Trump? The answer is they can't. He works from early morning to late evening. Yes, he plays some golf too. But that's also pure business. Every minute he's on the golf course, he's putting political deals or relationships together.

So, following Trump's lead, I've been a workhorse my entire life. I work from dawn to Midnight. And whenever things look bleak, whenever my business is down, whenever I've just lost a deal, I react by working harder—by hustling harder, by sacrificing more, by becoming more disciplined. I make more calls. I make more pitches. I follow up relentlessly. I get more creative. I go after new relationships like a madman. And after sixty to ninety days of that kind of hustle and maniacal intensity, my fears, worries, and negatives are gone. Vanished. History. A thing of the past. It works every time.

This could be why guys like me and Trump laugh and shake our heads at liberal protest rallies. We're too busy to protest. If you just out-worked, out-hustled and out-pitched the competition, you'd have nothing to protest or complain about. Just shut up and do it. Take action. Start pitching. And you'll never feel the need to protest again.

It's that simple. It's that automatic. Hustle and pitch 24/7 and the world becomes your oyster! Just another TRUMP RULE that changed my life.

NEW YORK MINUTE

Nike says, "Just Do It." They are partially right.

Trump believes in, *Just Do it . . . NOW!* Trump and I are both New Yorkers. There is a reason so many of the wealthiest Americans and so many of the most successful business titans are from New York. The numbers are staggering. It sometimes seems the richest, most powerful business moguls in *every* city in America are from New York. There's a reason for that.

New York is a 24/7 town. New York's streets are mean, rough, tough, and unforgiving. New York is dog-eat-dog. New York never sleeps—it's always moving at top speed. In New York, when you ask your CEO when he wants the project finished, he always replies, "yesterday."

That's where the saying "New York Minute" comes from. A New York Minute is not like any other minute. A New York Minute contains 30 seconds or less. You either do it fast in New York, or you lose . . . you're fired . . . you're a failure. Whoever hustles the most, whoever is the most aggressive . . . whoever is the most driven . . . whoever takes the initiative . . . wins.

Nike should change their saying to, Just Do It . . . *NOW!* As in, this minute. This second. Today. Don't wait. If you wait, someone else will beat you to the punch or steal your idea. That's what you learn in New York.

This all describes Trump. Trump is aggressive, combative, driven, demanding. He wants it done *yesterday*. New York does that. It hardens you. It makes you competitive and ambitious.

Pretty much every successful CEO I've ever met in New York, or is from New York, is just like Trump. They don't let grass grow under their feet. They want success and they want it N-O-W. And it works.

Nice guys really do finish last. I've never met a "nice guy" running a successful business in New York. You ever watch *Shark Tank*? Every successful business owner in New York is a *shark*. There is no room for minnows. They get eaten for breakfast.

The irony is this is exactly why so many liberal Democrats despise Trump. Because he is grumpy, demanding, has sky-high expectations, won't accept excuses, and suffers no fools. They want a nice guy . . . like Obama. Well Obama wrecked the US

★ ★ ★

economy, killed jobs, ruined healthcare, killed small business. It was eight years of misery and malaise. It was the worst economic growth in history—the first time since 1776 that we experienced eight straight years of less than 3% economic growth. The most people on welfare ever, the most on food stamps ever, the most on disability ever, the most government spending ever, the most debt ever.

Obama had never started a business, run a business, built a business, or created a job in his life. He knew nothing about how business works. So much for nice guys. He damaged and ruined a lot of lives. Trump is grumpy, rude, offensive, short-tempered, and demanding. But that's because those are the traits, like it or not, of a winner. If you don't play to win, you automatically lose.

If you want to win, you better be competitive, you better keep score, you better take action. You better Just Do It . . . *NOW!* Not tomorrow. Not next week. NOW. Otherwise, shut up and stop complaining. That's an important lesson.

If you want to move slow, stall, delay, procrastinate, or stay in bed until noon—fine. Just don't expect to be a winner.

If you want to be graded on a curve, or get "participation trophies"—fine. Just don't expect to be a winner.

If you don't want to be offended, if you want political correctness, if you want to never have your feelings hurt—fine. Just don't expect to be a winner.

If you want a "nice" boss, or "nice" business partner, or "nice" president of the United States—fine. Just get ready for failure, misery, decline, and bankruptcy.

Nice guys do finish last. Look at Obama and Jimmy Carter. If you want to succeed, get used to a grumpy, demanding, competitive, offensive boss or leader who will ask you to Just Do It . . . *NOW!* In a New York Minute.

CRISIS, CHAOS, CONTROVERSY: "YOU'RE FIRED!"

As a superstar business mogul, leader, and, of course, now president of the United States, Donald Trump recognizes one of the primary tasks of a CEO is to build a team of superstars, each of whom is great at what he or she does.

Remember the chapter about #WINNING"? That was so important, I made it the first TRUMP RULE. And while I've made the point that attaining success and wealth is all about you the individual (i.e. *If it is to be, it is up to me* and The Law Firm of *Me, Myself, and I*), the reality is . . . no matter how talented, smart, and charismatic you are, you'll still need a team of supporting players around you.

Even Trump needs a support staff. Even Trump needs executives. Even Trump needed business partners. Even Trump needed Mark Burnett to create *Celebrity Apprentice* with him. Even Trump needs a chief of staff. Even Trump needs a cabinet around him.

For you to be a winner, you must surround yourself with winners. Everyone must see the same big picture. Everyone must aim high and accept nothing but number one. Everyone must wake up excited to attack the day and win. No one in the inner circle can accept mediocrity.

In Trump's world, if the people you hire turn out to be mediocre or subpar, they aren't around for long. Hence Trump's favorite catchphrase from *The Apprentice*: "YOU'RE FIRED."

While many, if not most, great business CEOs operate this way, almost no one in politics before Trump has ever lived by this philosophy. By their very nature, politicians hire staff based on:

1. Patronage—They owe jobs to donors and campaign staff simply because these individuals helped elect them. *How*

absurd. Are they any good? Can they perform? Are they the best at what they do? Will they do a great job for America? Sadly, these questions are only a secondary consideration.

2. Diversity—Now we've hit upon the entire strategy of hiring by liberal politicians. It's all about *fairness, equality,* and *social justice.* Their hiring decisions are based first on diversity. They desperately want a team of diverse ethnic backgrounds, sex, and even sexual orientation. *Triple absurd.* Isn't hiring based only on sex or color of skin the very definition of sexism and racism? Shouldn't the question be, "Can they perform?" If not, they shouldn't be hired. Or worse, if they are hired and don't perform, it is almost impossible to fire them without the person doing the firing being labeled as "sexist" or "racist." Liberals either don't get it, or simply don't care, simply because it's OPM (other people's money).

3. Participation Trophies—Liberal politicians and government bureaucrats rarely ever fire anyone, lest someone's feelings be hurt. Regardless of how poorly they perform, politicians will pat them on the head and give them *participation trophies.*

We can all learn from this valuable TRUMP RULE on hiring. First, it's not about "diversity" or "patronage." It's about PERFORMANCE. Either you can do the job well or you're fired.

It's called "performance-based" because, well, performance is what matters. Not "feelings." Not "equality, diversity, and fairness." Not "being nice." Not being "compassionate." Not "doing the best you can." In Trump's world of excellence, if your best isn't good enough, bye bye, "YOU'RE FIRED."

Liberals and DC swamp bureaucrats don't understand this.

Not only do they not understand it, they are angered by it. It confuses them. It frightens them. They say, *"It isn't fair."*

This reminds me of a famous quote, when in 1970, G. Harrold Carswell was nominated to the Supreme Court. At the time, critics charged that he was, at best, mediocre and therefore unqualified to sit on the Supreme Court. Senator Roman Hruska leapt to Carswell's defense. In a statement that could only be made by a politician, Hruska declared: *"Even if he were mediocre, there are a lot of mediocre judges and people and lawyers. They are entitled to a little representation, aren't they ... ?"[78]*

NOT IN PRESIDENT DONALD J. TRUMP'S WORLD.

Trump doesn't give a damn about the ways of DC or government employee unions. Based on whether they perform to his high standards of excellence, President Trump is constantly firing top aides, staffers, even Cabinet Secretaries. To liberal snowflakes, this is madness. This is chaos. Trump's presidency is *in crisis.*

Nope. To Trump, this is business as usual. Trump just doesn't accept mediocrity, or under-performing. And Trump's got plenty of confidence and ego (ya think?), so he's not afraid to admit he hired the wrong person and start over.

What seemed "nice" and "compassionate" about Obama or Hillary (or substitute any other DC swamp politician, Democrat or Republican) keeping staff employed for perpetuity is actually a major weakness. It's easy to say they don't have the guts to fire an employee. They don't have the guts to tell someone they hired: "You suck at this job, so I'm letting you go." They don't have the guts to admit that they hired the wrong person.

But, it's even worse than that. They don't even recognize they are being a total failure to the American people as CEO of the world's largest economy by not demanding the absolute best employees in the world at each important position.

Trump knows what his job is and he knows how important it is that he does it right. When it comes to hiring and firing, he knows he can't give a damn about hurting someone's feelings. He knows the

American people hired him to get the job done right and that is what he's going to do!

So, yes, the Trump presidency is a revolving door. Yes, people get fired quickly, or leave quickly, because they can't take the crisis, chaos, controversy, competition and intense pressure to perform at the highest levels, or lose their job. That's a lot of stress. Only the best can handle it. Trump tests them under fire and quickly decides if they pass muster. If not, "You're Fired!"

To the liberal mainstream media, government bureaucrats, and political hacks, this is heresy. They say: "This is no way to run a White House. It's mean spirited." But a big-time CEO like Trump knows this is *exactly* how you run a successful business and knows it is time to run government the same way.

The private sector is based on performance. No one cares if you're a "nice fellow." No one cares if "you tried your best." No one cares if your feelings are hurt. Poor baby. It only matters that you get the job done better than anyone else. If not, you gotta go. Now. In a New York Minute.

The question arises: "Why do politicians and people in government care so little about performance (i.e. results)?

The answer is easy—**it's not their money.** They are playing with OPM—*Other People's Money.* The politician or DC swamp agency head isn't paying the salary or absorbing the losses out of his or her own pocket. They have no shareholders or board of directors to answer to. So, they can afford to be "nice" and "compassionate" and keep people employed forever.

In Trump's dog-eat-dog private sector life, before the White House, a CEO only survives if he produces great results and a profit. If not, he loses his own job. In other words, failure and mediocre performance are personal. If the people you hire fail to perform, not only do they get fired . . . you do too.

In Trump's world, there is no time to rest on your laurels. It's not about the color of your skin. It's not about kissing your ass. It's not about what you did yesterday. In Trump's world, after a big victory, you get to celebrate for one night. Tomorrow you start with a fresh slate. Tomorrow you have to prove yourself all over again. Yesterday is *yesterday's news.*

This is the mindset Trump brought to the White House.

Is this bad? Well, it's certainly stressful for the executives, staffers, and employees in Trump's orbit. But it sure keeps them on their toes. It sure molds them into the best executive, salesperson, or leader they can be. Trump's hyper-competitive world molds winners. There is no grey area. You're either the best, or you need to find another job because you are soon to be fired.

But just like a tough Marine drill sergeant, I'm betting Trump's harsh environment makes most of the employees (even the fired ones) better employees for the rest of their lives.

That's why the crisis, chaos, and controversy around Trump are no coincidence. It's purposeful. Trump is a very special man. He loves crisis and chaos. He thrives on controversy. Personally, I think he loves to get himself in trouble. He does it on purpose. First, he knows it will attract media headlines. Which means he is the center of the world's attention. Secondly, it gives him a chance to dance out of trouble. This is a man who flirts with disaster, twenty times a week. And yet he always makes a comeback. Every time he's almost dead, he comes back to life. I think he challenges himself to come back every day from a near-death experience, thereby proving he is super-human.

That's how Trump measures others. Can you survive and thrive under that kind of crisis, chaos, controversy, and competition? Trump wants it *dog-eat-dog* so he can test your mettle, quick thinking, competitive spirits, creativity, and courage under fire. He wants people who thrive under that kind of intense stress, who can survive in *war-like* conditions in perpetuity.

No one working for Trump is sitting around waiting for their twenty-year anniversary so they can collect a gold watch and pension for the rest of their lives. That's how government has been run forever. But anyone with lifetime job security and a pension is highly under-motivated. Meaning, they don't give a damn.

Government employees are guaranteed a safe weekly paycheck, top-of-the-line benefits and a pension for life. They also get a ton of paid vacation time. Most government employees can't be fired. And there is no bonus for doing a great job, saving money, or producing record profits. So, who cares? What's their incentive to be the best? Why give a damn about saving money or making money for Uncle Sam? As long as you show up—no matter how bad you are at the job—you get paid. You might as well do the minimum required.

A close friend told me he gave the following fatherly advice to his children: "If you find a passion in life, pursue it to the end. If you love what you do, success and wealth will come. But, if you don't find a passion, then take a government job. You'll get paid well, have little stress, and retire ridiculously young with an excellent pension for *not* working for the rest of your life."

What would happen if government employees were held accountable and demanded to produce results? The first time we ever tried that experiment was under President Trump. No wonder millions of bureaucrats, politicians, political hacks, and DC swamp rats hate Trump and want to frame Trump. They're in shock. They want him out—whether it be defeat in 2020, impeachment, or a perp walk. Some even dream out loud about assassination. They have to get rid of Trump before he fires them or kills their gravy train.

Of course they want him gone. He's upsetting their cozy life of minor effort, a guaranteed job, safe paycheck, and a pension for life.

Trump demands those he hires actually perform at the highest levels. Can you imagine the nerve? Trump expects them to work hard, cut costs, and produce a profit. He expects government employees to give a damn—like those who worked for him in the private sector do. To spoiled government employees with little or no incentive or need to ever prove positive results, this is blasphemy.

And instead of showing up for a cushy, no work, no stress job for twenty years and then retiring, Trump wants his employees to experience intense pressure, crisis, chaos, controversy, and competition. He actually expects the cream to rise to the top. He wants you to fight for your job. Like a nasty, mean Marine drill sergeant. This is how Trump gets the most out of each employee.

No wonder Trump is hated by the bureaucratic swamp. No wonder he is loved by so many hard-working, taxpaying, ordinary American citizens.

Does *Trump's way* work? Trump built a multi billion dollar empire. He dominated New York real estate in one of the toughest competitive environments in the world. He built the Wollman Ice Skating Rink at Central Park under budget and in record time, versus government bureaucrats who got nothing done in six years and wasted $12 million for nothing.[79]

Then he dominated Hollywood with one of the most successful franchises in TV history. Then he dominated politics and beat a field of the seventeen best GOP candidates in history. Then he beat Hillary Clinton, the most famous brand name in the history of US politics. Trump's prize? He became one of forty-five men in the history of the world to become the leader of the free world.

All of these fields are the hardest and most competitive in the world. Yet Trump dominated in *all* of them. He thrived under crisis, chaos, controversy, and competition. Trump's philosophy is a proven one-in-a-billion winner, and I believe applying this philosophy to government will result in him being one of the, if not the, best Presidents in history. The G.O.A.T. (greatest of all time).

There is no higher, harder, or more demanding CEO position in the world than that of president of the United States of America. Demanding outstanding performance by every employee should be just as high a priority running a country, as a company. Trump understands that.

But, change doesn't come easily. While Trump is demanding performance from his close staff and those he appoints, as well as changing how they are hired and fired, the career politicians and government bureaucrats (who hate Trump) are still making decisions based on DC *politics as usual*. They're undermining Trump. They still want to keep mediocre, poor-performing employees employed *forever*. That way they can lecture to everyone how wonderful they are, versus that *mean, nasty Donald Trump* who fires everyone and runs the government by crisis and chaos.

The sad examples of terrible political appointments are endless, although none more so than Obama's appointment of John Kerry and nuclear physicist Ernest J. Moniz, then Secretary of Energy, to negotiate the Iran nuclear deal. Neither had a clue as to what they were doing, or even a rudimentary knowledge of how to negotiate. Their only mission was to sign a deal with Iran, no matter how ridiculous the terms. What else could account for agreeing to give Iran more money back than they even asked for? Obama and his "negotiators" gave Iran the interest on the billions we had frozen for decades, based on their acts of terrorism around the world. Iran's negotiators never asked for the interest on the money held for decades. But Kerry and Moniz offered. *Pathetic.*

How about sending a plane loaded with pallets of US and international hard currency totaling hundreds of millions to Iran as a "thank you" to the mullahs for agreeing to perhaps the worst, most one-sided debacle in American history? Everyone involved should have been fired, then prosecuted. But no one cared. After all, it was OPM—*Other People's Money.*

Trump is changing the culture of government slowly. But now you understand why so many government bureaucrats despise Trump.

It turns out, chaos, crisis, and controversy aren't crazy. There's a method to Trump's madness. This is how you mold average employees into battle-hardened performers.

While none of us will probably ever be at the level of President Donald Trump, there is much we can learn and apply to our own success from this Trump Rule.

I've spent my entire career doing my best to surround myself with great people who perform at the highest level. I hire only people who have proven positive performance results in the private sector. I hire people who I believe can give me (their boss) a run for the money. That's what makes me stronger and sharper. Competition is great for everyone. Mediocrity pulls everyone down.

That's the only way to gain fame, fortune, and record-breaking success. *The Trump way.*

DRESS FOR SUCCESS

I'll be brief here. This TRUMP RULE is simple. If you're going to become a millionaire (or billionaire), you better dress like one first! If you're going to be a brand, be the best dressed brand that screams class and success.

Today's youth think it's ok to have tattoos all over their bodies, body piercings, and dress like a casual slob. Good luck with that one. You're defeated before you ever walk in the door. A) Most bosses will not hire you. B) Even if they do hire you, they'll never think of you as a top executive or lieutenant.

If you don't wear the uniform of success and leadership, you have very little shot of becoming a leader or achieving mega-success. Sure, there are a few exceptions—in Silicon Valley, or in the old Internet boom in the early 2000s. But those are few-and-far-between exceptions to the rule. And why fight an uphill battle? Why have to fight ten times harder to convince a boss or investor you're worthy, versus the guy in the $2,500 tailored pinstripe suit.

Why not walk into a room and exude success and wealth? I learned from the best—Donald J. Trump. Trump never goes anywhere (other than the golf course) without looking presidential, or like the billionaire CEO mogul. He's won and intimidated the competition just by walking in the door looking like a billion bucks.

Like Trump, I try to always look like a million bucks (at least). Everyone that meets me meets a stylish dresser, wearing almost exclusively bespoke European suits, hand-tailored for me. I aim to be the best-dressed man in every room. I aim to give off an image of success and wealth. On my Newsmax TV show, I always aimed to be the best-dressed man on American television. My wardrobe of twenty-five of the finest hand-tailored suits in the world (most pinstriped), over 200 colorful silk ties, and a collection of a dozen dress shoes is unmatched on TV. Because I believe *the clothes make the man.* I invested in me because I believe in me.

Remember in *The Trump Ego Rules,* how I pointed out, "if you don't believe in you, no one else will." Believing in you starts with dressing for success well before you achieve it. Others will believe in you when they see someone who looks like a #WINNER.

Thank you, President Trump, for teaching me to always aim for number one—in everything I do. It starts with dressing for success.

FREE MEDIA

Although I touched on this previously, I saved going into it in depth as the last of these valuable TRUMP RULES because it's such an important, valuable, and misunderstood trait. It also may be Trump's most valuable political rule. Because this is the rule most responsible for getting him elected president, against all odds.

Where would Trump have been without *free media*? Trump and I hate the mainstream media for their liberal bias and prejudice. But ironically, we've both figured out ways to use the media to make us successful. For me, that primarily means making me one of the most well-known, high-profile conservative talk show hosts in America. And soon, once again, "the King of Vegas Sports Gambling." In Trump's case, in addition to success and wealth, it was also critical in his becoming president of the United States.

We may both hate the media and their terrible bias, but we understand its value. As usual, I learned about *free media* by studying and modeling Trump. Everything I've done to use the media has mirrored what I learned from President Trump.

One great article in the media can make a business, movie, album, book, or political career. Who needs to spend money when the media can provide you with millions, or in the rare case of Donald Trump, billions of dollars in free publicity?

When I wrote earlier in this chapter about Trump's remarkable understanding of branding, guess who provided the platform to make that branding a success? *The media.*

When I wrote about Trump's use of celebrity to sell his products, guess who provided the platform to become a celebrity? *The media.*

When I wrote about Trump's salesmanship and nonstop pitching of deals, guess who provided the platform that he used to sell and

★ ★ ★

pitch everything from his real estate and his television show, to his presidential campaign? *The media.*

When I wrote about *Trump's Ego Rules* and P.T. Barnum-like, nonstop promotion, guess who provided the platform that he used to promote himself and his products? *The media.*

When Trump beat Hillary, it wasn't the Russians who gave him the edge. Russia spent a grand total of about one hundred thousand dollars on social-media ads, and it's an open question if they were intended to help Trump or Crooked Hillary. Ironically, it was the American mainstream media who gave Trump several billion dollars of publicity (a.k.a. *free media*).

The Trump brand goes hand-in-hand with *free media* the way America goes hand-in-hand with apple pie, motherhood, and Chevrolet.

Before he entered the political arena, Trump became famous and rich with the help of "Page Six" of the *New York Post* gossip columnists like Cindy Adams, talk show host Oprah Winfrey, the *National Enquirer, People, Us,* TMZ, *Access Hollywood,* and *Entertainment Tonight.* Trump was their favorite topic. They gave him billions in free advertising. It is not exaggerating to say they created the Trump brand. Trump, of course, gets an assist because he's the one who figured it all out and fed them the nonstop PR.

From Trump the business mogul, to Trump the billionaire playboy, to Trump the TV star, to Trump the President, it's always been about the free publicity provided by the media. Trump understood early in life that there's no need to spend billions of dollars on advertising when you can get the advertising, promotion, and branding *free* from the media.

Everyone can learn from Trump. Anyone can use the media machine, and used properly, can become rich and famous because of it. Just look at and ask the Hollywood PR machine how to utilize *free media* to create celebrity and build a brand name. Ask Kanye

West. Ask George Clooney. Ask Madonna. Ask Floyd "Money" Mayweather. The list is long. If they're famous, if they're a household brand name, you can bet they used *free media* to build their brand and earn a fortune off it. Free media is worth its weight in gold.

I'm a prime example. From day one, I used media to promote my careers. I used the media at age sixteen to brand me as *the next* Jimmy "The Greek." I used the *New York Post's* "Page Six" to promote my career as a young hotshot nightclub owner at age twenty-three. I used the media to get my first six-figure gig on NBC Radio at the age of twenty-five. I later became Jimmy "The Greek's" television partner at age twenty-seven, thanks 100% to nonstop media and PR. I became a successful businessman and CEO of a public company because of nonstop media. I became the Libertarian vice presidential nominee in my first try at national politics because I generated more media articles and TV appearances than all of my competition combined. And you can be positive I made sure the 1,000 delegates to the Libertarian convention knew it.

I then parlayed all that free media from my vice presidential run into thousands of guest appearances on television and radio shows nationwide. I appeared on all the biggest talk shows in America. I then parlayed that *free media* into hosting my own national TV and radio talk shows.

I used *free media* to help my oldest child (my brilliant and beautiful daughter Dakota) gain admittance to Harvard. She was the star of many stories in the local Vegas media as a teenager. We made sure Harvard saw them. And, after being accepted, Dakota appeared on Fox News with her proud dad to share her amazing accomplishments.

Approximately forty thousand brilliant students apply to Harvard each year. A mere eighteen hundred or so are accepted. Only one told her story on Fox News. Dakota learned well from her dad, just like I learned well from Donald J. Trump. *Free media* is worth its weight in gold.

I used *free media* to make my adopted Grandpa Norm famous at age ninety-two. Grandpa's experience of a lifetime was literally priceless. We spent zero dollars promoting it. Free media did the job for us!

Free media has been the centerpiece of my life for decades. Thanks, President Trump.

The message of this section . . . for that matter, the message to every reader of this book . . . is that you can use the media machine and the other TRUMP RULES to build a business empire, make a fortune, or change your life.

Remember the section of this book on *storytelling*? Let me use *storytelling* here now to show you a few examples of how *free media* changes lives and creates fortunes.

I've used this story at many of my business speeches for years. It is a remarkable, heartwarming, tear-jerker, *only-in-America* story.

Davion Navar Henry was born in prison to a criminal mother. He was an orphan, alone without parents for the first fifteen years of his life. I can't imagine what that's like. I grew up with two great, loving parents. My mom and dad had little money and no big titles, but they both told me they loved me every day of my life. I can't imagine what it would be like to grow up with no one to tell you they loved you for the first fifteen years of life.

In 2013, at the age of fifteen, Davion Navar Henry decided to change his life. *Free media* was his weapon of choice. It was a brilliant decision. He stood in front of a church in Florida and gave a heartfelt speech. He said . . .

> "I know God hasn't given up on me, so I'm not giving
> up either . . . I'll take anyone [to love me]. Old or young,
> dad or mom, black, white, purple. I don't care. And I
> would be really appreciative. The best I could be."[80]

The church knew Davin was going to make this plea and had notified the media—the same way I notified the media about Grandpa Norm's skydive. The media always needs a good story, because good stories raise ratings. It's all about money. No matter what you think about the media, they are predictable. They'll cover any story they think will bring a bigger audience. That's how anyone can trigger millions of dollars in *free media*.

The media covered Davion's heartfelt speech. And the story exploded. It made headlines across the globe.[81]

How powerful is *free media* exposure? This kid was alone for the first fifteen years of his life. No parents ever chose to adopt him. Then came the media exposure. Within days, more than ten thousand parents requested to adopt Davion. TEN THOUSAND. Davion received requests for adoption from a dozen countries.

Without the self-promotion and the exposure provided by *free media* this kid remains an orphan for the rest of his life. Sadly, there are millions like him. But with the help of the media spreading his heartfelt story, he winds up with a mom and dad.

But what about the millions of other orphans who don't get the media exposure? The answer is . . . nothing changes. They never get parents. Media was the difference, the only difference. I call it "the celebrity factor." It made Davion a media celebrity. And everyone loves a celebrity.

Davion changed his life. What's the dollar value on *free media* for Davion? *Free media* is priceless. Even a hundred million dollar fortune doesn't compare to having a mom and dad who say, "I love you."

Isn't that what this entire book is about?

The TRUMP RULES are not just about making money, they are about changing lives! *Free media* can work for anyone. For businesses, individuals, even for animals. Take the story of the Las Vegas "Arson

Puppies." A terrible, greedy, Las Vegas pet-store owner hired an arsonist to burn down her store—with puppies in it.

Thank God the fire department got there in the nick of time to, just barely, save these puppies from a fiery death. As luck would have it, this pet-shop owner had a video system in the store. It, too, was saved. So, the whole episode was caught on video. Society is fortunate that so many criminals are so stupid. She was arrested and sent to prison.

The twenty-seven purebred puppies were saved. They were not just kept safe and sound, but thanks to media exposure, these puppies were made famous celebrities themselves. The Animal Foundation announced a raffle. Anyone who donated one hundred dollars would get a chance to adopt these puppies.

Because of the media publicity, the response was enormous. It became a feeding frenzy. Thousands of pet lovers paid for the chance to own one of these puppies. Why these dogs? A combination of *free media* and the *celebrity factor* the media firestorm created. These lucky puppies became instant media celebrities.

Everyone wanted to save these *specific* twenty-seven dogs. They all wanted to be part of the story—a story they could tell everyone they meet for the rest of their lives. This was their chance to grab a piece of celebrity. Which is fantastic. I'm a dog lover and I love the happy ending for these puppies.

Because of my love of dogs, allow me a paragraph or two to go "off script." The tragic reality is . . .

Three to four million dogs and cats are put to death annually in just the United States. That's about eighty thousand per week. One dog or cat is euthanized every eleven seconds in this country. That doesn't even count how many are killed or die terrible deaths out in the streets each year. None of them are any different than these twenty-seven puppies. Almost all would make wonderful pets, if only someone would give them a home. But no one ever does.

An executive from The Animal Foundation was quoted in a Las Vegas television news interview after this whole "Arson Puppy Raffle" phenomenon. He said, "The hoopla has not resulted in increased adoptions. People wanted these twenty-seven dogs . . . no interest in any others. It was 'the celebrity factor.'"

Indeed. Nothing changed for all the lonely dogs and cats in America, or the rest of the world for that matter. No one wants them. But everyone wanted "the Arson Puppies" of Las Vegas. That's the amazing power of publicity, *free media*, celebrity, and branding.

One more story about the power of *free media*. But this one is *all business*. I assume that's why most of you bought this book . . . to learn how to turn the TRUMP RULES into wealth and financial freedom.

This story is emblematic of the power of *free media* to radially empower any business. The fact is, no amount of advertising could do for Maker's Mark Whiskey what *free media* did.

Maker's Mark went twenty-nine years with no promotion or media exposure. It was *America's best kept secret*. Then, the son Bill Samuels Jr. took over the business from his father, the founder of the company. The dad knew nothing about the value of promotion and media. He didn't think that was important. He had no interest in "commercializing" it.

But Bill Jr. was ambitious. He understood the value of promotion. He used PR and media to power this small whiskey company. Soon, Maker's Mark was on the front page of the *Wall Street Journal*. The date was August 1st, 1980.[82]

Overnight, business exploded. The company received thousands of orders the day after the *Wall Street Journal* story. The company received 35,000 letters after that article. Suddenly, every high-end restaurant and every liquor distributor in the country wanted to carry

Maker's Mark. The rest is history. In 2014, they began a $67 million expansion. Maker's Mark now sells over one million cases annually and does over one hundred twenty million annually in sales.[83]

With the power of *free media*, a small business was transformed overnight into a big business. Without promotion and media exposure, it would never have happened. The proof? It didn't happen for twenty-nine years, since the company was founded. Then it happened overnight as a result of *free media*. One story by the national media exploded the business and changed the course of its history.

Isn't that what this entire book is about? Those are the TRUMP RULES.

These rules can make you a millionaire or a billionaire. They can turn a small business into big business. They can turn dreams into reality. They can get a lonely orphan adopted by loving parents. They can turn a ninety-two-year-old man into a celebrity. They can help get a home-schooled girl into Harvard. They can save puppies from almost certain death. And, they turned this author into a radio, television, newspaper, publishing, and sports gaming brand. The TRUMP RULES are that powerful.

NEVER forget . . . these TRUMP RULES also prove being humble is *greatly* over-rated. Believe in yourself with every fiber in your body. Toot your own horn. "It ain't bragging, if you can back it up." Find a way to shout from the highest mountain about your talents, your value. Because if you don't, no one else will.

Brand yourself—then find an interesting angle to attract *free media*. Don't be shy, don't be afraid to sell—because *everything* is sales.

Make sure you always have a great emotional story to tell. Don't be afraid to pitch twenty-four hours a day. "Always pitching, never bitching." Don't waste a minute protesting or complaining. Use every minute for hustling and pitching.

Aim for the stars—sell yourself with passion and pitch—with chutzpah.

Ignore the failures and screw the critics. Stick to your gut. What the critics think doesn't matter and it's usually wrong.

Trust me, you can't go wrong with the TRUMP RULES.

Thanks, President Trump for empowering all of us.

SECTION IV

*Proof the Trump Rules
Work for Anyone*

─────── CHAPTER FIFTEEN ───────

My Fairy Tale Life: The Trump Miracles

"If you have an important point to make, don't try to be subtle or clever. Use a pile driver. Hit the point once. Then come back and hit it again. Then hit it a third time—a tremendous whack."

───────

Sir Winston Churchill

Much of this book is focused on planning for success, seeing it clearly before you actually achieve it, developing the mindset of a #WINNER, becoming comfortable taking risks, and overcoming failure. Those are the foundations of Trump's success. Those have been the foundations of my success. Those are the keys to success for anyone, anywhere, at anything.

Because I modeled my life after Trump, I became a financial risk-taking riverboat gambler, just like Trump. We both failed and crashed and burned our fair share. Like Trump, my life has been filled with ups and downs, peaks and valleys, the luxury of wealth and turning dreams into amazing reality—as well as a bankruptcy and multiple financial flops.

Like Trump, one day I was up, then I was down. Just like Trump, it changes on an almost daily basis. I still swing and miss all the time. Such is the life of a riverboat gambler and gunslinger. But, they are also the wild swings of a Hall of Fame home-run hitter. The greatest all-time home run hitters almost always top the charts for all-time strikeouts too. The key is to keep swinging.

Like most of you reading this book, I started at the bottom. Quite frankly, from where I started, I had little chance of achieving significant monetary success. The truth is, it usually takes money to make money.

My friend and business partner Doug told a great story about his days earning his MBA at Stanford:

"Perhaps my best learning experience at Stanford was our noon economics class, when entrepreneurs would come to talk about their success," Doug said. "The story was invariably some version of, 'We started in a garage, struggled, invented, changed, and are now worth millions . . . aren't we smart!' Then the floor was opened to questions. The first question was always the same. 'Where and how did you get your seed capital?' About half the time, the response was 'Well, my dad countersigned a million dollar note.' That was followed by a rustle, as half of us got up and left because the presentation had been a waste of time. We all knew if someone gave us a million dollars, we were smart enough to turn it into a success, too. The question we were all looking for an answer to was 'how do you get that first million dollars needed to build the business?'"

That was certainly the situation in my case. I faced impossible odds and had little chance to achieve what I have, as often as I have.

The life I've lived can only be described as a *fairy tale*. Thank God for America, for economic freedom, for capitalism, and for Donald Trump and those TRUMP RULES.

Every step of the way, I was empowered by the TRUMP RULES. These rules didn't make me a billionaire. They didn't guarantee success in everything I tried. But they allowed me to overcome tough (and often impossible) odds, again and again. When I did fail, they lifted me from the ashes. These TRUMP RULES gave me a fighting chance . . . a relentless spirit . . . a hunger and passion . . . a faith in my success . . . an energy and enthusiasm without bounds . . . and the chutzpah to dream big dreams, overcome big failures, and screw the critics.

I didn't reach the pinnacle of success and fame—like Donald Trump. I didn't hit grand-slam home runs—like Trump. I didn't become president of the United States and change the world—like Trump. But I sure did change my life for the better. I sure did empower and super-charge my world. I hit lots of singles, doubles, and triples. And as I write this book, I'm on the verge of my first home run at the age of fifty-nine. I have gone places and achieved successes I never imagined possible.

It doesn't matter where you start—the penthouse, the outhouse, or the gutter. It doesn't matter if you have the connections or financial backing of a Donald Trump. My success proves these TRUMP RULES will work for anyone, at any level, in any league. You don't have to start a millionaire, or end a billionaire, or even become president of the United States and leader of the free world.

These TRUMP RULES work for big dreams and little dreams. They work for big business or small business. They work for business, career, politics, or life. Study the TRUMP RULES and model Trump. I promise you a wild ride, a journey of a lifetime.

MY LIFE IS PROOF POSITIVE
THE TRUMP RULES WORK.

Following is a list of my life's miracles that I've laid out in simple, short, easy-to-understand bullet points. I call them *The Trump Miracles.* Because these TRUMP RULES empowered my journey every step of the way. As you will see, you are in the right place at the right time. Because, if this dead-end street kid from the mean streets of the Bronx borderline, with no money, no connections, and few talents or skills can pull off miracles like these, then ANYONE can!

Think I'm kidding? Let me first lay out my shortcomings.

I stink at math. Anything beyond 2 + 2 or 2 x 2, I need a calculator.

I have no mechanical ability of any kind. If a lightbulb needs changing, I pick up the phone and call the handyman. If my computer or laptop or iPad isn't working, I call my young sons for help.

To use any fancy feature on my iPhone, I need those young sons again. Fix a clogged drain, or change the oil in my car? You've got to be kidding!

I drive fancy, $100,000 cars. But on the day I sell them, I haven't used 99% of the car's fancy features. Why? Because I have no idea what the buttons are for. And if someone showed me, I'd still be afraid to touch them.

On Christmas morning, I can't put the toys together. I break whatever I touch.

I can't dance. I can't sing. I have absolutely no artistic ability—not a single bone in my body.

I'm a lousy athlete—because I'm uncoordinated with terrible hand-eye coordination. Although I was one heck of a football player . . . because all I had to do was aim at the ball carrier like a laser guided missile and knock his head off. That, I'm really good at!

I can't sit still for more than a few minutes—I'm the poster boy for ADD (Attention Deficit Disorder). Which is why I can't go to an office to work a traditional job. I've never done that in my life. I've always worked from my home office.

I don't take orders well. That's why I've never worked for others (except for a short stint as an anchorman and TV host at CNBC). I've always started and owned my own businesses. Most wealthy businessmen I've met have a similar story. They all made lousy employees, so they made themselves the boss!

So, I must repeat this point . . .

If this dead-end kid from the mean streets of the Bronx borderline, with few talents or skills and far too many weaknesses, can pull off miracles like the ones you're about to read, then ANYONE can!

Read on. Here is a list of the miracles in my fairy-tale life. Once you see how my life has been changed by making the TRUMP RULES an integral part of my very being, I think you will soon be convinced you can do the same and make your own dreams come true.

MIRACLE #1:

This is one of two miracles that came before I ever studied Donald Trump. But Trump would have been proud. I may not have known it, but at the age of sixteen I was already channeling *my inner Trump*. I had somehow grasped the crucial idea that everything is about sales, promotion, and *free media*.

I innately understood the importance of standing out from the crowd and the need for an "angle" that gets people's attention. I knew I needed to promote myself 24/7—because this is New York and that's the only way to stand out from the crowd. As a bonus, I learned you don't need to be a millionaire if you can get a million dollars of free media. The media will make you famous, and eventually rich.

At age sixteen, I made my first miracle come true with an early version of the TRUMP RULES. Jimmy "The Greek" Snyder was the most famous sports gambler and Vegas oddsmaker in the world. I decided to aim for his job. I wrote a press release (yes, at age sixteen) and sent it to the media, boldly announcing that I was the new Jimmy "The Greek." It got the media's attention. My hometown Mt. Vernon's *Daily Argus* headline read, "Meet the Betting WhizKid."[84] The article branded me as "the next Jimmy 'the Greek'." Soon, media across the USA picked up on the story. I was already using Trump's concept of *free media* to change my life.

MIRACLE #2:

Again, I had no idea who Donald Trump was at this point, but I was already utilizing the TRUMP RULES subconsciously. First, I always had chutzpah. I aimed for the stars. I knew I had to get out of my blue-collar life. I knew that getting accepted to Ivy League Columbia University was my ticket. I ate, slept, and dreamed 24/7 about gaining acceptance to Columbia U.

Then comes "the pitch." Everything in life is sales. But closing the deal requires a unique, exciting, compelling sales pitch.

I needed a plan to separate me from the tens of thousands of others applying for just a few openings, most of whom came from wealthy families, or whose parents were powerful Columbia alumni. How would a son of a butcher beat them at their own, rigged game?

The splash I'd made with my Jimmy "The Greek" media campaign had given me a shot of confidence. Why couldn't I do it again? Donald Trump would have been proud of my plan.

Just as I had successfully branded myself "the new Jimmy 'The Greek,'" I now branded myself as a S.O.B—Son of a Butcher. I walked confidently into Columbia's admissions office and told the admissions officer, "I am an SOB— Son of a Butcher. You'll accept hundreds of rich kids into Columbia University today from wealthy, powerful, connected families, but only one blue-collar SOB. I will be your one 'American Dream' story to brag about. I am your one-in-a-million. I am your needle in a haystack. Years from now, you'll look back at this moment, and I will make Columbia proud."

It worked!

I delivered that sales pitch like a pro. Donald Trump would have been proud. I was accepted into Columbia. I'm guessing I was the only son of a butcher admitted into that Class of 1983.

MIRACLE #3:

Soon after graduation from Columbia, I was back on "the campaign trail." I was marketing, promoting, branding, and selling myself for the role of *the new* Jimmy "The Greek." That dream started in 1977 with media coverage of my Jimmy "The Greek" plan. I fought for twelve long years, from moment of conception, to moment of victory. Twelve years is a long time to keep a dream alive. Especially a one-in-a-million dream. What are the odds a street hustler from Mt Vernon, NY would become the new Jimmy "The Greek?" Well I did it.

It took twelve years of failure, rejection, disappointment, challenges, humiliation on multiple occasions, and multiple failed businesses and careers along the way. But eventually, this relentless pursuit of my dream, combined with the help of the TRUMP RULES, paid off with another miracle. This was a doozy.

With no money, no connections, no prior education or experience in TV journalism, I talked my way into replacing the lead sports host and anchorman for Financial News Network (now CNBC). His name was Todd Donoho. He left FNN Sports to become the lead sports anchor for ABC TV in Los Angeles in 1989. That announcement changed my life.

In those days, Financial News Network covered business during the week and sports on the weekend. I had never before appeared on TV in my life—not even on a local cable access show. I had never taken a single course in broadcast journalism. Yet, I was competing with hundreds of veteran broadcasters for the job. These were men and women who had worked at a dozen different television jobs.

I had no clue what I was doing. I didn't even understand what a host or anchorman did. But I knew I was born to star on TV. I took a page from Trump. I walked into my audition like I owned the place. I was brimming with confidence. No one had a clue I didn't know what I was doing.

Talk about a miracle. I got the job. I became Financial News Network's Network Oddsmaker, NFL Analyst, and host of five shows—including the network's premiere NFL pre- and post-game shows starring myself and . . . drumroll please . . .

Jimmy "The Greek" Snyder.

What are the odds? Three hundred million people in America and I become the one who partners with my childhood idol and TV legend, Jimmy "The Greek."

As an aside, in one of the newspaper articles from a decade before about my goal to become my generation's Jimmy "The Greek," they interviewed Jimmy and asked what he thought about this kid, Wayne Root, who wanted his job. The Greek responded, "You tell Wayne Root that in every city in America there are a hundred guys who want my job. Get in line!" Well, I had just moved to the head of the line.

It was quite a journey. And the TRUMP RULES made it happen every step of the way. It was all about confidence, bravado, promotion and "the pitch." To put it in today's vernacular, this would be like a brash 16-year-old kid bragging to the media that he will someday replace Dr. Phil, Judge Judy, or Oprah, and winding up, a decade later, as their television partner.

After about three months of Jimmy and Wayne starring together, FNN/CNBC decided they didn't need Jimmy anymore and they fired him. It became my TV show. I actually replaced my childhood hero Jimmy "The Greek." The story played out exactly as I'd always dreamed.

MIRACLE #4:

While at FNN/CNBC I came up with a crazy dream. One even crazier than thinking I could become Jimmy "The Greek." The problem was, it meant leaving the job at the network. At the time, I was the host of five shows on national TV. Who walks away from that? No one ever just leaves the TV business at the height of his career and celebrity. But I did. Why? Because I sensed a fortune was just waiting to be made in the sports gambling business.

Like my hero and mentor Trump, I took a huge gamble. Everyone at FNN/CNBC thought I was stark raving mad. They were sure I'd just ruined my life. I proved them wrong—another important TRUMP RULE. Ignore the critics. Do what's in your gut. It wasn't easy, but I turned my talent for predicting pointspread winners into building the leading sports gaming advice company in America. I starred on a sports gaming television show that lasted for two decades. Over three million American sports gamblers called for my advice. The media dubbed me "America's Oddsmaker" and "The King of Vegas Sports Gambling." I was awarded a 180-pound granite star on the Las Vegas Walk of Stars alongside Elvis, Liberace, Wayne Newton, Frank Sinatra, Dean Martin, Sammy Davis Jr., and Siegfried & Roy. It was designated "Wayne Root Day" in the city of Las Vegas and the state of Nevada.

As boxing promoter Don King would say, "Only in America." I'd change it to, "Only in Donald Trump's America."

MIRACLE #5:

I created a TV competition show to crown the greatest casino gambler in the world called *King of Vegas.* It took me sixteen years of rejection in Hollywood to sell it to a TV network. But sell it, I did. The executives of Spike TV liked my *sales pitch* so much, they asked me if I'd co-host the show. Eventually I sold three reality TV shows to major television networks. One of them became the biggest hit series in the history of Travel Channel. To this day, I know of no one in Hollywood history to go three-for-three selling hit TV series as a part-time hobby. I'm very proud of my track record and I'm confident there will be more hit TV shows to come.

MIRACLE #6:

I was known for sports gambling, but the love of my life has always been politics. So, what did I do? I decided to radically change careers and become a politician. The sports gambler and Jimmy "The Greek" of his generation decided to run for the Libertarian presidential nomination.

I was laughed at. I was told I had zero chance. I was told to go back to my "day job." I was told I was in the wrong party. I was told to get off drugs, because I must be high to think a Vegas gambler could become a leading politician. With the help of the TRUMP RULES, I proved the critics wrong again.

I traveled to 50 state events. For over a year, I worked my tail off within the party and beat out a United States Senator (Mike Gravel) and a half dozen lifelong, high-profile Libertarian activists (heroes in the party). I almost beat a United States Congressman who led the impeachment of President Clinton (Congressman Bob Barr of Georgia) for the Presidential nomination. In the end, I fell short by a few delegates, but, won the vice presidential nomination. The next morning, I was a guest on Fox News, talking national politics with Neil Cavuto. I never looked back. A political career was born.

MIRACLE #7:

It was pretty cool to win the vice presidential nomination and spend the next five months campaigning across the USA, making TV and radio appearances. But the reality is, vice presidential candidates who lose are rarely heard from again—let alone a third party VP candidate. But none of the others understood the TRUMP RULES of nonstop sales, marketing, promotion and branding. I did.

I used my sudden media platform and "15 minutes of fame" to build a career as a political commentator, syndicated columnist and best-selling author. In short order, I wrote: *The Conscience of a Libertarian, Millionaire Republican, The Ultimate Obama Survival Guide, The Murder of the Middle Class, Angry White Male,* and *The Power of RELENTLESS.* And, my first book in Japan, *The Indomitable Art of Success.* Like Donald Trump, I understood how to capitalize on a small window of opportunity—with a combination of bravado, brash promotion, and hustle. It's a winning combination.

MIRACLE #8:

Like Trump, I figured if I had the talent, bigger-than-life personality, and communication skills to promote myself to all these amazing positions, why not promote other people's products? Trump is paid to put his name on buildings. So, I offered my personality to sell products. LOTS of products.

Today I am spokesman, TV pitchman, and *rainmaker* for a broad range of national and international companies. I estimate I've sold about half a billion dollars of different products on TV, radio, and the Internet. Just on my local Vegas radio show and national radio show, I am spokesman for over twenty-five to thirty different companies and products at any one time.

Donald Trump is a brand. But Wayne Root? How the heck did I become a spokesman for over 100 companies in the past five years? Can you explain to me how that's even possible? The answer is simple: I applied the TRUMP RULES. When you hustle, pitch and promote 24/7/365, anything is possible.

MIRACLE #9:

This is one of my favorite miracles of all time. I made a ninety-two-year-old man's dream come true. You already know this story from the earlier chapter about *The Trump Ego Rules*. But it's worth listing here because I'm so proud of this story. It's the most powerful story in this book. Pitching Wayne Root 24/7 is one thing, but pitching a ninety-two-year-old man who's been retired for twenty years, and turning him into a celebrity in the final days of his life? Now that's one-in-a-billion! That's perhaps better proof of the success of the TRUMP RULES than even my own story.

This is, of course, the story I named, "THROW GRANDPA FROM THE PLANE." A star was born that day. A retired print-shop operator became an overnight media sensation. I'm not a billionaire like Trump, but I sure felt like a billion bucks knowing I'd made a ninety-two-year-old man's dream come true.

Grandpa Norm's story is living proof that the TRUMP RULES work for anyone, anywhere, at any age!

MIRACLE #10:

Grandpa Norm is my favorite story. But this one is my *proudest*. Once again, the TRUMP RULES were at work every step of the way. This is the miracle that makes me the happiest and the proudest. This is the story of my oldest child, my daughter Dakota Root. Dakota was homeschooled from birth. Never in one classroom, for one minute, in her life. Her only "classroom" was being schooled by dad on how to be successful in the real world. She watched, listened, and learned like a sponge. The result? Drumroll please . . .

She applied to the top twelve universities in America including Harvard, Stanford, Columbia, Yale, Duke, Penn, Brown, Chicago. She was accepted to ALL of them. She chose to attend Harvard. Soon, she was sitting in the first classroom of her life, in the hallowed halls of Harvard University. She went on to graduate magna cum laude from Harvard, and also achieved top of her class honors at Oxford University.

What's most impressive is that she was first accepted at Yale before any other college. Yale recruited her, not for academics, but for her fencing skills. The Yale fencing coach offered her instant acceptance. A lifetime of hard work had paid off. Who in their right mind would turn down Yale? Dakota had no idea if any other elite university would accept a homeschooler. But Dakota had the audacity to tell Yale "NO."

I argued with her. Her reply sounded like Donald Trump himself. Dakota said, "Dad you were the one who taught me to always aim for number one. You said never settle for number two. Harvard is #1 in the world. I'm not settling. I'm going for it." My girl has world-class chutzpah. Actually, that decision was a level above chutzpah. She had Trump-level audacity!

But, at the time, I was sick to my stomach. I thought Dakota had thrown away an amazing opportunity. Who turns down Yale?

Especially if you don't know if any other college will appreciate your homeschool background?

But Dakota had faith. Two weeks later, every college said "YES!" She had her choice of the best colleges in America.

After graduation from Harvard, Dakota went on to earn her master's degree in economics and political science at the University of Hamburg, Germany, and is now studying for her PhD at one of the finest universities in the world. Is that a Trumpian story of achievement, or what?

How did she accomplish all this? It started with focus, intensity, and world-class levels of work ethic. Dakota achieved near-perfect SAT scores and won the prestigious National Merit Scholarship. And she was also one of the finest athletes in the country. As a high school senior, she won the Pacific Coast Fencing Championship and fenced in the Junior Olympics and Nationals. She represented the USA at World Cup events all over the world. Eventually fencing for the elite Harvard team, she earned Second Team All-Ivy League honors. She was the perfect all-American combination of scholar and athlete.

Dakota's story is extra remarkable because she was educated in Las Vegas, the same city that produces some of the worst public education results in America.

Dakota's success is yet more proof that the TRUMP RULES work for anyone, anywhere, at any age. Dakota proved it at eighteen years of age. Grandpa Norm proved it at age ninety-two. WOW.

MIRACLE #11:

There are 330 million people in America. Almost all of them want their "fifteen minutes of fame." Tens of thousands, maybe hundreds of thousands, are fighting to be TV, radio, and/or Internet stars. My dream was to turn my books, political speeches, and media appearances into a new career as a nationally-syndicated conservative talk show host.

I could, and perhaps will someday, write an entire book about this journey—especially about all the critics, hate, disappointment, rejection, and failure along the way. But none of that matters. In Trumpian fashion, I laughed off the critics, learned from the failure, overcame the rejection, and turned my dreams into reality.

Today, I not only host *Wayne Allyn Root: Raw & Unfiltered* on USA Radio Network, but I also pulled off a double miracle and got a second bite of the apple on television. I left FNN/CNBC in 1991, my last job as a national TV host, to start my career in sports handicapping. In June 2017, Newsmax TV hired me to host *The Wayne Allyn Root Show*. You do the math. That's twenty-six years between TV host jobs. I left TV when I was just turning thirty and made my comeback at age fifty-six.

As you probably know, it is very rare to be hired to host a TV show at age fifty-six. But I know of no one else who has *ever* made his or her TV comeback twenty-six years between gigs. But hey, when you have the TRUMP RULES as your foundation, anything is possible.

Then in the summer of 2018, Bill O'Reilly decided to make his TV comeback on my Newsmax TV show. Are you kidding me? Bill O'Reilly? Bill was the unchallenged "King of Cable TV News" for sixteen consecutive years. Like President Trump, that's an unheard-of-record of being number one. Getting on TV is always one-in-a-million. But try being number one out of *everyone* on TV. Now try doing it sixteen years in a row. Remarkable.

Bill is another rough and tumble New Yorker. Maybe that's why he felt comfortable making his comeback on my television show. But either way, it was the honor of a lifetime to have him by my side several nights a week for almost three years. I'm a blessed guy. That's twice in a lifetime that I've sat on national television next to a television legend. First, Jimmy "The Greek" Snyder, then Bill O'Reilly.

Who does that? Who gets that lucky twice in a lifetime? Well when you live by the TRUMP RULES, anything is possible.

Or as I like to say, **LUCK IS THE RESIDUE OF DESIGN.**

MIRACLE #12:

A closing miracle that has just started as this book was being finished. Just more proof of the power of the TRUMP RULES. One dream I had given up on because politics, political books, and political talk radio and TV have taken over my life . . . I never imagined this dream would be back in play. But my biggest lifelong dream was always to be a "King of Vegas." To become a CEO or top executive in the gaming business like Steve Wynn, Sheldon Adelson, or drumroll please . . .

Donald J. Trump.

As this book was being written, I just closed a deal to become CEO of a publicly-traded gaming company. My baby is named VegasWINNERS Inc. It's a startup. But I believe this company has a great opportunity to become one of the great online sports gaming companies in America. At my age, and with my political career, I thought my Vegas dream was dead. Yet, at the age of fifty-nine, it's just getting started. A new adventure. A new journey. Yet another exciting career. I think President Trump would be proud.

Who knows where it will lead? But the fact that I got this shot, for the first time at the age of fifty-nine, is another miracle. Perhaps I should call each of my accomplishments *The Trump Miracles!*

THE END

That's my story. This book is about President Trump, and his TRUMP RULES for success, not about me. But there is no doubt that to get the full value of this book, and the confidence to understand that these special rules can change your life, it is important, instructive and inspirational to hear the miracles achieved in the life of this nobody, this son of a butcher, this dead-end, blue-collar kid who started with nothing. I'm living a real-life fairy tale. Yet I made twelve real-life *Trump Miracles* happen. I turned crazy, impossible dreams into reality.

It all happened because I embraced and modeled these Donald J. Trump rules.

I'm no Donald Trump. But, if I can make miracles like this happen with a foundation of the TRUMP RULES, then anyone can turn their dreams into reality. Then no dream is too big. Then anything is possible . . . for each of you!

God Bless America. God bless freedom. God Bless capitalism. God bless Donald Trump. And God bless the TRUMP RULES.

WAR
Wayne Allyn Root
August 20, 2020

* * * * * *

———— ACKNOWLEDGMENTS ————

My thanks always go first to **God.**

Then to family. Thanks to my beautiful, brilliant, perfect children **Dakota, Hudson, Remington,** and **Contessa**. Daddy loves you with all my heart.

Thanks to my fiancée and love of my life **Cindy Parker**. Thank you for putting up with my sixteen-hour work days, 365 days a year. Thanks for always making my life better and easier. I love you.

Thanks to **Doug Miller**, my lifelong mentor, who helped edit this book. And has been a great partner and given me wise counsel for thirty-five years.

Thanks to **Lee Sacks**, my attorney and trusted friend for thirty years. You've always protected me and guided me.

Thanks to **Chris Ruddy** for being the first to recognize the idea of TRUMP RULES and nurture this book from inception. And thank you Chris for three great years on national television.

Thanks to **Sara Stratton** of Redwood Publishing for taking this book the rest of the way home. Chris Ruddy gets the assist, but you get the goal!

Thank you to **Fred Weinberg** of USA Radio Network for hearing my local Vegas radio show, recognizing my talent, and having the brilliance to syndicate my show across the USA.

Thank you to **Edward Stolz** for giving me my start on Vegas radio at KBET 790 AM five years ago. What a journey we've been on. You started it all!

Thank you to **Andrew Paul**, my right-hand man in everything I do nowadays. You are a Godsend and a great friend and ally.

Thanks to a few special friends who are always there for me to provide counsel and wisdom—**Lee Lipton, Lenny Tucker, Hollis Barnhart, Matt Schiff, Monte Weiner, Richie Sklar, Ron Coury,** and **Lt. Randy Sutton**. You guys are great friends and my guardian angels.

And finally, thanks to **President Donald J. Trump** for being the G.O.A.T. Not just the greatest president of all time for America. But for being my greatest inspiration of all time. I owe my business success and achievements in large part to the TRUMP RULES I learned from studying and modeling you for the past thirty-seven years.

God bless President Donald J. Trump. God bless the TRUMP RULES. God bless capitalism. God bless America.

——— CONTACTING WAYNE ———

Wayne speaks at GOP and conservative events and conferences throughout the USA. If you are looking for a dynamic, high-energy speaker for your next event, please contact Wayne at the phone number or email below. Or see **www.ROOTforAmerica.com**

Wayne is available to speak at business conferences, personal development events, and corporate conventions across the globe. If you're looking for a dynamic, high-energy speaker for your next event please contact Wayne at the phone number or email below. Or see **www.RelentlessROOT.com**

Wayne is the spokesman/RAINMAKER for many companies— big and small. He is the face, voice, and host of their TV, radio, and online advertising campaigns. If you'd like to engage Wayne to promote your business or products, please contact him at the phone number or email below. Or see **www.WayneRoot.com**

Finally, Wayne believes empowering and educating young people is his greatest gift. Contact Wayne below to arrange for the most dynamic TRUMP RULES presentation your college Republican or young conservative group has ever experienced.

WAYNE ALLYN ROOT

WayneRoot.com
ROOTforAmerica.com
RelentlessROOT.com

EMAIL:

Wayne@WayneRoot.com
WayneRoot@gmail.com

PHONE:

Toll Free (888) 444-ROOT (7668)

Parler:

@RealWayneRoot

Twitter:

@RealWayneRoot

Facebook:

@WayneAllynRoot

★ ★ ★ ★ ★ ★

—————— ENDNOTES ——————

CHAPTER 2: My Story—How I Met Donald J. Trump

1   Blaskey, Sarah, Nicholas Nehamas, Caitlin Ostroff, and Jay Weaver. "Chapter 8: The Gatekeepers." *The Grifter's Club: Trump, Mar-a-Lago, and the Selling of the Presidency*, 101-107. London: Hodder & Stoughton, 2020.

CHAPTER 3: Proof Positive You Are in the Right Place at the Right Time

2   Root, Wayne Allyn. "Donald Trump for President? The Race Just Got Fun." FoxNews, June 16, 2015. Re-published by Douglas Schoen. http://douglasschoen.com/donald-trump-for-president-the-2016-race-just-got-fun/.

3   Durden, Tyler. "Part-Time Jobs Surge By 161,000; Full-Time Jobs Tumble By 349,000." Zero Hedge, July 2, 2015. http://www.zerohedge.com/news/2015-07-02/part-time-jobs-surge-161000-full-time-jobs-tumble-349000.

4   Cox, Jeff. "Record 46 Million Americans Are on Food Stamps." CNBC. CNBC, September 4, 2012. http://www.cnbc.com/id/48898378.

5   Bennett, Jonah. "HHS: Record Number Of Americans On Welfare." The Daily Caller. The Daily Caller, July 9, 2014. http://dailycaller.com/2014/07/08/hhs-record-number-of-americans-on-welfare/.

6   Boyer, Dave. "That's Rich: Poverty Level under Obama Breaks 50-Year Record." The Washington Times. The Washington Times, January 7, 2014. http://www.washingtontimes.com/news/2014/jan/7/obamas-rhetoric-on-fighting-poverty-doesnt-match-h/?page=all.

7   Meyer, Ali. "Record 93,626,000 Americans Not in Labor Force; Participation Rate Hits 38-Year Low." CNSNews.com, July 2, 2015. http://cnsnews.com/

news/article/ali-meyer/record-93626000-americans-not-labor-force-participation-rate-declines-626.

8   Rucker, Philip. "As Donald Trump Surges in Polls, Democrats Cheer." The Washington Post. WP Company, July 1, 2015. http://www.washingtonpost.com/politics/donald-trump-surges-and-democrats-cheer/2015/07/01/895d9e9e-1f5d-11e5-84d5-eb37ee8eaa61_story.html.

9   Root, Wayne Allyn. "Donald Trump: The First Hispanic President." Fox News. FOX News Network, July 2, 2015. https://www.foxnews.com/opinion/donald-trump-the-first-hispanic-president.

10 Root, Wayne Allyn. "Explaining Why Trump Will Be President- Up Close & Personal." Townhall. Townhall.com, December 17, 2015. https://townhall.com/columnists/wayneallynroot/2015/12/17/explaining-why-trump-will-be-president-up-close--personal-n2094511.

11 Root, Wayne Allyn. "A Message For Christians About Donald Trump By Wayne Allyn Root." thespiritnewspaper.com, June 30, 2016. http://thespiritnewspaper.com/a-message-for-christians-about-donald-trump-by-wayne-allyn-root-p9573-94.htm.

12 Root, Wayne Allyn. "- Advice to Donald Trump From a Fellow Big-Mouthed New York Businessman & Politician." Townhall. Townhall.com, August 6, 2015. https://townhall.com/columnists/wayneallynroot/2015/08/06/advice-to-donald-trump-from-a-fellow-bigmouthed-new-york-businessman--politician-n2035274.

13 Flint, Joe. "Republican Debate Audience Was the Biggest Ever for a Nonsports Cable Event." The Wall Street Journal. Dow Jones & Company, August 8, 2015. http://www.wsj.com/articles/republican-debate-audience-was-the-biggest-ever-for-a-nonsports-cable-event-1438992539.

14 https://twitter.com/ianbremmer?lang=en

15 Olson, Kyle. "VIDEO: Diamond and Silk Warn Megyn Kelly: Back off Trump!" TheAmericanMirror.com, September 14, 2018. http://www.theamericanmirror.com/video-black-women-defend-donald-trump-shred-megyn-kelly/.

16 Root, Wayne Allyn. "Exclusive Wayne Allyn Root: Trump Is 'Relentless'." Breitbart, August 10, 2015. https://www.breitbart.com/politics/2015/08/10/exclusive-wayne-allyn-root-trump-is-relentless/.

17 Root, Wayne Allyn. "Donald Trump: Welcome Back, Ronald Reagan." Breitbart, July 22, 2016. https://www.breitbart.com/politics/2016/07/22/donald-trump-welcome-back-ronald-reagan/.

18 Ain, Stewart. "Trump's Jewish Giving Rubs Against Tenor Of His Campaign." Jewish Week, March 30, 2016. http://www.thejewishweek.com/news/national/trumps-jewish-giving-rubs-against-tenor-his-campaign.

19 Root, Wayne Allyn. "Trump Is Headed to the White House. Did We Just Elect Our First Jewish President?" Fox News. FOX News Network, November 19, 2016. https://www.foxnews.com/opinion/trump-is-headed-to-the-white-house-did-we-just-elect-our-first-jewish-president.

CHAPTER 5: TRUMP RULE #2—Failing Your Way to the Top

20 "George Clooney Net Worth." Celebrity Net Worth, July 10, 2020. https://www.celebritynetworth.com/richest-celebrities/actors/george-clooney-net-worth/.

21 "Sylvester Stallone Net Worth." TheRichest, June 7, 2011. http://www.therichest.com/celebnetworth/celeb/actors/sylvester-stallone-net-worth/.

22 "Sylvester Stallone Net Worth." Celebrity Net Worth, February 24, 2020. https://www.celebritynetworth.com/richest-celebrities/actors/sylvester-stallone-net-worth/.

23 Weisman, Aly. "14 People Who Failed Before Becoming Famous." Business Insider. Business Insider, February 20, 2014. http://www.businessinsider.com/people-who-failed-before-becoming-famous-2014-2?op=1.

24 "Oprah Winfrey Net Worth." Celebrity Net Worth, August 8, 2020. https://www.celebritynetworth.com/richest-celebrities/actors/oprah-net-worth/.

25 "Steve Jobs Net Worth." Celebrity Net Worth, September 2, 2020. https://www.celebritynetworth.com/richest-businessmen/ceos/steve-jobs-net-worth/.

26 Rockwell, Dan. "How Blowing up a Factory Changed Jack Welch." Leadership Freak Blod, May 7, 2017. https://leadershipfreak.wordpress.com/2011/10/13/how-blowing-up-a-factory-changed-jack-welch/.

27 "Jack Welch." Wikipedia. Wikimedia Foundation, August 23, 2020. http://en.wikipedia.org/wiki/Jack_Welch.

28 "Jack Welch Net Worth." Celebrity Net Worth, March 2, 2020. https://www.celebritynetworth.com/richest-businessmen/ceos/jack-welch-net-worth/.

29 Johnston, Theresa. "Charles Schwab's Secret Struggle." Stanford Magazine - Article, March 1999. https://alumni.stanford.edu/get/page/magazine/article/?article_id=41436.

30 "Bloomberg Billionaires Index." Bloomberg.com. Bloomberg, March 1, 2017. https://www.bloomberg.com/billionaires/profiles/charles-r-schwab/.

31   Walt Disney's Failures Could Inspire Entrepreneurs. Accessed September 30, 2020. http://www.hollywoodstories.com/pages/disney/d3.html.

32   Weisman, Aly. "14 People Who Failed Before Becoming Famous." Business Insider. Business Insider, February 20, 2014. http://www.businessinsider.com/people-who-failed-before-becoming-famous-2014-2?op=1.

33   Tate, Amethyst. "Celebs Who Went from Failures to Success Stories." CBS News. CBS Interactive, July 25, 2012. http://www.cbsnews.com/pictures/celebs-who-went-from-failures-to-success-stories/15.

34   http://blog.megafounder.com/blog/most-famous-failures/.

35   "Colonel Sanders." Wikipedia. Wikimedia Foundation, August 29, 2020. http://en.wikipedia.org/wiki/Colonel_Sanders.

36   "Clinton Bores His Audience." NBCNews.com. NBCUniversal News Group, July 20, 2004. http://www.nbcnews.com/id/5470323/ns/msnbc-msnbc_special/t/clinton-bores-his-audience/.

37   Kurtus, Ron. "Failures of Abraham Lincoln (1800s)." Failures of Abraham Lincoln (1800s) by Ron Kurtus - Lessons Learned from History: School for Champions, October 11, 2011. http://www.school-for-champions.com/history/lincoln_failures.htm.

38   "Christopher Columbus." Wikipedia. Wikimedia Foundation, September 28, 2020. http://en.wikipedia.org/wiki/Christopher_Columbus.

39   "George Washington." Wikipedia. Wikimedia Foundation, September 29, 2020. http://en.wikipedia.org/wiki/George_Washington.

40   "Winston Churchill." Wikipedia. Wikimedia Foundation, September 29, 2020. http://en.wikipedia.org/wiki/Winston_Churchill.

41   Klein, Christopher. "Winston Churchill's History-Making Funeral." History.com. A&E Television Networks, January 30, 2015. https://www.history.com/news/winston-churchills-funeral-50-years-ago.

CHAPTER 6: TRUMP RULE #3—Screw The Critics

42   Blaskey, Sarah, Nicholas Nehamas, Caitlin Ostroff, and Jay Weaver. "Chapter 8: The Gatekeepers." *The Grifter's Club: Trump, Mar-a-Lago, and the Selling of the Presidency*, 103. London: Hodder & Stoughton, 2020.

43   Novak, Matt. "Nate Silver's Very Very Wrong Predictions About Donald Trump Are Terrifying." Paleofuture. Paleofuture, November 4, 2016. https://paleofuture.gizmodo.com/nate-silvers-very-very-wrong-predictions-about-donald-t-1788583912.

44   Arrieta-Kenna, Ruairí. "The Worst Political Predictions of 2016." POLITICO Magazine, December 28, 2016. https://www.politico.com/magazine/story/2016/12/the-worst-political-predictions-of-2016-214555.

45   Sargent, Greg. "Opinion | Can Trump Ride White Anger into the White House? A New Analysis Suggests It's a Fantasy." The Washington Post. WP Company, April 6, 2019. https://www.washingtonpost.com/blogs/plum-line/wp/2016/06/02/can-trump-ride-white-anger-into-the-white-house-a-new-a nalysis-suggests-its-a-fantasy/.

46   Needham, Vicki. "Election Model: Clinton Will Win Easily." TheHill, July 1, 2016. https://thehill.com/policy/finance/economy/prediction-hillary-clinto n-easily-wins-beats-donald-trump-moodys-presidential-election-model.

47   Shepard, Steven. "GOP Insiders: Trump Can't Win." POLITICO, August 12, 2016. https://www.politico.com/story/2016/08/donald-trump-electoral-vote s-gop-insiders-226932.

48   Sargent, Greg. "Opinion | Obama's Campaign Guru: Don't Fret about Polls. Clinton Is Winning, and She Can Finish the Job Tonight." The Washington Post. WP Company, April 6, 2019. https://www.washingtonpost.com/blogs/plum-line/wp/2016/09/26/obamas-campaign-guru-dont-fret-about-polls-clinton-is-winning-and-she-can-finish-the-job-tonight/.

49   Larry J. Sabato, Kyle Kondik. "SABATO'S CRYSTAL BALL." Sabatos Crystal Ball. Accessed September 30, 2020. https://centerforpolitics.org/crystalball/articles/our-final-2016-picks/.

50   Wang, Sam. "All Estimates Point toward HRC>50% Probability. What Determines the Exact Number?" Princeton University. The Trustees of Princeton University, November 6, 2016. https://election.princeton.edu/2016/11/06/is-99-a-reasonable_probability/.

51   Jackson, Natalie. "HuffPost Forecasts Hillary Clinton Will Win With 323 Electoral Votes." HuffPost. HuffPost, November 8, 2016. https://www.huffpost.com/entry/polls-hillary-clinton-win_n_5821074ce4b0e80b02cc2a94.

52   Rothschild, David. "PredictWise: 89% Chance of Hillary Clinton Winning." Bloomberg.com. Bloomberg, November 8, 2016. https://www.bloomberg.com/news/videos/2016-11-08/breaking-down-the-odds-of-the-u-s-presidential-election.

53   Katz, Josh. "2016 Election Forecast: Who Will Be President?" The New York Times. The New York Times, July 19, 2016. https://www.nytimes.com/interactive/2016/upshot/presidential-polls-forecast.html.

54 "2016 Election Forecast." FiveThirtyEight, November 8, 2016. https://projects. fivethirtyeight.com/2016-election-forecast/.

55 Milbank, Dana. "Trump Will Lose, or I Will Eat This Column." The Washington Post. WP Company, October 2, 2015. https://www. washingtonpost.com/opinions/trump-will-lose-or-i-will-eat-this-column/20 15/10/02/1fd5c94a-6906-11e5-9ef3-fde182507eac_story.html.

56 Silver, Nate. "Election Update: Women Are Defeating Donald Trump." FiveThirtyEight. FiveThirtyEight, October 11, 2016. https://fivethirtyeight. com/features/election-update-women-are-defeating-donald-trump/.

57 Posted By Tim Hains On Date October 7, 2016. "Bob Beckel: This Race, Effectively, As Of Tonight, Is Over." RealClearPolitics. Accessed September 30, 2020. https://www.realclearpolitics.com/video/2016/10/07/ bob_beckel_this_election_is_over.html.

58 Bump, Philip. "Donald Trump Is Facing an Apocalyptic Election Scenario, Thanks to Women Voters." The Washington Post. WP Company, April 29, 2019. https://www.washingtonpost.com/news/the-fix/ wp/2016/10/13/donald-trumps-facing-an-apocalyptic-election-scenario-th anks-to-women-voters/.

59 "Cook Political Report Electoral College Race Ratings." 270toWin. com. Accessed September 30, 2020. https://www.270towin.com/maps/ the-cook-political-report.

60 Borchers, Callum. "The Wrongest Media Predictions about Donald Trump." The Washington Post. WP Company, April 29, 2019. https://www. washingtonpost.com/news/the-fix/wp/2016/11/09/the-wrongest-medi a-predictions-about-donald-trump/?noredirect=on.

61 Heer, Jeet. "Donald Trump Will Be Buried in an Electoral Avalanche." The New Republic, June 17, 2016. https://newrepublic.com/article/134366/donal d-trump-will-buried-electoral-avalanche.

62 Fallows, James. "How the Press Should Handle a Candidate With No Chance of Winning." The Atlantic. Atlantic Media Company, July 13, 2015. http://www. theatlantic.com/politics/archive/2015/07/3-truths-about-trump/398351/.

63 White, Ben. "Trump Won't Win, but Yes, He Matters." CNBC. CNBC, July 17, 2015. http://www.cnbc.com/2015/07/17/trump-wont-win-but-yes-he-matters. html.

64 Chait, Jonathan. "Donald Trump Is Going to Lose Because He Is Crazy." Intelligencer, August 26, 2015. http://nymag.com/daily/intelligencer/2015/08/ donald-trump-is-going-to-lose-because-hes-crazy.html.

65 Schwartz, Ian. "Scarborough: Trump 'Knows He Is Going to Lose'; Supporters Are Wondering 'Does This Guy Want to Win?'." RealClearPolitics. Accessed September 30, 2020. http://www.realclearpolitics.com/video/2016/08/15/scarborough_trump_knows_he_is_going_to_lose_supporters_are_wondering_does_this_guy_want_to_win.html.

66 Nelson, Jim. "Hack Trump!" GQ. GQ, May 25, 2017. http://www.gq.com/story/trump-will-lose-election.

67 Magary, Drew. "Donald Trump Is Going To Get His Ass Kicked On Tuesday." The Concourse. The Concourse, November 6, 2016. http://theconcourse.deadspin.com/donald-trump-is-going-to-get-his-ass-kicked-on-tuesday-1788618628.

CHAPTER 7: TRUMP RULE #4—The EGO Rules

68 "P. T. Barnum." Wikipedia. Wikimedia Foundation, September 29, 2020. http://en.wikipedia.org/wiki/P._T._Barnum.

69 "Mother Teresa." Wikipedia. Wikimedia Foundation, September 21, 2020. http://en.wikipedia.org/wiki/Mother_Teresa.

70 Van Biema, David. "My Take: The Mother Teresa You Don't Know." CNN. Cable News Network, September 10, 2012. http://religion.blogs.cnn.com/2012/09/10/my-take-the-mother-teresa-you-dont-know/comment-page-1/.

71 Tani, Red. "Mother Teresa: Blessed Billionaire, Holy Hypocrite : Filipino Freethinkers." Mother Teresa: Blessed Billionaire, Holy Hypocrite | Filipino Freethinkers, December 31, 2011. http://filipinofreethinkers.org/2011/12/31/mother-teresa-blessed-billionaire-holy-hypocrite/.

72 "Joshua Chamberlain." Wikipedia. Wikimedia Foundation, September 28, 2020. http://en.wikipedia.org/wiki/Joshua_Chamberlain.

CHAPTER 13: TRUMP RULE #10—Chutzpah (a.k.a. Becoming More Jewish)

73 Sharkansky, Ira. Essay. In Governing Israel Chosen People, Promised Land and Prophetic Tradition, 20–22. New Brunswick, NJ: Transaction Publishers, 2017.

74 Cha, Ariana Eunjung. "Sold on a Stereotype In China, a Genre of Self-Help Books Purports to Tell the Secrets of Making Money 'the Jewish Way'." The Washington Post. WP Company, February 7, 2007. https://www.washingtonpost.com/archive/business/2007/02/07/sold-on-a-stereotype-span-classbankheadin-china-a-genre-of-self-help-books-

purports-to-tell-the-secrets-of-making-money-the-jewish-wayspan/
da06370a-5c28-4220-8d4c-cdb03edbc449/.

CHAPTER 14: More Valuable TRUMP RULES

75 Adams, Susan. "Optimists Become CEOs, Study Finds." Forbes. Forbes Magazine, November 15, 2012. http://www.forbes.com/sites/susanadams/2012/11/15/optimists-become-ceos-study-finds/.

76 "Study: CEOs Are More Optimistic, More Open To Risk." Study: CEOs Are More Optimistic, More Open To Risk | Duke's Fuqua School of Business, November 5, 2012. http://www.fuqua.duke.edu/news_events/news-releases/ceo-personalities/.

77 "Study: Optimistic MBA Grads Have Better Career Prospects Than Pessimists." Duke Today. Accessed September 30, 2020. https://today.duke.edu/2011/01/optimistic_mba.html.

78 "G. Harrold Carswell." Wikipedia. Wikimedia Foundation, September 28, 2020. https://en.wikipedia.org/wiki/G._Harrold_Carswell.

79 Cuozzo, Steve. "Saving Wollman Rink Made Trump a New York City Hero." New York Post. New York Post, January 22, 2017. https://nypost.com/2017/01/22/saving-wollman-rink-made-trump-a-new-york-city-hero.

80 "An Orphan's Plea." FamilyLife®, April 7, 2018. https://www.familylife.com/articles/topics/parenting/foundations/adoption-and-orphans/an-orphans-plea/.

81 DeGregory, Lane. "More than 10,000 Families Want to Adopt Orphan Davion Only." Tampa Bay Times. Tampa Bay Times, June 17, 2020. http://www.tampabay.com/features/humaninterest/more-than-10000-families-want-to-adopt-orphan-davion-only/2149190.

82 "Family: Our Story: Maker's Mark." Family | Our Story | Maker's Mark. Accessed September 30, 2020. https://www.makersmark.com/history/truths/the-wall-street-journal.

83 Acitelli, Tom. *Whiskey Business: How Small-Batch Distillers Are Transforming American Spirits.* Chicago, IL: Published by Chicago Review Press Incorporated, 2017.

CHAPTER 15: My Fairy Tale Life: The Trump Miracles

84 The Daily Argus Mount Vernon, N.Y. -1994. Newspaper out of print.